COVERT SKIES

Ron Sutphin's
Road to Civil Air Transport (CAT)
and
Covert Operations in Laos

Ronald J. Sutphin

CS Norwood, Editor

Copyright © 2022 by CS Norwood
All rights reserved.
U.S. Copyright Office Certificate of Registration Number: TXu 2-319-007

PUBLISHERS CATALOGING-IN-PUBLICATION DATA

Sutphin, Ronald J. / Author; Norwood, CS / Editor
Covert skies: Ron Sutphin's road to civil air transport (CAT) and covert operations in Laos /
by Ronald J. Sutphin and edited by CS Norwood

Memoirs of a pilot who loved to fly and lived to fly, no matter where it took him around the globe--even if that place was the dangerous world of flying covert operations in war-torn Laos.

BIOGRAPHY & AUTOBIOGRAPHY / Aviation & Nautical / Memoirs
HISTORY / Asia / Southeast Asia

Regional themes - 2.4.0.0.0.0.0 Southeast Asia - 2.4.5.0.0.0.0 Laos

Large Print Edition

304 pages / 17.78 x 25.4 x 1.5 cm / 60 illustrations
Includes biographical references and index.

ISBN: 979-8-9884470-0-9

Library of Congress Control Number: 2024911170

Cover design by: Sylvia Lynne Malvoso
Illustrations were enhanced using Topaz Gigapixel AI for clarity.
Printed in the United States of America

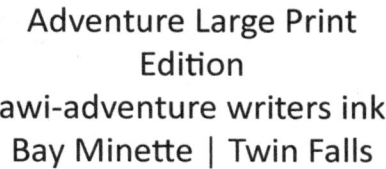

Adventure Large Print Edition
awi-adventure writers ink
Bay Minette | Twin Falls

Aderholt's Inscription

Dear Lynn[e] - It's an honor to sign this book for Ron's sister. FYI Ron is one of the greatest pilots in the history of aviation—Rates with Jimmie Doolittle, Bob Hoover, Chuck Yeager. As a combat pilot he is the best I have ever known. Can do anything and is totally fearless. A great American and my dearest friend. You can be proud.

Sincerely.

Heinie Aderholt, Gen. U.S.A.F. (Ret).
Inscription in his book "Air Commando One"

Lynne's Poem

I watched the dark-night skies
Where planes like stars crossed by
Where the war was not a victory
But my brother passing by.

—Lynne

C-47
I spent many
hours in them
wish I could tell
you a lot about
this picture

Included in a letter home to Mom...(Family Photo)

Acknowledgments

Larry and Kat Teufel
Always Family, Thank You!

Sylvia Lynne Malvoso
Sister; Confidant, Artist, and Manuscript Curator

Kathleen Sutphin
Sister; Confidant and Proofreader

Loraine Kingston
Sister; Confidant and Family Photo Curator

Joanna Moseley Bailey
Librarian Advisor

Ken Kahn
Aircraft Editor; Webmaster of Seaboard & Western

Seaboard World Airlines

Jerry J. Jacques
Alaska Master Guide #110, Bush Pilot, Author, and Friend

For all those who dare to fly and
those who keep them flying.

Contents

Aderholt's Inscription, iii
Lynne's Poem, iv
Introduction, xi
Foreword, xii
Preface, xvii

        FIRST FLIGHT, 1
        TSINGTAO, 12
        FLIGHT, 22
        NAVAL CADETS, 29
        KOREA, 54
        AMERICAN FLYERS, 72
        THE ROAD TO
        CIVIL AIR TRANSPORT, 77
        CAT, INC., 97
        INDONESIA, 110
        TEST PILOT, 120
        LAOS AND AIR AMERICA, 128
        COVERT SKIES, 156
        HELIO OVER LAOS, 167
        PAK KADING, 175
        VIENTIANE BURNING , 187
    DROP SITES OVER VIETNAM AND LAOS, 190

Afterword, 202
Addendum, 203
Capt. Ronald J. Sutphin, 211
Endnotes, 214
Bibliography, 246
Index, 263

Photos

iii, Aderholt's Inscription
iv, Included in a letter home to Mom...(Family Photo)
1, Taylorcraft Plus D (McIntyre-Collection)
2, Grumman - F4F-3 Wildcat
8, Curtiss C-46 Commando in Flight (Photo by USAF)
10, Northrop P-61 Black Widow night fighter
16, Martin PBM Mariner water takeoff
20, Scout plane catapulted from carrier
25, Fairchild PT-23 (Golden Wings Museum)
29, Naval Cadet - Ronald J. Sutphin (Family Photo)
31, Boeing Stearman Model 75 (Stearman Kaydet)
32, Cessna AT-17/UC-78 Bobcat Crane Model T-50
35, Retired Lt. Gen. Frank E. Petersen Jr., the 1st African American Marine Corps aviator, and the 1st African American Marine Corps general, served during the Korean War in 1953 and Vietnam in 1968. He flew more than 350 combat missions. (U.S. Marine Corps File Photo)
39, Aeronca Model 7 Champion
43, A U.S. Navy Consolidated PB4Y-2S Privateer (BuNo 66304) of Patrol Squadron VP-23, circa 1949-1953. This aircraft is today on display at the National Museum of Naval Aviation, Pensacola, Florida (USA)
48, Grumman F6F-5N Hellcat night fighter assigned to NAS Jacksonville, Florida in 1944/45
50, Beech SNB-5 Navigator Model 18
51, Navy Douglas AD-4 Skyraider taking off from USS Princeton during Korean War
53, Vought F4U-4 Corsair
54, K-6 Airbase, Pyeongtaek, South Korea 1952-53 - Long before

it was called Camp Humphreys or later, U.S. Army Garrison Humphreys, K-6 airfield south of Seoul, Korea was home to U.S. Marine Air Group 12 during the Korean War. [Photo] courtesy of J.R. Boyer, a Marine who served at K-6 during the war. (Color image to grayscale)/ (U.S. Army, USAG Humphreys; Boyer, J. R. 2019)

56, Douglas AD aircraft with wings folded. Photo taken at K-6 (No. 15 sits to the side of the folded-wing AD, with tailfin letters AK showing.) Photo was taken by J.R. Boyer (c. 1950-53), K-6 Marine. (Color photo to grayscale)/ (Boyer, J.R.; USAG-Humpherys 2009)

62, Cessna L-19 Bird Dog

62, Douglas DC-3 (C-117D) United States Marines at the Pima Air & Space Museum. (Photo from aeroprints.com)

63, Douglas F3D Skyknight

64, Grumman TBM (GM-built TBF) with Sto-Wing folding wings, 1945

77, CAT, Inc. Pilot Capt. Ronald J. Sutphin (Family Photo)

81, Howard DGA-15P (FlugKerl2 2013)

82, Grumman F9F-6 Cougar in flight, c. 1952

83, Pan Am DC-6B at London Heathrow in September 1954 on a transatlantic tourist flight. (RuthAS)

84, Seaboard & Western Douglas DC-4

86, Seaboard Connie, Lockheed L-1049D Super Constellation

91,Goodyear-built FG-1D (USN - U.S. Naval Aviation News March 1953)

93, Capt. August Harvey "Augie" Martin, Seaboard Airlines

97, CAT large baggage sticker

100, CAT Curtiss C-46D Commando in Indochina (USAF - National Museum of the U.S. Air Force photo 110224-F-XN622-005, Public Domain 1950-54)

104, Captain Robert E. Rousselot (Photo by Stephen Pingry / Tulsa World)
111, Lockheed T-33 Shooting Star (U.S. Air Force Photo/Alejandro Pena)
112, Douglas A-26 Invader
115, Brig. Gen. Harry C. "Heinie" Aderholt
116, Helio Courier (Photo Credit Tom Lum)
118, North American F-100 Super Sabre
121, Emblem of USAF 80th Fighter Squadron
123, Toss- or loft-bombing with Auto LABS (U.S. military diagram of the over-the-shoulder bombing technique)
131, Kong Le (Lair, Bill; Ahern, Thomas; Undercover Armies, 1961-1973; Washington 2006 (Center for the Study of Intelligence, CIA) 1960s)
133, Sikorsky S-55/H-19 Chickasaw in flight
135, Gen. Phoumi Nosavan
137, Hmong leader Vang Pao
138, Sikorsky UH-34D helicopter (Photo Credit Tom Lum)
147, Boeing B-52 Stratofortress
148, Lockheed C-130 Hercules (Photo Credit Tom Lum)
148, Turbo Beech Volpar (Photo Credit Tom Lum)
149, Fairchild C-123 Provider (Photo Credit Tom Lum)
151, Pilatus Porter (Photo Credit Tom Lum)
154, Ron's sketch of air routes over Laos
155, Ron's sketch of highway routes through Laos
161, "Helio B-833 on the Tarmac" (Digital Painting by Sylvia Lynne Malvoso)
167, "Helio B-835 in Flight" (Digital Painting by Sylvia Lynne Malvoso),
186, Ron (with walking stick) on or about 18 November 1960. Heinie Aderholt is next to Ron, and surrounding them are

the Thailand Special Forces soldiers, sent to bring him in. (Family Photo)

186, Ron wrote on the back of the photo: Northern Laos, Moung [sic] Soui. This was taken right after I walked out after being shot down. I lived on the jungles for 2 weeks evading the enemy so I was very sick & no food. I live 1000 years in 14 days. (Family Photo, back)

201, Capt. Ronald J. "Ron" Sutphin Handwritten on the back: me VTE, Laos 1960 I picked up 231 holes this flight. (Family Photo)

> Please note that, although every effort has been made to render these photos as sharp and clear as possible, many photos included here are still somewhat blurry.

Introduction

Capt. Ronald J. "Ron" Sutphin was a Marine, Naval Cadet and commercial aviator, CAT, Inc. and Air America pilot, test pilot, instructor of pilots, rancher, adventurer, and my brother.

This work is written and adapted from his unfinished, first-draft, original manuscript. While every effort has been made to verify all information and correctly cite all sources included in Ron's original work, the manuscript itself was obtained, and my work was begun, several years after he was killed in the crash of his Piper Super Cub. Considering this, every effort has been made on my part to verify such things as the correct spelling of names and places, as well as dates and event timelines. The original manuscript contained no citations or photographs and did not detail the aircraft or other pictures included here. Unfortunately, then, this leaves me with some gaps in the record, along with a few unfinished stories, perhaps a few misspelled names, or even Ron's vague recollection of a few events. I pass all this along to the reader in the hopes that, even so, this narrative is the best account of the life he really lived. My apologies if I got something wrong.

CS Norwood (csn 2022; 2019)

(Some hyperlinks listed may be no longer be extant. A few names have been changed for various reasons.)

Foreword

By Jerry Jacques

Ron Sutphin was a U.S. Marine fighter pilot who served in both the Korean and the Vietnam Wars. When shot down one November night along the Mekong River in Laos, with Pathet Lao (Laotian communist) forces actively trying to capture him, he evaded the enemy and survived alone in the treacherous jungles for fourteen days. His everyday life is the stuff of legends. Ron was not only a fighter pilot, but he was also a test pilot, flight instructor, commercial airline pilot, and a bush pilot. He was a gold miner in Alaska and a cattle rancher in Oregon. Ron helped many young pilots—including me—become special ops pilots operating in war zones or in covert missions around the world.

As a flight instructor Ron was calm and patient but demanded the best from his students while pushing them to learn to fly to the extreme edge of their plane's limits. He taught many of us how to operate Helio Couriers, Pilatus Porters, Super Cubs, and similar aircraft in extreme situations. His lessons helped us come back alive and, in my case, they helped me save another life.

This is a story I pried out of him—one that he really didn't want to tell:

Ron was flying a Helio Courier on one of his covert

missions in Southeast Asia, in an area where, according to the enemy, he was not supposed to be. He had completed his assignment and was headed back to base, flying low at about fifty feet above the treetops along one of his routine flight paths.

Suddenly the dense tree canopy disappeared as he crossed over a newly built airstrip in the middle of the jungle. It wasn't there a few short weeks before, so he was surprised to see it fully functioning with planes on the runway. As he flew directly over, he identified two MiG fighter jets at the end of the airstrip with pilots already scrambling to get airborne. He knew that if those jets got into the air, he would be dead. His little Helio had absolutely no chance against an airborne MiG. With its top speed perhaps 140-160 miles per hour, the Helio was no match for those MiGs with well over three times the speed. He knew his life depended on what he did now—on his skills as a fighter pilot, his aircraft, and his aim. He had to engage or die. They knew he had seen them, and there was no way he could outrun them.

Fortunately, Ron's Helio was armed with rocket pods that day, so he turned and banked the Helio as tight as he could, lined up, and fired a rocket at one of the MiGs on the ground. His rocket hit the MiG, completely disabling it, but he still had that second MiG to worry about.

Again, he turned the Helio tight in order to line back up on the second jet. But by the time he came around, the second MiG was already starting down the runway. As the MiG accelerated, just beginning its takeoff roll, Ron fired his remaining rockets. To his horror, he missed—his shots landed directly in front of the MiG! The rockets did, however, blow a big enough hole in the runway that as the MiG rolled into the crater its nose-wheel collapsed. Now along with number one, MiG number two wasn't going anywhere that day; it came to a grinding halt on the runway. He told me he felt incredibly lucky that his second round of rockets had disabled that second MiG.

Unanticipated MiG-mission accomplished, Ron turned tail and ran back for home base, hoping more MiGs weren't already airborne in his vicinity.

Fighter pilot in a Helio Courier versus MiG jet fighters— kind of unbelievable, but I know it's true. Ron was an amazing man and one of my heroes. I am proud to have called him my friend.

Covert Skies is a must read for every person with an interest in aircraft and aviation in the 1950s and '60s, as well as flight in the shadowy world of covert operations.

—Jerry J. Jacques, Alaska Master Guide #110, author of "No Sequel to Life: From the Heart of a Bush Pilot"

By Ken Kahn

When I was hired as a pilot by Seaboard World Airlines in 1967, I did not know Ron Sutphin or that he had flown for Seaboard & Western (the company name changed in 1961) in 1955-56. Even long after I created a website to preserve the history of Seaboard, Ron only appeared as a name on a long list of pilots. Recently, however, I learned from his autobiography, *Covert Skies,* about his remarkable life in aviation.

After graduating NAVCADs at NAS Pensacola and returning from his tour of duty in Korea, he flew as a pilot in the U.S. Marine Corps Reserves and as an airline pilot flying war-surplus transport planes across oceans. This was sufficient adventure for many pilots, but Ron wanted more. He still wanted to fly commercially, but he wanted to fly in Southeast Asia. He resigned from Seaboard in 1956 to sign on with Civil Air Transport (CAT), an airline he soon realized was deeply involved in covert operations in Southeast Asia. The airline was controlled by the Central Intelligence Agency. This is a book for anyone interested in that part of history. Some readers will doubtless have a dim view of U.S. policy in Southeast Asia in those days, particularly with the wisdom of hindsight, but men like Ron believed they were patriotically serving their country and trying to protect the Lao and highland tribespeople against brutal communist incursion. He did so with great courage, flying dangerous missions on an almost daily basis. Ron, as well as all those like him who flew in the "secret war" in Laos, risked their lives many times over with little reward and no recognition.

From correspondence with Ron's sister, CS Norwood, I know that she is a diligent researcher and has worked exhaustively to ensure that the book is as accurate as possible. As a commercial airline pilot, someone who has been interested in aviation my entire life—I flew airplanes for 32 years—I found Ron's story fascinating. His experience was much more varied than that of most pilots, having flown more than 35,000 hours in aircraft from covert-duty light planes to military F-86s and F-100s, and, eventually, to Japan Airlines' Boeing 747 jumbo jets.

The 76-year-old retired pilot and rancher was killed while checking cattle with his Piper Super Cub. To borrow a line from the obituary of one daredevil pilot who crashed during a 1931 air show, Ron died as he lived, with *a roar and a flash.**

I recommend this book to anyone interested in aviation history in general, and to pilots in particular. The spotlight is on the U.S. involvement in Southeast Asia of government owned/CIA controlled CAT and Air America, but, above all, it is a story of an unusually adventurous pilot's life.

—Ken Kahn, Webmaster, avian photographer

*The New York World-Telegram reported at the time, that Charles "Speed" Holman "...died as he lived, with a roar and a flash at three hundred miles per hour."

Preface

For years, literally, the thick white ring-binder containing the typed, ink-stained, double-spaced lines lay stacked among the piles of books and papers in my house, accumulating dust, garnering only an occasional glance from me. Still, I didn't want to lose track of it. When it came in the mail in 2008, I had read through a couple of chapters, with my first thoughts being, "... My brother wrote this...It needs some work." It was an unfinished manuscript of recounted adventures from a storied career. I read a little more, about halfway, and put it down. It was a very rough draft, and Ron (Ronald J. Sutphin) was not a writer, he was a pilot—a pilot who was gone now, killed in the crash of his Piper Super Cub while checking cattle at his ranch in Oregon. He died of blunt-force trauma on my 59th birthday, exactly one month shy of his 77th birthday. My profound sadness over the loss of a brother I had never known kept me at a distance. I believe I really did not want to read more, especially since he was no longer here. I wanted him to say, "pick up the manuscript; take a good look at it," and then tell me we could work together finishing it—Ron the pilot, telling his own story, me the writer, polishing it all off.

Ron was no longer here, though, and I had my life to live, too. My husband had dementia, and I felt like I was swimming upstream against my own personal rip tide.

Years passed and, in early 2019, with my husband now safely residing in a local veteran's home, I had some time to think of other things. I still had not fully read the manuscript that I fully intended to read someday, when my sister told me of an inscription in a book she received years before from Ron's lifelong friend from CAT days, Heinie Aderholt (Trest, Air Commando One: Heinie Aderholt and America's Secret Air Wars 2000). She read the inscription to me, and I was impressed. I located the manuscript in those ever-changing piles of books and papers and dusted it off—I was ready to read it all, and what I read now was amazing.

Aircraft design was still in its formative years when he was a boy, and piloting airplanes was still only for the bravest adventurer. Daredevils of the sky like Eddie Rickenbacker, Charles Lindbergh, and Amelia Earhart were all legends in their own time. They had only recently made names for themselves when nine-year-old Ron took his first airplane ride in the small, single-engine Taylorcraft. Soaring above it all was where he truly wanted to be. So, like the legends before him, his fate was sealed.

Throughout his life, his passion was flying. He loved to fly and lived to fly. He spent his life studying flight and teaching countless others to fly. He flew any and every fixed-wing aircraft he could talk himself into, from the single-engine Cub to the twin-engine C-46 Curtiss

Commando to the Douglas A-1 Skyraider. Ron flew STOL aircraft, fighter jets and supersonics, cargo transports and luxury airliners—he was a man for his time.

Ron was a Marine first—one of the last of those who became known as the *China Marines*—as well as a Naval aviator. He went to war as a combat pilot but traveled the world as a commercial pilot. As a combat pilot, he flew several sorties in the Korean War, arriving in Pyeongtaek only one month before the armistice was signed. As a civilian pilot, he flew Rhesus monkeys out of India for the Polio Foundation as well as flying SAR, humanitarian, and CIA covert operations in Indochina with CAT and Air America.

He helped perfect the Helio Courier for Brig. Gen. Harry C. "Heinie" Aderholt, the two remaining lifelong friends, each writing their own separate legends in covert aerial operations. He crashed in numerous airplanes only to walk or hobble away and fly again. He was shot down in his aircraft, evading the enemy for weeks, making his way through the treacherous Laotian jungles.

And so the story goes from a clouded leopard in the jungle to Helios over the Mekong River. I read on and discovered a brother who lived for the adventure of flight. Even before I finished reading, I knew this story, his story, was worth telling. Now adventure was calling me—I would finish the autobiography he had only begun.

—CS Norwood, one of Ron's sisters

Chapter 1.

FIRST FLIGHT

I vividly remember my first airplane ride that sunny summer Sunday. Dad took me and my younger brother into Laurel Fork, Virginia, where a barnstorming pilot was offering airplane rides in one of the nearby fields. The ride lasted maybe five minutes. I think the plane must have been an early Taylorcraft[1] or a J-5 type Cub. As soon as they came out in 1940, I started collecting Wings cards from WINGS Cigarettes *Modern American Aircraft* series[2] and began building wooden and model airplanes. My soon-to-be-realized life as an aviator had begun.

During the winter of 1940 -41, our family packed all our belongings in suitcases and moved away from Virginia,

Taylorcraft Plus D (McIntyre-Collection)

headed for York, Pennsylvania, moving finally into the village of Mt. Royal. The moving trip was quite an event for me. By that time, Mom had five kids in tow, the oldest twelve, I was eleven, and the youngest at the time, a toddler. The highlight was a stopover in Pulaski, Virginia, with a long wait for the train. It was then and there that I saw my first movie. It was Tailspin Tommy.[3] There was a lot of flying in that movie and, even before the ending, I was even more convinced that I should fly someday.

US Navy Fighter Grumman F4F-3 Wildcat

These were WWII years, and I spent much of my time learning to build and building model airplanes, mostly Navy bombers and fighters, as I thought them to be the best. I read all I could find on airplanes and desperately wanted to be a Navy pilot. I read Joe Foss's book[4] about Guadalcanal and decided the Grumman F4F Wildcat[5] must be the best fighter made.

In high school, I spent much of my time studying the

Weems Air Navigation manual[6] and, at age seventeen, I went up to Harrisburg and enlisted in the Marine Corps. Staff Sergeant said I did well on my test, and that I was to report back on 12 November.

And so, on November 12, 1947, I was on my way.

If someone had told me ahead of time what Marine boot camp on Parris Island, South Carolina, would be like in the year 1947, I probably would have deserted right then and there; but no one had.

My older sister and her husband drove me to Harrisburg, Pennsylvania. There I met the friendly staff sergeant again, and he gave me a train ticket to Philadelphia, escorted me to the train and, while we waited at the station, gave me a lecture on how to get through boot camp.

"Be very careful what you say or do," he said. "Obey orders and observe everything that takes place within your sight or hearing; and, above all, try to avoid trouble."

Well, I had all that memorized by the time I arrived in Philadelphia. Along with other recruits and re-enlistees, I underwent a brief physical exam, then boarded a train for Washington DC. We all had to wait until quite late at night for a connection to Parris Island, so we did a tour of the White House and Capitol grounds under the supervision of an ex-staff sergeant who was signing up for another tour. He told me that he was an ex-Marine pilot, and, for a short time, I believed him. It was not until later that I learned to know who pilots were and who was dreaming of being a wheel. I soon realized that he was one of the latter.

I don't remember much about that train ride south to Port Royal, South Carolina, but I sure remember the shock that hit me and the others upon arrival. The staff sergeant had a lot of young Black men gathered around him, and the language that came out of his mouth was vile. The strangest part of this scene, however, was that the more he swore at us the larger the smiles he evoked. He lined us up in three rows and read us the *riot act* out of his Marine Corps manual. By the time he finished, we had all decided that it was the end of our world as we had known it. After that, it was the ferryboat ride to Parris Island and a new life.

Once we disembarked from the ferry, we were bussed to the mess hall and told to eat everything on our tray, and not to dare speak or look up. The next day was no brighter. It started with getting our heads shaved, being issued our uniform, shoes, water bucket, and brush. All this took until about 2:00 p.m. or 1400 hours. Then we sort of marched to our new barracks and became members of 2nd Recruit Training Battalion, Parris Island, South Carolina. I had become Private Sutphin, Serial Number 649840. Even my rifle had a number; I think it was 118727922.

Our DIs (drill instructors) were PFC Jenkins, Corporal Sundin, and Staff Sergeant Broom. Sundin and Broom sure worked the hell out of a lot of recruits in our battalion!

During the first few weeks, we learned close-order drill, rules and regulations, general military procedures, and the Ten General Orders[7] for walking post. Almost every night we had to scrub down the barracks completely, and woe to the recruit caught smoking! The punishment was to put about ten cigarettes in the offender's mouth, light them up, put a bucket over his head, and make him smoke them down short. Bed wetters were the ones who had it the worst, though. The recruit who had the night barracks watch had to wake them every hour and escort them to the head. After a while, I think they all left the class on a medical discharge.

Despite the sudden immersion into a harsh and foreign way of life—almost like falling off a bridge into a dark, frigid body of water—those first few weeks did not seem that hard to me. We were all kept so busy that time just went by without my realizing when and how it went. I had so many new things to learn, all my focus was on adjusting to the system. But what I learned above all else was to go with the flow. Those who didn't or couldn't were moved out. Recruits left the class for various reasons, but I never knew if they were put in other classes, got medical, or were discharged for other reasons. Anyway, that was not my concern at the time. Me, I soon realized that military life wasn't all that bad.

We marched in soft sand, across glades, and through water. It did not matter, we marched. Finally, we transferred to the rifle range, walking there with our packs on. I enjoyed this phase of training and still have an ongoing love of the M1 rifle. It was then that I picked up good habits that have stayed with me to this day. Whenever I take up the trigger slack, hold my breath and squeeze off a round, I think of my shooting instructor at Parris Island. My new-recruit training remains with me always. I think all young men would benefit from a stint on Parris Island.

After completing rifle and ordnance training, we were marched back to the old barracks for various tests and schooling to assess each recruit's aptitudes. In one of the sessions, a recruit asked the instructor if any of us would ever become officers. The instructor said if any of us ever made it through the ranks, Private Sutphin would be the most likely. I was so encouraged by what he said that it changed my whole outlook on the future. Now I decided that just going with the flow was not enough.

At the end of my basic training, I had the chance to enroll in the MCI (Marine Corps Institute). This was a good deal; I could go as far as I wanted. I enrolled in the science curriculum and completed two years of college with MCI.

On 29 January 1948, I completed training at Parris Island and was promoted to PFC (Private First Class) by W. M. Kessler, Lt. Col. USMC. I believe two other recruits were also promoted at the same time. I also heard rumors that we were on the draft for replacements in China. I wanted to see China and the Pacific, so I made up my mind I was going to make it all the way there without being pulled off at Hawaii or Guam. The pull-offs were also part of

Chapter 1. FIRST FLIGHT | 7

the rumor. The pull-off at Guam was to track down some troublesome remaining Japanese soldiers.

On 1 February 1948, the China and Guam draft was sent to Port Royal by ferry, then loaded aboard a troop train headed for the West Coast. Over the five-day trip, we stopped at different places in the country, and I had my first good look at the western states. I especially loved the open country in Colorado and New Mexico.

After disembarking the train, we were transported to Treasure Island Naval Base in San Francisco, where I got my first good look at the Pacific Ocean. We referred to the Marine personnel there as Hollywood Marines, because they were from the Marine recruit battalions in San Diego, California. Although Parris Island and San Diego undoubtedly had the same training methods and thus should have been regarded as equals, we Parris Island graduates didn't seem to think that was the case.

I was put on a light work detail for the Navy Commissary shuffling crates and boxes around. This short-term duty was good for me.

After about ten days, the complete draft, made up of roughly four hundred personnel, departed from Oakland aboard the USS Mann.[8] I soon became seasick and remained sick for the duration of the trip. Troops were berthed at the fantail, which, in addition to the crowding, did not help matters. I was put on a paint-chipping detail but had to be taken off because of my seasickness. That was one trip I did not appreciate, but it did somehow cure me. I never again got seasick on a ship.

The USS Mann disembarked the Marine draft at Honolulu, and we went to Catlin. The weather was warm, and I enjoyed the rain. The light duty there was good, and I got to go on liberty in Pearl Harbor. I made the tour of the USS Arizona and some interesting sites. I loved travel and sure felt as though I was getting my money's worth out of the USMC.

The Curtis C-46 Commando in flight. Photo by USAF)

Some of the Marines were cut out from the draft at Camp Catlin.[9] Their names were posted on the bulletin board, but I was one of the lucky ones—I would be moving on.

Once again aboard the USS Mann, we headed for Wake Island and Guam. I got a good look at World War II wreckage the day we spent at Wake Island. A damaged Japanese tank was still parked near the enlisted mess hall. Even with the effects of wartime still visible, what a beautiful island that was.

While en route to Guam, I had worried I might be pulled off the China draft and left there. Once there, we were trucked to a supply depot to patrol the area for any Japanese troops that had never surrendered, even though the war had ended. The surrender speeches on the loudspeakers did no good. The Japanese were creeping into the Marine depot (even into the Quonset hut area) almost every night and stealing from us. Our pants, shirts, money—you name it, they took it. We knew there were a good number of them in the area, and our job was to catch them if we could. I did manage to see one of them, but he was quick to get away into the jungle. It was Marine policy not to hurt them, just to catch them.

After about a month, I saw my name on the bulletin board for airlift to Tsingtao, China. Added to my elation was excitement about getting to ride in an airplane. Evidently, the Marines flew a regular shuttle between Guam, Iwo Jima, Okinawa, and Tsingtao. They used the Curtiss C-46 Commando transports.[10] I was in awe of this airplane and the pilot who flew it.

We were briefed by the pilots before departure and told about the stops at Iwo Jima and Okinawa, as well as the route of our flight over Southern Japan. We breakfasted at Iwo Jima and saw a lot of Mustang P-51s, as well as transports parked on the airfield there. Cargo parachutes covered the top of the mess hall and made for pretty good decoration. Lunch at Okinawa was a box lunch for all hands, including the navigator and all forty-two Marines. There I got a good look at some Black Widow night fighters,[11] some more Mustangs and four-engine R5D transports.

Northrop P-61 Black Widow night fighter

It rained the entire way from Naha, Okinawa, to Tsingtao. We passed over Southern Japan, but the rain obscured my view from the window. Arrival over Tsingtao was late in the evening of 20 April 1948. The first things I noticed were the countless rice paddies. Even on the hillsides, they managed to have small rice paddies or gardens. The rain had continued all the way from Okinawa, and everything looked very green and very wet. I was thrilled to be in China. I wanted to see the place where people lived on three cents a day. At least, that's what my grade schoolbooks had told me.

About 10:00 p.m. that night, we all reported to the

2nd Battalion Headquarters for assignment to Charlie Company, 3rd Marines.

Chapter 2.

TSINGTAO

Resting on tree-covered hills, its streets and buildings made of stone, Tsingtao[1] was a beautiful city. In fact, I regard it as the loveliest of all Chinese cities. Once a German colony, the German people had certainly left their mark on the city. The streets were paved with small square stones, and they looked like some of the streets of Hamburg, Germany's older sections.

What more could I ask for? The climate was mild, and Tsingtao beer was good. I had always liked to read about the Chinese people, so I made up my mind almost as soon as I arrived to extract the most from my new life and my tour of duty here.

The Marine compound (called by what sounded like *Doshilu* in Chinese) covered about eighty acres in an area of Tsingtao city with many large trees and was mostly surrounded by a stone wall. The Chinese Army had used it before the Marines took it over. It had a large parade field and a two-story, well-designed, and well-built barracks.

Life in Charlie Company was quite relaxed and, though

I had little use for the Platoon Guide (he seemed to be all Marine Corps twenty-four hours a day), I got along well with my squad members.

I was assigned to serve as the BAR man. Some Marines did not like to carry the Browning automatic rifle around. Empty, it weighed twenty-one pounds and seven ounces, but I liked the idea of a lot of firepower. Rumors placed the Chinese Communist Army quite close to Tsingtao, and I got the impression that someday I might be using my BAR.

Training for C-Company meant marching out of the main gate and going to the nearby woods and hills to play war. Usually, this would last all day. We saw many poor or displaced Chinese in those hills gathering twigs, leaves, and scraps of wood for cooking. Most of them were elderly women or very young girls.

One morning, our platoon was reconnoitering a remote gully in the woods when I accidentally stepped on the body of an older Chinese woman. Her body was just lightly covered with leaves. She had probably been there for several weeks. The other Marines told me to not mind, that she was left there because no one wanted to claim her or cared. I did notice that her feet had not been bound as a child,[2] contrary to the foot binding of most of the older women I saw there. This woman had somehow escaped that barbaric practice.

At times we were assigned guard duty both inside and

outside the city: at the Marine airbase and the Navy dock yards, as well as various storage areas and ammo dumps. There were close to one hundred posts covering over thirty miles that the enlisted Marines had to walk in the Tsingtao area. Though I did not like standing guard duty, it did give me the opportunity to see virtually all the area. I learned to guard my post the Marine Corps way, keeping in mind the second general order: "Walk my post in a military manner, keeping always on the alert and observing everything that takes place within sight or hearing." One of my first tours of guard duty was in the dock's supply area. I had about a five-acre area of supplies to guard including vehicles, road equipment and poles, as well as thousands of miscellaneous items. I had the 0800 to noon watch and, of course, started by walking around my post in a military manner. On one occasion, I saw a Chinese man trotting off with one of the large poles. I was amazed he could lift it, much less trot away with it. I shouted the necessary *yamu* (halt or stop) and fired a warning shot. He dropped the pole and ran away. I did not purse.

After that, I decided to walk my guard duty posts in a military manner for only one or two rounds. The rest of the watch, I would then play a game of hide and seek with the Chinese thieves. The result was astounding. The thieves had an organized system for pilfering. They would use children to observe how the sentries acted or walked their post, timing their rounds. They dug crawl spaces under the wire or walls and had hidden lookouts while using all sorts of signals and methods to attract and distract the guards. Only by playing and winning their own games could they be truly outfoxed. I would have to spot their lookouts, pretend to walk my post at right shoulder arms in a true military manner then suddenly run around my post at port arms, all the while keeping my eyes on the lookout for their reactions. If they got frantic, I could almost bet that I had infiltrated their system. Then I could run to wherever they had come in and block their way out. When that happened, I could hear the lookouts yelling and screaming as they realized their pilfering foray had gone from bad to worse. I usually got my thief—almost always a child—and kicked him or her off the post while cursing them in Chinese.

Scuttlebutt is the word for rumor, and Marine scuttlebutt was that if you shot or killed one of the Chinese people, you would receive a General Court Marshal for the sake of the record, then be transferred to another station. I certainly was not about to go that route, but I did come close. During one of my posts at Tsingtao docks, I almost shot a young girl who would not stop at my warning. I chased her from the post area once I assumed the guard, but she insisted on coming back into my guard area. I could see that she had already taken a great deal of government property, and I was already irritated by the number of lookouts around this post. After about an hour of this, I aimed at her. I was so angry that I almost pulled the trigger before I stopped myself. I was much more careful after that and kept my emotions in check.

Martin PBM Mariner water takeoff

Seaplanes had always held a great fascination for me, and the Navy had the big PBM (Patrol Bomber Martin) flying boats (patrol planes),[3] in the harbor along with their tender ships. When I had guard duty on or near the harbor, I could watch their graceful takeoffs and landings on the water. They always took about a mile-and-a-half to get airborne. One time, I was assigned to the docks when a Curtiss Commando transport plane had been salvaged and towed out of the nearby harbor. The pilot, en route from Okinawa, had arrived over the Tsingtao airbase but could not land due to the fog that had moved in. Apparently, after several unsuccessful approaches to the airbase, he elected to make a water landing in the harbor and have the Navy stand by for rescue. He certainly made a fine water ditching because, even after being towed in and lifted onto the docks, there was little damage to the plane. Now I was able to get another good look at the C-46, initiating my personal love affair with this airplane. It was streamlined with a large cockpit area and big engines. Little did I know then that I would be flying it just a few short years hence.

The U.S. Navy Hospital Ship Repose[4] was parked at Tsingtao Harbor for a time, and it was while on guard duty in front of this ship that I met Capt. John Plank of Civil Air Transport (CAT). I asked him about the Curtiss C-46 transport that had ditched in the harbor and inquired what kind of aircraft he was flying. We only talked for about five minutes, and I was grateful that he took the time to even say hello to me, being a lowly sentry on guard duty. I met him twice more while at Tsingtao but did not speak with him again. A few years later, I was to save his life, or at least keep him from certain capture at the *Plaine des Jarres* (Plain of Jars) in Northern Laos.

During the autumn and winter of 1948, I was moved from the compound to the airbase[5] about fifteen miles inland from Tsingtao. I was still a private first class, and my duties were to guard the Marine airbase, ammo dumps, vehicles, compounds, and so forth. But this assignment put me near the airplanes! I watched countless CAT flights arrive and depart during that winter.[6]

On my off-duty time, I went to Operations and asked the enlisted personnel there lots of questions. I also talked to the Chinese Mustang pilots based there. One of the Chinese captains even let me sit in his cockpit while he answered all my questions about his P-51 Mustang. Col. Lansen Scribner was the airbase commander, and he was curious why a PFC was spending so much off time hanging around Operations. He even had the operations officer call me in so he could ask me how I proposed to become a pilot, so my intentions now were no secret. It was at Tsingtao that I met Capt. William "Bill" Gaddie and his copilot. Bill became my good friend. When I told him that someday I too wanted to be a CAT pilot, he just laughed. I reminded him of this some years later, but he had forgotten all about our encounter.

At that time, it took a million Chinese dollars to equal one U.S. dollar. Money there was always a problem. The situation was getting worse as Chiang Kai-Shek's armies were losing[7] to the Communists in all the provinces, especially those around Tsingtao and the northern parts of China. Things were getting so bad that our guard duty shotguns were replaced with M1 rifles.

Sometime during March 1949, I was transferred back to the compound in Tsingtao. All of Charlie Company, 3rd Marines were doing live ammo firing on the rifle range, practicing infantry tactics, and making long marches into the nearby mountains. I especially remember one week that we were driven north of Tsingtao in 6x6 trucks for our maneuvers. From our drop-off point, we marched to a beach and boarded a naval transport ship. These maneuvers lasted about two weeks and climaxed with us hitting the beaches, regular Marine style, from LCVPs (landing craft, vehicle, personnel, or Higgins boats).[8] Admiral Badger, the Commander of Naval Forces, was putting on a demonstration for the Chinese Communists who, by this time, were in the vicinity. When the LCVPs hit the shoreline, we climbed down the sides using net ropes, rendezvoused in a circle, and then drove for the beach simultaneously. I was wet up to my waist when I hit the beach.

We remained in bivouac for a few weeks after the maneuvers and then returned to Tsingtao where I was assigned as a guard to Admiral Badger's headquarters at Edgewater. The admiral, staff and their dependents all lived at headquarters. The Marines called the compound the Edgewater Hotel. It was painted all white and fenced off by huge walls and barbed wire. One guard station walked around the outside of the compound walls, and another patrolled the main house. Inside the house was a large safe room. I usually had the inside guard duty, and I think it was due to a staff request. While on duty, I got to meet Admiral Badger and some of the other staff members.

In April of that year, I was pulled off guard duty and, with about forty other Marines, assigned a special project. We were to go into the interior and bring some important people out of China. We were given several briefings about the Communist and Nationalist troops we might encounter.

Our group departed in early May[9] and arrived in Hong Kong around 3 May 1949, flying in a Nationalist C-46 aircraft. In Hong Kong, we were berthed with the British Navy for a few days before being boated out to the harbor to join the U.S. Navy fleet who were in maneuvers near the Quemoy-Matsu Islands, very close to Mainland China proper. While ashore in Hong Kong, I had ample time to go on liberty, eat some Chinese food and hike up and down the steep hills just behind the main street.

Scout plane catapulted from carrier

After completing the project, a cruiser took us back to Tsingtao around 9 May.[10] I made friends with one of the sailors in the Aviation Department. His ship had an amphibious scout plane on board which could be catapulted off when necessary. He was either the Enlisted Sailor in Charge of Maintenance or Plane Captain. (Enlisted maintenance men were called Plane Captains if they oversaw a particular plane.) I spent a lot of time with him while he was working on or around the scout plane. He had obtained a student license while in port at Pearl Harbor and explained that if I ever had any extended stay there, I could learn to fly as well.

All the Marines in Tsingtao were getting ready to board ships to return to the United States. C-Company, 3rd Marines, was scheduled to go to Camp Pendleton, California.[11] Now that I was reassigned to the unit, I was able to watch an amphibious scout plane take off to go on patrol just inland from Tsingtao. It was rumored that the Communists were about to enter the city itself. After the scout returned, it landed in the sea close by the ship and I watched as it was hoisted on board.

The fleet sailed to Yokohama, Japan, and I managed to get three days liberty there. Making the most of it, I took a train to Tokyo on my first day and went to the main Post Exchange. Personally, I found the Japanese people very different than the Chinese people. At the time, they seemed more industrious. From that short liberty in Yokohama, I formed a very favorable opinion of the Japanese people.

From Yokohama, we traveled to Pearl Harbor. There I spent about five days before departing for Long Beach, California. Our whole Tsingtao group was taken to Camp Joseph H. Pendleton Marine Base at Oceanside, California. I was still with C-Company, 3rd Marines, 1st Marine Division; however, I was now a Corporal. My new rank meant no more walking posts.

Chapter 3.

FLIGHT

I loved the weather at Pendleton—hot, dry days and cool nights. We practiced war every day, usually at company level. On the third day there, I ran into a large rattlesnake. Most of the squad was afraid of it but, since I was familiar with snakes from my youth, I killed it quickly.

I was again enrolled in MCI for my second year of college. I had completed my first-year courses while in China through correspondence school.

We were authorized to wear civilian clothes while we had liberty, which was from Friday evening to Sunday midnight. I wasted no time in buying some new duds and heading to the nearest civilian airport. In August 1949, I met the owner of the Oceanside airport, Mr. Neil. He had two J-3 Cubs and one Fairchild PT-23 available for student training. I met Staff Sgt. Brown there, and he told me that it was a good place to learn. He schooled me on the ins and outs of Oceanside Airport and about people there.

It took me some time to begin flight training, as I wasn't always able to get weekend liberty, plus, I had to complete ground school first. Finally, though, my first flying lesson was scheduled for 10 October with Mr. Atkinson, although he really did not seem very happy about taking me up.

He did not explain anything; he just took me up in a J-3 Cub (N3613K) and gave me an aerial tour of Oceanside. He did introduce me to turns and both straight and level flight but, once we landed, he just got out of the aircraft and headed home. At the time, I thought it was me—that I hadn't done so well in my first lesson.

I was scheduled for my second flight the very next day, which was a Sunday. This time, I learned to make climbs and glides and practiced level flight and turns again. Still, after we landed, Mr. Atkinson had nothing to say. I decided it was either due to his nature or a lack of enthusiasm for his job. Whatever the reason, a new instructor was at the airport for my third flight. His name was George Brusch, a former U.S. Government employee assigned to train Army Air Force Cadets during WWII. He had a lot of instructor hours under his belt and spent quite some time just talking before we took off. Furthermore, once we were airborne, he talked to me most of the time: reviewing details, critiquing my turns and glides, as well as other basic maneuvers. Then, after landing, he continued by debriefing the flight. I was so elated and pleased with George that I went to the flight school's owner and asked if George could be assigned as my permanent instructor.

George had rented a building at the Oceanside airport and was working on, and trying to get a patent for, a bomb sight. When not teaching, he was there in his shop. I met his wife and children at this building, and George and I spent many off-time hours together there.

On my seventh flight, I got airsick while learning to do spins. I feared that I might not be able to be a pilot after all and even considered discontinuing my lessons. But I was smart enough not to tell George that I had been airsick. To my good fortune, I did not experience any airsickness at the next spin training session. That was a relief because I was so eager to solo.

After seven hours of dual training, George let me solo the Piper Cub. I recognized my takeoffs and landings were quite expert for a novice and, on that day, 22 October 1949, I decided I was going to become a commercial pilot.

I went to the Pan American Navigation Service located on Ventura Blvd. in San Fernando Valley, Los Angeles and purchased some of their flying manuals. Like some people carried Bibles, I carried commercial pilot and navigator manuals. I studied them religiously, day-in and day-out for the next year.

In November 1949, I was recommended for Aviation Training School, NAS Pensacola and was detached from my company to attend schooling at Camp Pendleton. So, the rest of my time at Camp Pendleton was spent attending school and flying on the weekends.

George gave me a checkout in the Fairchild PT-23[1] and, from then on, I logged most of my flights in that. It had a radial engine, 220 horsepower and open cockpits. I loved this plane. I could do loops, rolls, and spins, and it responded very well to control.

Fairchild PT-23 (Golden Wings Museum)

During October, November, and December 1949, I made a lot of cross-country flights around Southern California, though I made it a point to visit as many airports as possible, mostly going to Del Mar and San Marcos Valley. On New Year's Day 1950, I was going to go to Bellflower with Corporal Bickham in the back seat. It was a sunny day but a little chilly, generally perfect weather for Southern California. We taxied out of Oceanside for a southern takeoff and were airborne only about thirty seconds when my engine started missing. I continued to climb slowly until I was at about 1,000 feet. By this time, though, the engine was missing so badly that I knew I could hardly count on anything except a forced landing. I turned ninety degrees to the left and was going to attempt a landing on a nearby hilltop but, since I still had partial power, I continued my turn and headed back towards Oceanside. Just about half a mile from the runway, my engine completely quit. I crash landed about a quarter of a mile from the south end of the runway. The aircraft had only minor damage, but I broke my nose on impact and spent the remainder of New Year's Day (plus five additional days) in the Naval Hospital at Pendleton. Bickham wasn't injured at all and told me later that it was a good holiday for him.

In just a few days, the aircraft was repaired, and I was flying it again. The other two pilots at Oceanside later told me that they had had power troubles with this plane. Oceanside did change the engine before it went up again.

I went to Long Beach around the middle of January and bought my own Piper Cub, number NC42992. I needed 200 hours to get a commercial license and by 15 April, I had logged 150 hours. On that date, I transferred to Marine Corps School at Quantico, Virginia. I decided to fly NC42992 cross country to get there. En route, I encountered a heavy fog and was forced to land on a ranch about thirty miles west of Lordsburg, New Mexico, to wait for it to dissipate. I liked the ranch owner so much that I stayed there for two days helping him locate some cattle with my Cub before continuing my trip.

I went through Pine Bluff, Arkansas, and into Island Airport in Knoxville, Tennessee. I had planned to land at Laurel Fork, Virginia to see my Grandpa Jackson (my mother's dad), landing at the very airport where I took my first airplane ride. The field seemed much smaller than I remembered it, and it turned out not to be an airport after all, just a field, but I figured if the barnstorming pilots could make those landings, so could I. My Uncle Forrest met me there, and we spent a few nights visiting together.

While at Quantico, I had liberty every weekend with an occasional three-day pass, so I was able to fly my Cub to visit all the surrounding Civil War battlefields. I loved Civil War history, and I was building up my flight time fast and had passed all the written exams for my commercial pilot's license. In September 1950, I took my flight check from the CAA (Civil Aeronautics Authority)[2] in Washington DC and became a Licensed Commercial Pilot.

Also, about this time, I was promoted to the rank of sergeant and was transferred to the Fleet Marine Force.[3] War had started in Korea and, evidently, Uncle Sam needed all the Marines he could get his hands on. I was sent as a replacement.

I was laying phone lines to the front one night when I was almost captured by some North Korean soldiers. By almost, I mean that a knife cut across my left arm. I escaped capture but got cut off from my communications unit. My feet froze that night while sleeping out in the open with neither sleeping bag nor any survival equipment. The best I can say is that I had a close call. With the frostbite in my feet, as well as a few other ailments, I ended up in the U.S. Naval Hospital in Camp Lejeune, North Carolina. I didn't think it was so bad at the time (I still have no feeling in some of my toes), although I had been accepted to go to Naval Cadets on 23 May 1951, so I was anxious to be discharged from the hospital and depart.

I had time to kill after discharge, so I took leave and went to American Flyers in Fort Worth, Texas,[4] to complete my multi-engine and flight instructor's licenses. This was probably the number one civil aviation school in America at that time. It was founded in 1939 and run by Reed Pigman. I took so many courses there (both then and later), that I got to know Reed well. Besides my Instructor's, Multi-Engine, Single- and Multi-Engine Airline Transport ratings, I also took my DC-3 rating there from Reed, himself. We were airborne during a thunderstorm, but he maneuvered it so that I not only passed, but I also made a flight with him the next day as his copilot.

I returned to Camp Lejeune that July 1951. I picked up my orders there and headed to Pensacola, Florida, for Naval Aviation Cadet flight training.

Chapter 4.
NAVAL CADETS

Naval Cadet Ronald J. Sutphin
(Family Photo)

On the afternoon of 12 July 1951, I departed Camp Lejeune along with Corporal Martin who was going to Pensacola as well. It was about 5:00 p.m. when we left Jacksonville on the train. We arrived in Pensacola the next night.

Pensacola weather and climate were ideal for me. Of all the places I have been in the world, I like the Pensacola climate and area best. I sometimes regret that I could not have spent my entire life there.

I was assigned to NAAS Chevalier Field, Mainside, the Marine barracks at the main base for the first few days. The area consisted of several outlying auxiliary air stations which provided various training phases for the Naval Aviation Cadets. Besides Chevalier Field, Mainside consisted of a seaplane harbor, a deep port for ships and aircraft carriers, and a main maintenance base. The auxiliary stations were NAAS (Naval Auxiliary Air Station) Whiting Field North and South, Corry Field, Saufley Field, Barin, Bronson, and Bagdad. There were a few other outlying fields but, except for things like practice flights, they were not used very much.

While waiting for my discharge, I bought a Harley-Davidson 70 motorcycle in Pensacola. It was a big motorcycle and responded well. I kept it all through Cadets. It was a pleasure to ride it around Pensacola.

I became a Naval Cadet on 17 July 1951 and moved a short distance away to the cadet barracks. My new roommates were Noble Stark, Warren Comer, Bob Lokker, and Tom Spurr. We were assigned and uniformed to Class

16 of '51. I maintained contact with Warren Comer long past the Korean War, Tom Spurr and Bob Lokker until the end of the conflict, and Noble Stark only until we left Pensacola. He was killed in a Hellcat upon takeoff while in the Caribbean.

No females were in the Naval Cadets at that time. There were a couple of Black cadets, but none in Class 16. There were about sixty-five cadets in Class 16. We were initially taught how to march and handle swords for parade purposes. We were instructed in minutia about the demerit system and given general indoctrination; afterward, we commenced ground school.

Boeing Stearman Model 75 (Stearman Kaydet)

We sometimes had five or six days of duty, but we always had Sundays free for liberty. During our indoctrination phase, I went to Pensacola Municipal Airport and asked for a part-time job as a flight instructor. The two owners were quite receptive to the idea and the full-time instructor, Mr. Sackett, graciously gave me a checkout in their Stearman PT-17, a biplane of WWII vintage.¹ I fell in love with it and continued to fly it during all my stays at Pensacola. I enjoyed its responsiveness to flight and had many students wishing to fly it. Mr. Sackett also checked

Cessna AT-17/UC-78 Bobcat Crane Model T-50

me out to instruct and fly in their Cessna T-50 twin-engine trainer, better known as the Bamboo Bomber.²

After indoctrination, ground school began in earnest. Initially, I feared I would not be able to keep up with the class, at least in terms of grades. All the cadets had at least two years of college and most had a degree of some kind.

Two of my favorite courses were Naval Orientation and Navigation. After a couple of weeks, I found myself at the head of the class in these two courses! That should not have surprised me, though. In addition to the instructor's ability to hold my attention, I had been studying navigation and the naval aspects of the Civil War on my own for a very long time. The highest grade available was 4.0, and I considered myself lucky to have a 3.8 GPA.

Each Sunday morning, I presented myself to Chevalier operations and asked for a ride in the SNJ trainer. Once personnel learned I was a commercial pilot, they arranged for me to take a flight with one of the Naval pilots. I usually got to fly from the back seat. Everyone was curious why a Naval Cadet in Preflight was out bumming rides. I just explained that I wanted to know all about the SNJ and how it responded to flight.

Sometime during this phase of training, we started PT (physical training) and swimming courses. Swimming and ditching lectures were my favorite parts of PT. All the Naval pilots had to be qualified swimmers. At the end of the course, we were given a test and awarded a Triple A card if we qualified. Part of the test was to demonstrate our ability to escape from an airplane—upside down, underwater—with shoulder harness, parachute, and all our flying equipment on. The Dilbert Dunker, a dummy aircraft seated on a track, was launched from above the water. It impacted the water at a high speed, turned over and sank. Each cadet had to demonstrate that he was able to successfully escape.

Once we completed the Dilbert Dunker test, our PT classes focused on running and gym training.

Stark and Comer both had motorcycles as well, and we toured Pensacola on Saturday nights. The local Harley shop introduced us to the local Harley-Davidson gang of Pensacola which included civilians and some sailors; about sixteen guys in all. For many years, the San Carlos Hotel[3] served as headquarters for the gang. One Saturday evening, I was to meet Stark and Comer there with the cycles. As I was waiting on my cycle by the traffic circle, I saw them coming at high speed. Evidently, Comer's brakes had failed. He shot through the red light at the intersection and, to avoid collision, went under a moving semitruck, coming out the other side with his cadet uniform in shreds. The whole thing was pretty exciting, and, except for some scratches, Warren was okay. It was a really close call—he always did have a knack for getting in and out of trouble.

I already had my room reserved, as we usually spent Saturday nights at the San Carlos. At that time and probably during WWII, as well, the San Carlos was a real Saturday-night hangout for a lot of cadets. An old friend of mine from Civil Air Transport told me he got washed out of cadets for urinating on the sidewalk by the San Carlos.

Sometimes we went to the ACRAC, a recreation building at Mainside. On weekend nights a busload of young ladies would site-visit the center to dance and meet cadets and just have a good time in general. It was at the ACRAC that I first met Cadet Pete Petersen,[4] probably the first Black Aviation Cadet, and the first Marine Corps pilot. Pete served in MAG-12 in Korea the same dates as I did but in another squadron.

Chapter 4. NAVAL CADETS

Retired Lt. Gen. Frank E. Petersen Jr., the 1st African American Marine Corps aviator, and the 1st African American Marine Corps general, served during the Korean War in 1953 and Vietnam in 1968. He flew more than 350 combat missions. (U.S. Marine Corps File Photo)

About midway through preflight training, I was awarded the rank of Battalion Cadet Adjutant (the second highest cadet officer rank) and given a 3-Bar to go on my cadet uniform. The Battalion Commander was a cadet from New York. He proved to be a nice guy and an able commander but later left the cadet program when it came time to fly. In fact, most of the cadets handled ground training well but, when the flying started, it was a different story. I doubt if even forty percent successfully completed that final phase. A lot of them went into the enlisted ranks; some went on to become naval officers without wings. Perhaps the Navy would have been better off to have each cadet fly in a Piper Cub a couple of hours before even going to Pensacola for cadet training.

After preflight training at Mainside, we were shipped

either to North or South Whiting Field, all part of one naval air station about fifty miles from Pensacola. Whiting was isolated and in good location for cadet flight training. Here we started ground school all over again and had quite a few different courses to complete before flight training: Morse Code, Blinker, Atomic Energy, Aircraft Recognition, etc. Afterwards, we started flying dummy SNJ-type aircraft.

The SNJ trainer[5] was manufactured by North American Aircraft for the Navy and was, in my opinion, a very good aircraft. It responded well to all phases of our training, including gunnery and aircraft carrier flights.

I was assigned to North Whiting Field, and my instructor, Lieutenant McClaugherty, knew his craft. On our first flight, he wasted no time asking me about my flight experience. As soon as I took the controls, he started to quiz me. After I told him of my experience and flight time, he asked if I had flown the SNJ before. Of course, I told him that the naval pilots at Mainside had let me take off and land it from the rear cockpit. From then on, I had to work. He immediately introduced me to advanced maneuvers—practicing aerobatics, crosswind precision landings, things like that. I was no longer taking things easy. I had to work just as hard as if I had never logged any flying time at all.

Whiting flying had stages, A, B, and C. A-Stage was primary flying, in which the cadet was allowed flights up to A-20 before solo flight. If a cadet did not make it through the first nineteen flights, he was washed out—

terminated—and moved out of naval flight training. B-Stage was precision flying and C was acrobatic training. If a cadet was going to wash out, it usually happened at Whiting. About a third of the class washed out, departing for other fields of venture.

Cadets Stark, Comer, Spurr, and Lokker all made it through Whiting with me and, except for Comer, completely through Naval Cadets. Noble Stark had a lot of trouble at Whiting, and they thought he was not going to make it, but the base commander evidently thought a lot of him and gave him extra flights. I also helped him by flying him in the PT-17 Stearman, figuring it would help him get over his main problem, motion sickness. We did aerobatics constantly, until, after three weekends and twenty-four hours, he was pronounced by both of us as cured.

Stark got more than just training and aerobatics, however. He also got a free parachute jump. He was not killed, but it scared both of us almost to death. I had turned the Stearman upside down, cut the engine off and started an inverted glide. The PT-17 has open cockpits, and, for some reason, Stark's shoulder harness and safety belt came loose. Out he went, into a farmer's field about ten miles north of the airport!

I watched him float down in his parachute, circled to make sure he was okay, marked the location, flew back to the airport, took off on my motorcycle, and picked him up. The jump went okay for him, and that was certainly lucky for me, as well. We both would probably have been kicked out of Cadets if the Navy had learned about our extracurricular flying. Although this cured Stark of his motion sickness, shortly after getting his wings, he died in his Hellcat. His Grumman F6F went out of control on takeoff, killing a good man who should never have passed Whiting Field.

I got this idea that I could get a job as copilot with a commercial airline and do better as a civilian. It was my good instructor at Whiting, Lieutenant McClaugherty, who talked me out of quitting Naval Cadets. He gave me a good pep talk when I needed it, and I am ever grateful to him for that. I did not realize then just how important it would be in my life to have that Naval Aviation background.

McClaugherty said he would immediately recommend me for a C-check. If I passed, I could graduate early from Whiting and move ahead of my class. I took the C-flight check ride with the commander of North Whiting, and I was able to transfer to the next stage of cadet training—D-Stage (instrument flying) at Naval Auxiliary Air Station Corry Field,[6] not far from Mainside and Pensacola.

When I arrived at Corry Field, one of the first cadets I met was Myron Schlung, a cadet officer with two bars. He was an ex-Marine sergeant originally from Iowa. I bunked with him at Corry and met him again later in my career, long after departing Corry Field.

We had to go through ground training (again!), as well

as instrument training. The simulator was used for blind flying. My instructor was a female pilot who had served in WWII and was now in the WASP (Women Airforce Service Pilots),[7] teaching simulated flight. I got to know her well and enjoyed that part of the course.

I graduated from Instrument Flying on 15 April 1952 and was transferred to NAAS Saufley Field. Saufley was close to Corry, and here we were taught formation, night flying and gunnery. Cadet life was not difficult for me, so I spent most of my time off flying as an instructor at Pensacola Municipal Airport, usually going on long cross-country flights with one of the other cadets.

Aeronca Model 7 Champion

On 30 May, another cadet and I went to Norfolk, Virginia, in an Aeronca[8] aircraft. It was a three-day weekend, so we had ample time. We stopped for the night in Fayetteville, North Carolina, before continuing to Norfolk to visit his parents. His older brother was a B-17 Flying Fortress pilot and had been shot down and killed over Germany during WWII. His parents still had all the pictures of their son and his crew on display throughout their home. They wanted this younger son to quit the cadets and stop flying, but he liked it too much to quit. He went on to become a Naval pilot despite their fears and pleas.

After learning to fly formation flights and getting the feel for relative motion, I was even more enthused about aviation. The Flight Leader would take off first, go to an IP (initial point) and start turning around this point in a circle. The other cadets were to approach and join on his wing. This was called a rendezvous.

Night flying at Saufley was routine for me as I had done it plenty of times before becoming a cadet. Gunnery was next in line, and it was done by shooting at a sleeve towed behind another aircraft. Usually, about eight SNJs in a formation would get ahead and above the tow banner and make a high-side dive on it. Each aircraft had a different-colored dye on its ammunition so we could tell how many hits each aircraft scored on the sleeve.

Assigned as leader of one of these flights, I took off first, went to my assigned altitude and IP and started my circle. It was then, while circling, that I came close to terminating my cadet career, just missing a midair collision. Another SNJ from another command missed my aircraft by only a few feet. He merely continued his course, straight and level. Because I was in a constant left turn, his approach had been blanked out. I did not see him until he was on me, and I think he was never aware that he had even come close to another aircraft. In my career, I've had three or four close calls involving midair collisions, but this was, by far, the closest and most dangerous of all. In naval terms, I would say that I almost *bought the farm*.

I do not remember what my gunnery score was, but I believe it was about average. I thought it was very exciting to shoot from a moving platform watching my tracer bullets find their target.

After completing the syllabus at Saufley, we cadets were transferred back to the Naval Auxiliary Air Station at Corry. The main goal here was to complete FCLP (field carrier landing practice). This flight training was performed at an outlying field close to Whiting Field. We would fly there each morning and spend the whole day in training and practice. First, we had to learn about the aircraft carriers. The main man here, as far as we were concerned, was the LSO (Landing Signal Officer), who was a naval aviator with a lot of carrier experience, special training, and the ability to roundly curse out juniors and Naval Cadets.

The LSO easily knew more about how the cadet was flying than the cadet knew himself. FCLP was to prepare the Naval Cadet for the real test: to land and takeoff on the aircraft carrier. A carrier deck was marked off at Bagdad for this purpose. The LSO gave the pilots about fifteen main signals, and it behooved one to respond to every one of his signals. In fact, failure to respond to a wave off or a cut, if given, were court martial offenses. The wave off was a no-land signal; the cut meant to cut your throttle and land—regardless.

After completing this landing practice at Bagdad, we went aboard the USS Cabot aircraft carrier. I first went aboard on 1 July 1952.

My friend, Draper, had a car during FCLP training, and we went to Mobile, Alabama for the weekend. We met two local girls at the USO Friday-night dance, and we spent the weekend running around town with them. I even considered getting married! I had second thoughts once the drinks wore off, though. It was against regulations for a cadet to be married, anyway. I did write to her a few times, but lost track of her after getting transferred to Advanced Training.

In August, I completed all work required in basic training and traded in my motorcycle for a car. I headed for Corpus Christi, Texas, via Galveston so I could spend a few of my extra days off checking out the notorious red-light district there. Other cadets who had come back after completing their training at NAS Corpus Christi had all recommended Galveston for R&R (rest and recreation), and they did not steer me wrong. I spent my time there with a girl who told me she was working her way through college.

Corpus Christi is where the warm winds blow—a beautiful city with ideal climate. My only regret about being there was that my stay was temporary. Corpus Christi

Naval Air Station was the main base with many outlying auxiliary naval air stations surrounding it. Cabaniss and Kingsville were the main auxiliary stations. At Mainside, Corpus Christi, the Navy conducted Advanced Training in the four-engine PB4Y-2, nicknamed the PB4Y Square.[9] It was a patrol bomber used by the U.S. Navy. There was also a seaplane harbor, and PBM flying boats were used there, as well.

A U.S. Navy Consolidated PB4Y-2S Privateer (BuNo 66304) of Patrol Squadron VP-23, circa 1949-1953. This aircraft is today on display at the National Museum of Naval Aviation, Pensacola, Florida (USA)

When I arrived at Corpus Christi, I asked for and was assigned to Multi-Engine Training. The Naval Cadet and Wave barracks were located on the far side of the base, next to Corpus Christi Bay. I loved the warm winds and being right on the Gulf of Mexico. I spent many evenings sitting alone on the empty wharfs, enjoying the sound of the water and the feel of the warm offshore breezes. It was here that I met one of the Waves.[10] We remained friends throughout the time I was in training.

Multi-engine training consisted of a long ground school and refresher courses in both dead reckoning and celestial navigation.

Brownsville, Texas, on the Mexican border, was also a hangout for a lot of naval personnel, and I headed there some weekends. I also went to Cuddihy Field (a private airport) and joined the local Civil Air Patrol as they had a squadron there, a couple of small Cub-type aircraft, and a Stearman biplane—the same type that I had been flying around Pensacola.

I had another one of my close-calls-in-life while at Mainside, Corpus Christi. Curfew for cadets was 2200 hours (10:00 p.m.) each night. One night, around the end of July, I didn't make it back to the base in time, so I decided to park my car and swim the bay to get around the main gate. It looked easy to do, so I put my wallet in my hat and tied my hat on with my necktie. My plan was to swim around to the left of the main gate and let the tide carry me all the way out to the cadet barracks. The water seemed warm and calm, and it was working well enough—at first. It wasn't until daybreak, though, that I arrived at my objective, the barracks. Not only was I deceived about the distance, but I also did not figure on the seawall. Covered in barnacles, it was difficult to climb. By the time I got to my barracks, I was covered with numerous cuts and bruises, had torn my uniform, and was totally exhausted.

Some of the Waves were up and about, staring at me as I passed by. I'm sure I looked a mess. I made it to my room without being stopped, although the real danger I had escaped was from the tide and either spending all night in the bay or even drowning.

I managed to clean myself up and make it to formation at 0830, and I thought I had it made until I fell asleep in my first class of the day. The instructor, a Navy Petty Officer, ignored me, and my classmates did not wake me. The class was on the PB4Y2 hydraulic system. A few days later, I was notified that I was to see the admiral. I was scared at first but, after thinking it over, decided there was no way he would have known about my swim.

I was told that, since I was a Marine, I was slated to go to Cabaniss Field to fly the F6F Hellcat.[11] At that time, the Marines needed replacements for Korea, and it was common to switch assignments to meet the Marine Corps demand.

Cabaniss was only a few miles from Corpus Christi and Mainside. I liked the base and was eager to fly the F6F. It was undoubtedly one of the Navy's best planes ever and proved a pleasure to fly. It was very rugged in construction, with adequate power for its time and purpose. Built by Grumman Aircraft, it was designed for shipboard handling and shooting down Japanese planes in World War II.

There were eight students in the class, and the Marine instructor was Captain Law. On my first flight in the F6F Hellcat, I was slow in getting my canopy closed after takeoff, making me slow to rendezvous with the others. This put me on Captain Law's bad side, and there I was to remain for the rest of my stay at Cabaniss Field. I sensed that he would give me bad marks if given the chance, so I was extremely careful around him. Flying was too important to me to risk getting into any trouble.

Despite my efforts to toe the line, however, I did get extremely drunk one weekend with my Waves friend. We had gone to Padre Island and started drinking on the beach that Saturday night. One of the other cadets drove us back to the base the next morning. We had plenty of time to sleep it off but, to this day, I don't know why I got so drunk. I couldn't even walk. It certainly was not a good idea for a Naval Cadet to be drinking and worse yet to get caught. Drinking has never been a big thing for me, and, after that, I spent my weekends at the civil airport with CAP friends.

We received instrument training at Cabaniss, then dogfighting, over-water/cross-country/night flights, and gunnery over the Gulf of Mexico. I was assigned to dogfight with Captain Law. I was eager to do it, sure that I could beat him. The idea was to fly parallel, at the same altitude and, at a prearranged signal, start a scissor pattern with my opponent. If I managed to get on his tail, I would be declared the winner. I lost. I really underestimated the man. I was overeager; he made no mistakes.

So eager was I to get him that I let my F6F stall in one of my steep turns. It wasn't a violent stall, just enough to give him an edge. I was amazed that he did not downgrade me after we landed. I checked my grades for the flight, and they were all average. Perhaps he did not dislike me as much as I originally thought. He knew I wanted to be a multi-engine Navy pilot now and not a Marine pilot. Looking back on it, he had a right to be less than overjoyed with one of his wild cadets.

Later, he did give me three below-average marks for night navigation flight. He complained that I was not flying close enough to him. On the next night after the bad marks, we had a different instructor, and I got all above averages from him. I complained to the naval commander about the disparity, and he told me not to worry, that Law would not be likely to give me any further hard time, and he didn't.

Five of the students in my class were already officers, not cadets. They were out of Annapolis or from the regular Navy and just undergoing flight training in the same program as the cadets. We finished training at Cabaniss and got our orders to return to Pensacola for Carrier Training and Qualifications in the F6F.

Three of us—two Navy ensigns from my class and one cadet—started out for Pensacola via Galveston, of course. We spent three full days in Galveston and had a good time.

Grumman F6F-5N Hellcat night fighter assigned to NAS Jacksonville, Florida in 1944/45

I tried to find my friend from before, but she was gone. I figured she went elsewhere for another job or was sitting in a college classroom somewhere.

When we arrived in Pensacola, we were based at Barin Field. We could do our FCLP at Bronson, another NAAS (Naval Auxiliary Air Station) not far from Barin. It was 1 December 1952 when I began FCLP training and, though winters were very mild, I did not exchange my car for another cycle. Even in Pensacola, it does get chilly on a Harley 70.

In mid-December, we went aboard the USS Monterey[12] for CQ (carrier qualifications). I had no troubles on the carrier, having enjoyed it while in the SNJ, but it was even more of a thrill in the Hellcat Fighter.

Even so, my first two attempts to land were waved off because I was blinded by the sun. I never could stand to fly with sunglasses on. The LSO did not seem to mind and didn't curse me out. He was a friendly LSO.

We all knew that the Navy washed a lot of cadets out of their program on Advanced CQ. A couple of mistakes in Advanced CQ, and you could either lose your life or get thrown out by the seat of your new uniform. We were all really alert during this last phase of training.

I received my orders on 10 November 1952. Addressed to Second Lt. Ronald J. Sutphin 058999 (NAVC), from Commandant of the Marine Corps. My orders read:

> When directed by the Chief, Navy Air Basic Training, Naval Air Station, Pensacola, Florida, you will stand detached from your present station and you will proceed to Marine Barracks, NAS, Corpus Christi, Texas, and report to the Commanding Officer for temporary duty in a flying status involving operational or training flights in connection with the U.S. Naval School, All Weather Flight. Upon completion of this duty involving flying, you will further proceed to the Marine Corps Air Station, Santa Ana, California, and report to the Commanding General, Aircraft Fleet Marine Force Pacific for Active Duty. You are authorized to delay ten days in reporting to the Commanding General.

From my previous talk with the admiral in Corpus Christi, I knew this meant air combat in Korea. It looked like I would not be flying multi-engines after all. Taking me further and further from my dream of becoming qualified for commercial flying. There was nothing to look forward to now, except Korea. I wasn't scared; I was disheartened. That airline job seemed extremely far off, somewhere in the distant future—if there was to be one.

After docking aboard the USS Monterey, we spent the next few days at Mainside, Pensacola, getting our U.S. Navy wings pinned on. I was happy to be the third of Class 16—third among all those who made it all the way through the Naval Cadet training program!

I got in my car and drove back to Corpus Christi for All Weather, not stopping in Galveston this time. Now I was a Marine officer, and a high-class Second Lieutenant. (Amen!)

I was almost arrested en route for reckless driving, though. I was so tired that the police officers behind me thought I might be drunk. They told me not to drive any farther until I had some sleep but, as soon as they were

Beech SNB-5 Navigator Model 18

out of sight, I drove on. It was not a very smart thing to do now that I reflect on it.

During All Weather Flight training at Corpus Christi, I flew the SNB-5, better known outside the Navy as the Twin.[13] Then on 27 January 1953, I finished All Weather Flight and was on my way to Santa Ana, California, prior to joining the Fleet Marine Force Pacific in Korea.

I spent some time in Port Isabella, Texas where I sold my old Packard automobile and then took a ride on a military plane to El Toro Marine Corps Air Station. I reported to Marine Attack Training Squadron 10, Fleet Marine Force (VMAT-10). At VMAT-10, I would be flying the Corsair[14] as well as the Douglas AD.[15] Incoming World War II reserves

Navy Douglas AD-4 Skyraider taking off from USS Princeton during Korean War

reporting for active duty would be checked out at the training base to fly both aircraft as they were both in use in Korea. A few second lieutenants like me were mixed in with them as well as ex-cadets who had skipped carrier duty at Corpus Christi due to the Marine Corps shortage of replacement flight officers for the Fleet Marine Force.

I made one lifelong friend while at VMA-10—Bob "Hoirt" Horst. Hoirt was a World War II Marine pilot who served on Okinawa flying Corsairs. We both went to Korea but were not in the same squadron. He was in VMA-212 in Korea, along with Pete Petersen.

Most of the trainees at El Toro were captains or first lieutenants. I lived in the BOQ (Bachelor Officers Quarters) for a while at El Toro. I also spent a few weeks with Tom Spurr, who had started out in Class 16 NAVCADs with me. I soon got my own apartment by the ocean in Laguna Beach. I really liked having access to the beach.

My roommate and former cadet friend, Second Lieutenant Schlung was killed in his Douglas AD on one of his training flights while at El Toro.

One of our instructors was Capt. "Cowboy" Reese, a Korea War veteran who had the job of teaching us how to bomb, strafe, drop napalm, and shoot rockets from the AD and Corsairs. He was also killed while I was in training at El Toro.

I was leading a flight of Corsairs one morning while at El Toro when we encountered a squadron of P-51 Mustangs from a nearby Air Force airbase. I saw a chance to find out which plane and which service was the best in a mock dogfight. I couldn't resist the temptation, so we jumped them. We were at about 12,000 feet; it would be a low-altitude hassle. As in all mock dogfights, you could hardly tell who won. I thought the aircraft were well matched at low altitudes. The Mustangs were good and so were their pilots.

Vought F4U-4 Corsair (Metzler 2012)

Chapter 5.

KOREA

K-6 Airbase, Pyeongtaek, South Korea 1952-53 - Long before it was called Camp Humphreys or later, U.S. Army Garrison Humphreys, K-6 airfield south of Seoul, Korea was home to U.S. Marine Air Group 12 during the Korean War. [Photo] courtesy of J.R. Boyer, a Marine who served at K-6 during the war.
(Color image to grayscale)
(U.S. Army, USAG Humphreys; Boyer, J. R. 2019)

After completing training at VMAT-10, I left the U.S. on 12 June 1953. We were flown to the Marine Corps Air Station at Itami, Japan, close to Osaka where the Marines from Korea usually spent their week of R&R. At Itami, I tried to have my orders changed to get in a transport squadron flying R4Ds. R4D was a two-engine Douglas DC-3 that was in wide use with the airlines at that time. I had checked out in it while based at El Toro, having met Master Sergeant Lurie upon my arrival there and being lucky enough to have him check me out and fly with me on weekends. I thought that if I became an R4D pilot, I would have an easier time getting on with the airlines after the war.

I wasn't so lucky this time, however. After three days at Itami, I was shipped off to Pyeongtaek, Korea. Marine Air Group 12, Pyeongtaek Airbase was known as K-6 Korea. The airbase was originally a Japanese military base (known as *Hetaku* in Japanese) and had extensive tunneling underneath its runway. Later, the base was condemned for this reason. The town of Pyeongtaek was near the airbase and had a railroad depot. Outside the premises of K-6, there were various Army units, including the tents for their personnel.

Upon arrival at K-6, on 17 June, I was assigned to VMA-121 (Marine Attack Squadron 121).[1] At the time, I did not hold the idea of being an attack pilot in very high esteem. I wanted to fly transport planes! I did realize, however, that second lieutenants don't always have their own way.

VMA-121 was a squadron of fellows who certainly did like their whiskey, so much so, that I have never since been with a group that could out-drink VMA-121. For initiation into the squadron, we had to chug-a-lug a large mug full of mixed whiskey. This wasn't hard duty for me, only because I had prearranged with 2nd Lt. Tom Spurr (the official drink mixer) to make mine about three-fourths water.

Douglas AD aircraft with wings folded. Photo taken at K-6 (No. 15 sits to the side of the folded-wing AD, with tailfin letters AK showing.) Photo was taken by J.R. Boyer (c. 1950-53), K-6 Marine. (Color photo to grayscale)/ (Boyer, J.R.; USAG-Humpherys 2009)

We were billeted in Quonset huts and had to build our own beds out of wood and inner tubes. Spurr, who had arrived in Korea before me, clued me in on the local area and procedures. It was not long after, on 30 June 1953, I was on my first and most memorable combat mission in Korea. Led by Flight Leader Captain Steed, eight aircraft flew to our target: a railroad marshaling yard in

North Korea[2] and the village nearby. Five of the Douglas Skyraiders each carried eight 250-pound bombs and three 1000-pound bombs. Three aircraft, including mine, were loaded with three 1000-pound bombs, but with only four 250-pounders each.

In the early morning briefing, intelligence informed us that there were a large number of troops billeted in the village and troop compound which was formerly a schoolhouse. Two train engines and a few cars were at the station. The aerial photo showed the target area very clearly. The troop compound was to be my specific target. I was to dive from 10,000 feet, skim across the ground a few hundred yards and wipe out the compound with bombs and cannons.

Mission No. 01 and my mission, No. 02, had the same time off, 0710. While on takeoff, the aircraft in front of me from Mission No. 01 jettisoned all its bombs (3x1000-GPs and 8x250-GPs) on the runway on my left side. We were using staggered takeoff at about ten-second intervals. All his bombs tumbled end-over-end, right in front and ahead of me on the runway. In that ten seconds, I considered aborting the mission but quickly judged that I could miss those tumbling bombs by moving fast. I steered my aircraft over to the right edge of the runway. I became airborne well before I got to the rolling bombs because I carried 1000 pounds less ordinance. My aircraft was relatively lightweight; I had been running at one-quarter flaps, but I went to half-flaps as soon as I saw the bombs. Quick thinking got me airborne fast.

The rendezvous was en route, and from there we climbed directly on course to Inchon. When I joined Captain Steed, my legs were still shaking from that takeoff ordeal. I was ashamed of myself for getting so scared. After the exit point, north of Inchon, we proceeded on course to the marshaling yards target area in North Korea.

I had plenty of time to see the target area before starting my dive. I rolled over and went down at 300 knots, barndoor open (speed brakes out). As I approached the troop compound, I saw people starting to run from the yard area. I hit the building dead center. I was so low, I thought I was going to clip a pole on the building—I missed the pole. I'm not sure by how much, but it was probably just inches. As I went over the target, I nearly ran into an antiaircraft emplacement shooting at me almost point blank. I was so intent in my dive that I had forgotten to shoot my 20mm cannons. It was only when I started pullup, jinks at full power, that I thought of this.

I decided to turn around and wipe out the antiaircraft emplacement. I circled the village and train station from about 200 feet. Taking my time, I expended all my remaining ammo on troops running down the side of the railroad bank.

All the while, I could hear the others talking on the radio about the flack and departing the area at maximum power. I could also hear the flight leader calling me on

VHF (very high frequency). He was asking the rest of the flight what had happened to "two dash two," my call sign. I answered as soon as I got clear of the area. I told them I was okay and that I would proceed to K-6 on my own.

I spent all my time en route home trying to figure out how to get away with what I had done—how not to get thrown out of Korea or court-martialed. By the time I had landed, I decided I would tell them I just got behind a little and play things down if I could. I missed the debriefing and was called to Operations of MAG-12 and asked to explain all the hits by small arms in the side of my aircraft. I had no choice at this point but to tell them what I did and why I did it.

About two weeks later, they had developed my gun camera film. A major asked me what 121 did to me as far as reprimand. I told him "nothing," that perhaps they thought I got disoriented on pullup. He said that I sure played "holy hell" with the Koreans that day and warned me to stay with the squadron. From then on, I did—except for one time later when I did not leave the target area with the rest of the flight. I saw a better target than assigned and lingered behind to wipe it out. On my third sortie, my aircraft, AK-17, was loaded with two napalm tanks. The chronological narrative shows that the mission expended all its ordinance.

I liked combat! This was something I discovered about myself that I hadn't realized before. It was exciting—that rush of adrenaline in a target area. I wanted to let the

North Koreans know that my Skyraider was going to hit more than once before heading home. Now I goaded myself to do the unexpected, sometimes even surprising myself.

We had a few so-called air raids while I was in VMA-121. It usually was a lone North Korean plane flying around at night, harassing the U.S. airbases south of and around Seoul. I was Assistant Navigation Officer and Assistant Engineering Officer, but I had no real ground duties.

On 27 July 1953, the armistice was signed, and we stopped flying combat missions in North Korea. I asked for and received R&R leave to Itami Marine Corps Air Station near Osaka, Japan. Some of the other officers on this leave included Captains Sledge and Gray (from VMA-121), Horst and Patterson from VMA-212, and a few officers from VMA-251, all from Marine Air Group 12.[3]

Upon arriving in Itami on R&R, the routine was to go to the Officers Club and order a large Kobe beefsteak and some wine, then go to the Takarazuka Dance Revue in nearby Takarazuka, winding up the evening at Ishibashi 258, the non-approved, unofficial officer's house of ill-repute. The street number was 258, hence Ishibashi 258. Ishibashi became quite famous as a premier cathouse and remained so until the Marines left Itami, Japan.

My roommate, Chuck Sledge, fell in love with one of the girls from Ishibashi 258 and bought her freedom. He received an assignment to Itami as a maintenance test pilot. On 1 July 1954, he burned to death while approaching Itami Airbase during one of his test flights. It was a matter of not bailing out in time. As a test pilot, he was probably trying to save the aircraft. Chuck was one of my closest friends, and I missed him sorely after that.

I spent one night at the opera in Takarazuka, then next day went to Osaka City where I met a Japanese girl by the name of Miki Nishihara. She and I spent the remainder of my R&R in the mountains near Gifu. Miki introduced me to a Japan I learned to love and still regard as one the best of all countries in which to live. She also began teaching me the Japanese language and, from that time on, I became a student of that beautifully expressive language. Very soon, I stopped studying Korean and concentrated on Japanese.

I also fell in love with Japanese food on that first R&R. I still consider it the best in the world. I certainly prefer it to both western and Chinese food. Except for a few European hotels that have Japanese chefs, true Japanese cooking can only be found in Japan.

I went to the maintenance and overhaul buildings in Itami and asked the Engineering Officer if I could fly a ship back to Korea after R&R. All he had available was an L-19 Bird Dog[4] that was to be delivered to the front lines at a small field (airport) site in Korea. So the next day I flew the Bird Dog as far as K-6. A few days later, I flew it north to the frontlines—there I met my brother. As a Marine corporal, he worked in maintenance on helicopters as well as Bird Dog aircraft. The reunion was short, but it was good to see him again.

Cessna L-19 Bird Dog

When I returned to K-6 after my R&R in Japan and delivering the L-19 aircraft to the 38th Parallel, I was detached from VMA-121 and assigned to base operations at Marine Air Group 12 (MAG-12). Here I started flying an R4D, the two-engine Douglas DC-3,[5] and made quite a few

Douglas DC-3 (C-117D) United States Marines at the Pima Air & Space Museum. (Photo from aeroprints.com)

trips to Japan. I also checked out in jet fighters. MAG-12 had one Lockheed T-33/TV-2 jet trainer, and I logged 30 hours in it before switching to the Douglas F3D,[6] a twin-engine jet night fighter nicknamed the Skyknight.

Douglas F3D Skyknight

A friend of mine, Dave Curtiss—a second lieutenant when I had known him from my enlisted days at Quantico—had gone through cadet training as an officer cadet and was now a first lieutenant and night fighter pilot in the Douglas F3D. Because I was in MAG-12, Base Operations, he agreed to give me a check out and let me fly with the squadron. I also flew the model Corsair AU-1 and got a check out in the COD turkey (TBM: Torpedo Bomber).[7]

During the fall of 1953, I took up hunting again. The countryside around us was full of Korean ring-necked pheasants, and it was also full of children who were master thieves. They would follow us on hunts or hide nearby and steal anything that we left unattended. They took my first day's booty—pheasants I had killed outside the nearby village. I thought I had hidden them in the large, jeep-style weapons carrier but, when I returned, both my sweater and the birds were gone. I didn't mind all that much, though; they were sure to have put them to good use.

Grumman TBM (GM-built TBF) with
Sto-Wing folding wings, 1945.

About the middle of October, the ducks and Siberian geese started to arrive in the estuary and on the small island at its mouth. At times the sky was almost filled with geese. At Asanman Bay, near a village on the shores of the estuary at Kongse-Ri, the Koreans had salt beds where they trapped the ocean water during high tides. When off duty, some of the other officers and I took the weapons carrier there to hunt geese and ducks.

It was on one of these trips that my Class-16 roommate, 2nd Lt. Lokker, now also stationed at VMA-121, made a serious hunting error. Just outside a small Korean village, he shot and killed two tame ducks and crippled two more. All its citizens were up in arms, so to speak. I could only understand some of their words—just enough to know it was time to get the hell out of there. We jumped in the jeep and left; that ended our hunting day before we really even got started.

That winter I graduated to Ardent Goose Hunter. With the geese remaining in the area all winter, I decided to kill some for the officer's mess—with my Douglas AD.

After all, I could see what seemed like millions of them on the small islands. In late November, I arranged with VMA-121 to have all my guns loaded and the enlisted men standing by with trucks in that area. The tide was low. It would be just like a turkey shoot only with geese.

Shooting geese from a dive bomber sounds easy, but it turned out to be more of a chore than I expected. I expended a lot of 20mm cannon ammo, exploding shells but getting few hits. The men picked up only about fifty geese by the end of the so-called massacre. It really was not a very sporting event. On the good side, however, a lot of children beat the men to the kill area. At least they enjoyed some of the spoils of my adventure.

One truly memorable goose hunt took place in January. Lieutenant Stuart, the ordnance officer, and I went into an abandoned house on the hillside to get out of the bitter cold. It had no windows but provided shelter from the fierce wind. We had to wait to start our hunt until just before nightfall when all the geese would start flying from the estuary to the rice fields nearby. They would feed in the rice fields all night before returning to their water sanctuary at dawn. As my eyes were adjusting to the darkness, I suddenly realized that we were in a house full of dead bodies. The Koreans stored their dead here during the winter months—we had taken shelter in a house of corpses! Stuart and I hightailed it out of there as soon as we realized where we were.

I figured it out later. With the ground frozen, grave digging and funerals had to wait for the thaw. Some years later, I returned to Pyeongtaek to hunt geese and again took shelter in that very same house of the dead. You can be sure that I ascertained it was empty before I went in.

Despite the snow that winter, I flew quite a few practice missions with VMA-121. Because most of the wartime pilots had been transferred out of the area, I usually served as flight leader. On one such flight, when I was in a steep dive, I heard a sound like a sharp crack in my wing area. I immediately cut my engine power, aborted the dive, and returned to K-6.

I wrote aircraft #21 up in the maintenance report as being unsafe for flight. Engineering checked it thoroughly, but they could not find anything wrong. They asked me to withdraw my report, but I refused. All the personnel in maintenance and operations were upset with me for causing this aircraft to be grounded for a month; they asked me to re-fly or test it, then re-sign off on it. I again refused. Finally, the commanding officer, Colonel Flater, informed me that he personally would fly this AD on a mission. It came apart on him in a dive; he was killed.

Shortly after this incident, I almost lost my life while on a training flight with VMA-121. Tom Spurr was to fly my wing on an instrument training flight. I was to put the hood over my canopy after takeoff and practice GCAs (ground control approaches) to K-6 airbase. With the wingman acting as a safety pilot and warning of any danger, the pilot could simply slip his white hood back in the cockpit in about a second to be flying visually again. I had made about four approaches with K-6 GCA talking me down. On my fifth and last approach, something went wrong with the GCA. I was reported to be on course and on glide path and was taking the approach down to about 50 feet before raising my hood. Making my approach to the south, I planned to the cross estuary just off the end of the runway. As pilots fly closer to the runway, the corrections get smaller, requiring more precision flying. The tendency is to concentrate mostly on airspeed and rate of descent.

When I was about 200 feet from the field, I cross checked my altitude—it showed 50 feet! I immediately jerked my hood back and found myself sitting directly in front of the estuary bank, racing toward it at 90 knots! I only had time to jam full throttle and pullup. I must have missed ground impact by just a few feet. It scared the living daylights out of me.

Once I got my voice back, I had a few choice words for my safety pilot, my wingman. And after landing, I went to the GCA and had a few choice words for them, as well.

I was promoted to first lieutenant around January '54. It was unexpected; I knew I was regarded as independent and, with my reputation as a wild officer, I figured I would stay a second lieutenant forever. Evidently, the Marines thought more of my officer capabilities than I did of myself. Despite my pleasure over this promotion, I still felt my life's direction was in commercial aviation or with a company like CAT (Civil Air Transport) of China.

As operations officer at Base Operations, MAG-12, I was called to the crash site of an Air Force plane just outside the airbase at the mouth of the estuary. The plane had gone in vertically and made a large hole in the middle of one of my goose-hunting areas. It was on this trip that I met Army Sergeant Bednekoff, who I would meet again several more times in later years.

I also met a young Korean girl by the name of Young-Ja. She was beautiful, and she spoke some English, as well. She helped me learn more of the Korean language, and her brother showed me the two ancient mounds[8] in a village near K-6. For the rest of my tour in Korea, I made her home my off-base headquarters. Through her, I got to know the Korean people and learn both how poor and how good-hearted they really were.

I spent a lot of my free time among the Koreans from January '54 on. I always carried a supply of hard candy for the children, as well as the grownups who sometimes got in line with them. I had an ample supply as I was flying the Douglas R4D to Japan, and the Base Exchange in Itami had all sorts of candy.

In February, I was scheduled for two weeks E&E (evasion and escape) training at K-46, an Air Force base; the actual training took place around Hoengseong and the Airdrome. After completion of the ground course, we were taken out in the hills in 6x6 trucks, dumped off and told to get back to the K-46 classroom within the next two days without getting caught. Army soldiers were detailed to get us if they could. Second Lieutenant Martin, my cadet friend, was also in Korea at that time and was with VMA-251. Lieutenant Martin and I got through the E&E training without getting caught by the U.S. Army aggressors. I regarded the training as a piece of cake. We were careful to only travel at night, stay off all roads and trails, not go near or through any villages, stay off the skylines, and obey all the other regulations taught in ground school. It was an interesting game which we all enjoyed at the time.

I continued my goose hunting exploits throughout the winter but, by this time, I was usually in the company of Korean farmers, natives around the estuary, who served as guides. Thanks to Young-Ja, I now had the essentials for the language and a great respect for the Korean people. I gave all my geese and ducks to them and, now that I really knew them, never had to worry about theft. Now that they knew me, they chose to steal from others.

That spring, I was assigned as bombing range officer for a while. I was transported (dumped off) by helicopter at or near Dangjin, where my job was to talk to various aircraft and units on the VHF radio to inform them whether or not there were any people in the range area and if it was safe to drop their bombs. I would relay their hits or misses by triangular sightings.

The range shack was near a very narrow gauge, push-type railroad track where Korean children pushed the carts to and from a local mine. The track passed right by us, and I welcomed the chance to talk with the children. One little girl had a very bad infection in her leg. I was able to get advice from our K-6 flight surgeons and had the chopper bring in some medical supplies. Before I finished my assignment there, her leg had healed.

It was here that I made the shot of my life with my .38 pistol. It was just after sunset one evening, and some of the children were with us. I had learned to speak pretty good broken Korean by this time, and we were talking about the birds flying around us and catching the bugs while they flew. To show off, I pulled out my .38 and shot at one bird, hitting it directly through the head. The Koreans gazed at me in awe. I didn't dare shoot again. The enlisted Marines knew why, but the children did not. I left it at that, content to be a hero in their eyes.

I continued flying the R4D and several other different fighters at K-6 until I received my orders to return to the USA on 2 June 1954, my tour of duty in Korea was over.

I had made many Korean friends and had learned quite a lot of the language and customs. I resolved to return to Pyeongtaek someday, which I did.

On 5 April 1954, I had requested assignment to a multiengine squadron and on 9 April my request was approved by the Commanding General, Aircraft, Fleet Marine Forces, Pacific:

> Forwarded, recommending approval.
>
> Lieutenant Sutphin has displayed excellent qualities as an attack pilot and the assignment to a multi-engine squadron is approved.

I spent a week at Itami Airbase before boarding an R5D four-engine transport back to the USA. I knew the Navy lieutenant who was scheduled to fly it as far as Honolulu, and he let me sit in the copilot's seat for most of the flight from Midway to Honolulu. I was looking forward to flying an aircraft like this one day soon, hoping it was forecast by the stars I saw in the sky.

Chapter 6.

AMERICAN FLYERS

On 10 June 1954, I arrived at Meacham Field, Texas. My orders directed me to report to the Marine Aviation Detachment at Pensacola, Florida. I had two months leave after my Korean tour and wanted to make the most of it at the American Flyers School, the most respected flight school in the USA at that time. In Korea, I had managed to fly more than the 1,200 hours required to obtain my airline transport license. The age requirement was twenty three, and I had turned twenty-three years old the previous November.

I checked in with Mrs. Ross, who, with another elderly woman, operated a boarding house for pilots at 620 South Street in Fort Worth, Texas. At one time or another Mrs. Ross had put up all the pilots going through American Flyers training. I had stayed there in 1951 when I was first at American Flyers getting my multiengine and flight instructor's licenses and received a warm welcome back.

Ed Cook was also enrolled at American Flyers in the commercial pilot course. His father owned some oil wells, was quite wealthy, and had given Ed a used PT-17 Stearman—in perfect condition—for his 18th birthday. The only hitch was that Ed could not fly it. I agreed to give him all the instructions needed for a good check out. We became good friends during my stay in Fort Worth.

Reed Pigman and his wife owned and operated American Flyers. Reed was a very experienced instrument pilot and had a small airline composed of two DC-3s at that time. He chartered them to various organizations, mostly colleges with football teams and usually on a call and need basis. Countless airline captains have graduated or received training, at one time or another, through Reed Pigman's school.

I was getting my training under the G.I. Bill and had to go through all the ground school courses before going to the CAA and taking the required written examinations on navigation, regulations, weather, etc.

Professor Albert Moore was my first instructor, and I was supposed to have his recommendation before reporting to the CAA for the written exams. About halfway through his course, though, I got bored, both with his teaching style and the fact that I already knew what he was presenting, so I went to the Feds and took the exam on my own. I did pass all the subjects, but it made Prof. Moore so mad—furious is more like it—that he tried to get me kicked out of the school.

Reed Pigman called me into his office, and I had to

explain to him that I was on leave from the Marines, and I could not afford to waste so much time on things I thought I already knew. Evidently, Reed agreed with my argument; after that, he invited me to his home for dinner two or three nights in a row, and my flight instructor, Jim Fletcher, accelerated my training and recommended me for my Single Engine Airline Transport Pilot rating.

One of the examiners, Chief Pilot Hamilton, gave me my single engine check ride. After that, I enrolled in their Multiengine Airline Transport course using the Douglas DC-3.

On our evenings off, Ed Cook introduced me to all the night life around Fort Worth. We would usually go to the late-night restaurants or dance places even though Mrs. Ross frowned on my late arrivals at 620 South Street. Ed also owned a boat and lake house north of Fort Worth, and he introduced me to waterskiing.

I started dating the daughter of a preacher while there and, wanting to make points, I agreed to go to church with her and her family one Sunday. Ed and I had stayed out late the night before, but I did make it to their home by 9:00 a.m.—in my uniform, of course, because I wanted to impress them. Unfortunately, halfway through the service I became the focus of attention because of my snoring; that ended that romance.

Chastened by my disgrace, I stopped night-hopping with Ed and settled down to getting my DC-3 rating. Toward the end of my training, Reed called me into his office. In dire need of a copilot for his next day's flight, then and there, he decided I was ready for my check ride. When the DC-3 arrived that night, he would personally give me the DC-3 type-rating check and, if I passed it, I would put on the former copilot's uniform and help him move a football team.

It was by far the most dangerous and unusual check flight I ever made in my life. There was a terrific thunderstorm—lightning and thunder filled the sky. It was really Donner and Blitzen. Off we went, though. Never once in the two-hour flight did Reed or I mention the wind, rain, or lightning. I figured it was not my place since he was the instructor, checker, and owner of both the airplane and the school.

We went through all the check-ride syllabus, and I landed and taxied to the hangar area. After the flight, Reed did not speak. He just got out of the plane, got in his car, and drove off. I didn't know what to think, but I showed up at 7:00 a.m. the next morning as planned.

Reed did not arrive until 9:00 a.m., however. He went right to his office, so I talked to Mrs. Pigman who had come with him and was at the desk. She told me I had passed the check ride and that Reed was typing the forms. She also told me that, due to weather—in this case, thunderstorms—in the area of our charter, our flight was delayed one day.

Years later, Reed Pigman died during the crash of a Lockheed Electra Airliner. There is some contention as to what actually happened, whether or not a heart condition killed him before he lost control. He had done so well in the school and charter business that he had been able to lease or purchase a four-engine airliner to haul military personnel around. At night, with a thunderstorm going full-blast, Reed was making a circling approach at low altitude to land. He was killed along with everyone onboard.[1]

After that, American Flyers was eventually sold. During his lifetime, though, Reed Pigman was regarded as one of the great pioneer aviators in America.

Before I departed Fort Worth, I received my Certificate of Competency from Capt. F. G. Burns, the Chief Pilot of American Flyers. I said goodbye to Mrs. Ross and drove my car to Pensacola to report to the Commanding Officer, Marine Aviation Detachment. It was 22 September 1954.

Chapter 7.
THE ROAD TO CIVIL AIR TRANSPORT

CAT, Inc. Pilot
Capt. Ronald J. Sutphin
(Family Photo)

I expected a flying assignment; instead, I was immediately detached for administrative duties. I was to interview all Marine officers in the training command and bring their service records up to date. Though I protested this assignment to the Marine commanding officer, he did not change his mind.

As it turned out, however, this was the best thing that could have happened to me, because the position enabled me to start flying again out of Chevalier Field. I was pretty much my own boss as my only requirement was to turn in my required records per week. I asked for and got an SNB-5 for my own use to travel to different bases in exchange for making VIP flights all over the country. I had ample time to do these VIP flights. I also got checked out in the R4Ds at nearby Corry Naval Air Station.

I asked the Navy operations commander for a special instrument (or Green Card) rating, and he consented to let me take a check flight for the Green Card once he saw how much civilian pilot time I had logged. So, I became a special instrument pilot and began giving instrument check flights to those Navy pilots who needed them. Only Green Card pilots were able to do this at the time. I was averaging over 100 hours flight time each month. I was so busy I had no more time for civilian flying or instructing.

I was billeted at the BOQ at Mainside, and it was here that I met Andy Hamlin from New Orleans. We became close friends, and I spent a few weekends with him at his home in Iberia, Louisiana, very close to New Orleans. Once I left Pensacola, I did not see him again until Vietnam.

While at Mainside, I started flying the F6F Hellcat again. They had a lot of F6Fs that needed shakedowns (test flights) and, since the F6F was one of my favorite aircraft, I eagerly volunteered.

During December '54, I went through the Instructors Basic Training unit, a school for flight instructors. I flew the SNJ and T-28 during this course and, when I completed the course, I was transferred to North Whiting Field to be an instructor. There I started flying the SNB Twin Beech, giving instrument check flights to the instructors. However, because I was always being requested for special VIP flights by Mainside, I only had three students during my whole stay at Whiting.

In the spring of '55, I was offered a regular commission in the Marine Corps. My choices were to accept it, extend my active duty as a Reserve officer for four more years, or decline both and become a weekend warrior, meaning that I would remain a reserve Marine officer subject to active-duty call at any time. The latter appealed to me the most, as Marine officers usually got to fly almost anytime they wanted and were only compelled to be on active status two weeks out of the year. I could probably get all the flying I wanted with some Navy or Marine reserve squadron and perhaps also hold down an airline position at the same time. It would afford me the best of both worlds, so I agreed to join the Reserves.

I had written to Capitol Airways in Nashville, Tennessee. They had a fleet of Curtiss C-46 Commandos, the ones I had so much admired on my tour in China. In my mind this would be the road to Civil Air Transport. Capitol Airways said that they would be glad to have me. I applied for special leave, and, on the first of May, I drove to Nashville.

Capitol Airways welcomed me like one of their own. After spending two days in Nashville, I was sent to Macon, Georgia, the location of their main Air Force contract. They made some long-range flights to Europe in their DC-4s, but their main source of revenue was hauling freight around the USA in the C-46.

In Macon, I was given the chance to study all about the C-46, and Charlie Jones gave me a check flight, which I passed without a hitch. The C-46 exceeded my high expectations as a superb aircraft. Then, and still to this day, I regard the Curtiss Commando as one of the finest transports ever invented.

I did most of my flying for the next two months with Captains Hosford and Jones. They both let me fly from the left seat (the captain's seat) and unselfishly made me feel like I was already a part of Capitol Airways. I believe young pilots should get left side flying experience and training for several reasons: first, transport takeoffs and landings are usually done from the left side; second, check rides were usually given from the left side; and finally, a pilot should learn the duties of a captain.

I flew most of the time to U.S. Air Force bases and especially liked Kelly in San Antonio, Texas.

However, after going off active duty in June, I did not return to Capitol and sometimes regret that. I often wondered how life treated Hosford and Jones.

I received orders to report to VMF-351 (Marine Fighter Squadron 351) at Floyd Bennett Naval Air Station, Brooklyn, New York, on 6 June 1955. I was to become a member of the reserve squadron and would be able to fly on weekends. As it turned out, I could fly anytime I wanted to if aircraft were available.

Howard DGA-15P (FlugKerl2 2013)

Before leaving Pensacola, I sold my car for $1,300, and I purchased a Howard DGA[1] from one of the local airports. Even in 1955, that was a good deal as far as I was concerned. The DGA was a small aircraft with 450 horsepower. It was high-winged, like the Canadian Beaver but not as well known. I found that it did not fly nearly as well, either. From my perspective, it just was not the outstanding airplane design that Howard intended.

Arriving in New York, I was lucky to find a good place to live with Mrs. Murphy and her family at 34-39 75th Street in Jackson Heights. The Murphy family rented me a room and I liked the children, even though they seemed to have a pact to never let me be alone in my room.

Grumman F9F-6 Cougar in flight, c. 1952

In Brooklyn, when I checked into VMF-351, I found out that I would have to go through a check out course in order to fly their jet aircraft, the swept winged Cougar F9F-6 and the later F9F-7 model.[2] Upon arrival, I noted that the U.S. Navy had a lot of Corsairs parked on the flight line. Since I had an ongoing love for the Corsair, I approached the Naval Commander, showed him the Corsair flight time in my logbook, and asked if I could fly it. He readily consented and said that the Corsairs were awaiting retirement, and, just to keep them in working order, I could fly all of them on test and shakedown flights. Elated, I continued to fly

Chapter 7. THE ROAD TO CIVIL AIR TRANSPORT | 83

the Corsair even after check out in the more modern jet fighters. Besides my squadron jets, while at Floyd Bennett, I flew the SNJ-5, the SNB, Corsair, and the R5D transports.

Pan Am DC-6B at London Heathrow in September 1954 on a transatlantic tourist flight. (RuthAS)

Upon arriving in New York, I had secured a job as copilot with Pan Am (Pan American World Airways), flying the four-engine Douglas DC-6.[3] I would fly copilot for two or three months and then go to celestial navigation school. It was essentially a navigator's job, forecast to last several years, and I did not relish the commitment. I decided that, after finishing navigation school, I would try to get another position.

While with Pan Am, I flew the South Africa route to Johannesburg with layovers in Lisbon. Sometimes I had trips to London and Shannon, Ireland. Pan Am was a good company, but I knew it could not last; I was slated for navigation school.

I met Paul Mlinar while flying into New York. He was the chief pilot for Seaboard & Western Airlines, a much smaller company than Pan Am, but there were certain aspects about them that I found attractive. First, they had professional navigators. Also, they carried all kinds of freight and ran charter flights, so their routes varied to all places in the world. Paul gave me a check out in the DC-4[4] and sent me off on my first flight to New Delhi, India. I found that I liked the people at Seaboard. The captains had concern for the copilots, and, indeed, they treated all crew members as equals.

Seaboard & Western Douglas DC-4

While in New York at Floyd Bennett Naval Air Station, a lot of my old friends arrived: Warren Comer, Lokker, and McKillop were with Pan Am. Dave Curtiss and Lem Stockum, both from MAG-12 in Korea, had also transferred to the weekend-warrior status and joined VMF-351.

Both Dave Curtiss and Lem Stockum were killed while flying at Floyd Bennett. It was a great loss to me when Dave died; I had been with him since I was a sergeant in the Marines, and he was my platoon leader.

Warren Comer had been fired by Pan Am for messing up

an instrument approach into New York and was looking for a job. I told him I was trying to get a job with Civil Air Transport in the Far East and that he should write them a letter as I had done. I had been writing Civil Air Transport for the past year because I wanted to return to the Far East. Their flight routes to Korea, Tokyo, Manila, Hong Kong, and Bangkok appealed to me.

In late December '55, Mlinar asked me if I would fly the C-46 out of Luxembourg for three months. He told me it would be temporary. Because I had flown the C-46 with Capitol, my doing so would mean no delay for them in replacing a sick pilot. So, I went to Luxembourg Airlines, which, at the time, had a wet lease with Seaboard. They had one airplane and three pilots.

I was issued Airline Pilots License No. 55 by *Le Commissaire du Gouvernement*, signed by Mr. Hamer. I flew inter-Europe with Captains Woody Wray and Bernier, both excellent pilots. We went to France and Italy and almost all the major cities within Germany, Scandinavia, and the British Isles. The weather was bad during those winter months, so we were almost always flying instruments. I really got to know the European weather during this tour of Europe which greatly helped me in years to come.

I lived at the City Hotel in Luxembourg and, during my free time there, I either went wild boar hunting with Mr. Gordon or deadheaded (hitched a ride) on our C-46 to Frankfurt where I had a girlfriend.

On 1 February 1956, I returned to Idlewild, New York, and moved into the BOQ at Floyd Bennett NAS. As he had previously promised me, Captain Mlinar promoted me to copilot on the most modern and largest airliner of that time, the Lockheed L-1049, better known as the Super Constellation.[5]

Seaboard Connie - Lockheed L-1049D Super Constellation

After a check out in the Constellation, I decided I really liked my job and temporarily forgot about trying to fly for Civil Air Transport. The captains were superb pilots and, when it came time to fly, I always flew from the left seat—a wise policy for any airline during those days.

After a while I was flying with the Navy as well as the Marines. I had no complaint from Major Clark in VMF-351. As a matter of fact, in terms of flight time, I flew many more hours for the U.S. Navy throughout my 21 years and 7 months as a Reserve pilot than for the Marines. The only time I was with the Marines was in MAG-12 and VMF-351.

The Navy always seemed to have some flight for me to take, and I was always eager to fly.

During 1956, I went to visit my old schoolmate, Will Landis who still lived in Mt. Royal, Pennsylvania. Will had not changed a bit. He had gone into the Army as a telephone line repairman, had a tour in Germany, and was back home now. Still single, he was living at home. Will, his brother Leonard, and I went pheasant and rabbit hunting while I was there. I used the Browning automatic shotgun I had purchased while in Luxembourg. Then, after about a week, I returned to New York to resume my scheduled flights with Seaboard.

On the Super Constellation flights, the schedule was usually from New York to Frankfurt, transporting military freight or passengers. I did make one flight in the 1049 to New Delhi, India. I also flew the Douglas DC-4 to haul Rhesus monkeys for the Polio Foundation (National Foundation for Infantile Paralysis). The polio vaccine was made from their livers.[6]

While in New Delhi, I had some time and went on a tour with one of our monkey handlers to watch the trapping. It was a day's ride north of New Delhi. The trappers put some food at a place near where the wild monkeys lived, and, invariably, a few monkeys would cautiously come to get the food. Then the trappers placed more food, and more monkeys would come. Finally, after about two weeks, hundreds of monkeys would be waiting for the food trucks to arrive. With enough numbers, the trappers placed a huge net above the food supply. At first, this scared most of the monkeys off. After a few days, though, they learned to live with, or ignore, the net. It did not seem to be a threat to them, and the food kept coming.

The net was sprung one day, however, and about 1,600 Rhesus monkeys were typically hauled in. Unfortunately, the plane trip was a terrible flight not only for the monkeys but also for the crew. The flight took at least two days, and the smell soaked into the lining of the aircraft, as well as our uniforms. Wherever we landed, people gave Seaboard monkey crews a very wide berth!

If any monkeys got loose from their flight cages during a flight, there would be hell to pay. On one flight, the aircraft stopped in Luxembourg for overnight maintenance, and quite a few monkeys escaped into the hangar, the airport area, and even into some nearby homes.

On one of my flights to India, we departed New York with a full passenger load of seamen from India returning to Bombay after a long charter voyage. As standard operating procedure, we had two stewardesses aboard. Our route took us through North Africa to Bombay where we dropped off the seamen and spent the night. The next day we were en route to New Delhi when we experienced engine trouble; we had to feather (shut down) one of our engines. Engine repairs dictated we spend a week off there. We made the most of our free time. The monkey handlers were English, lived in the city, and offered to show us all the city sights.

And did we ever see the sights! Our entire crew ended up in the New Delhi jail! We had gone into a local bar and night club where we received a less-than-warm welcome. Our navigator promptly got into a free-for-all brawl over one of the painted girls. Added to this was the argument over how much damage was done to the bar, and there we were—all of us locked up together in one jail cell—right out of an American western movie set—facing the sheriff's desk where we could see all the action.

After we were there for about an hour, a young police lieutenant came in with a mother and daughter and the daughter's boyfriend. They had a few words between themselves in the local dialect and then the lieutenant pulled off his belt and started whipping the girl's boyfriend. He really gave it to him. All the while, I kept wondering if we would be next. I hoped not.

Then the lieutenant came over to our cell and started to talk in perfect English. He explained that the boy had gotten overly fresh with the girl, and that he was just teaching him a lesson. When he discovered that we were Americans, his attitude toward us immediately changed. He explained in detail how America and India have so much in common because both countries had broken the yoke of oppression and obtained independence.

We explained what had happened in the cabaret, and he came up with a solution. We were to go back there with him and confront the villains. So, we were released to go back to the cabaret with him. Once there, he lined up all the locals and had a peppy talk with them. He slapped one of the waiters a few times, and the manager promptly returned all our money to him.

Back again at the jail, he tried to refund our money. Wisely, we told him that we would like to pay for all the trouble we caused. I think the total bill was all of 20 dollars, or about 320 rupees. We told him to have dinner on us, and he ever-so-kindly accepted. Off we went, ever-so-careful never to offend the New Delhi long arm of the law ever again.

When the week was over and the engine repaired, we departed New Delhi on our return flight. The two stewardesses were both sick from the water. So, between their travail and the stench of the 1,600 Rhesus monkeys onboard, it was a flight best forgotten.

Our first stop was Bahrain for refueling and then from Bahrain to Beirut. I had to make a rather steep approach into Beirut due to the terrain and air traffic control. The stewardesses were sleeping on the floor with blankets over them and, because of the steep angle, got doused with monkey urine running forward from the main cargo compartment. As a further indignity, this barred them from going into the Beirut Airport restaurant. I had to order and carry their food out to them.[7]

From Beirut, we stopped again for fuel in Brindisi in southern Italy before finally going on to Luxembourg. Once there, both stewardesses headed for a much-needed bath and change at the City Hotel, decided that was their last flight with Seaboard and, back in New York, promptly resigned.

I continued to live at Floyd Bennett NAS and fly with VMF-351 and the Navy. I made quite a few buzz jobs (high-speed dives) on and around my old home in Mt. Royal, Pennsylvania, mostly in the Navy Corsairs. I had been informed that all the model FG-1D Corsairs[8] were scheduled to be mothballed in Arizona, so I wanted to fly them as much as possible before they were gone forever.

Goodyear-built FG-1D
(USN - U.S. Naval Aviation News March 1953)

On 10 October 1956, I had an eventful flight in the Lockheed Constellation. We departed Idlewild, New York (later named JFK Airport) about 2000 hours (8:00 p.m.) bound for Frankfurt with a full load of Air Force personnel and dependents. During climb out, the policy was to idle all four engines at the same time to engage the super chargers. This was done at about 14,000 feet and always caused some concern among the passengers.

The flight progressed uneventfully, though, to Shannon for refueling. Then, after that early-morning takeoff and departure, we started losing fuel. The engineer alerted us but—even though he, the navigator, and I all thought we should put down in London—the captain decided it was only the gauges and had us continue to Frankfurt.

I was flying this leg of the ILS (instrument landing system) approach through the morning fog, when the number one engine caught fire. We continued the approach and landed with the engine still burning—then it dropped off the plane onto the runway!

To add insult to what was almost injury, a young Air Force captain slammed open the cockpit door and demanded to know who had gone to sleep last night and run out of fuel. He thought that when the engines were idled for the super charger engagement that the crew had run a fuel tank dry and that was what had caused the engines to die. We later had a most spirited conversation with this captain.

The investigation revealed that the PRT (power recovery turbine) in one of the engines had burned to pieces and had caused a high fuel intake. We had lost most of our fuel, flying on no reserve. It was a very close call for a very large commercial airliner.

In the summer of 1956, while flying with VMF-351, I had been promoted to Captain in the Marines and to Reserve Captain with Seaboard Airlines, two surprises! I was beginning to like New York. Despite my aversion to cities, New York seemed to grow on me.

In November '56, I received a letter from Warren Comer saying that Civil Air Transport, the company he then worked for in Taiwan, would be contacting me from their Washington DC office. He had put in a good word about me.

Capt. August Harvey "Augie" Martin
Seaboard Airlines

Then in December, Seaboard leased their four Constellations to Eastern Airlines and was planning to either put some of their crews on furlough or lease them as well to Eastern. A pilot's meeting was called at Idlewild

Airport, and it turned out that I was the cut-off man—the last numbered pilot who could remain with Seaboard. But, because of Capt. August "Augie" Martin,[9] [10] I went with Eastern anyway. Eastern would not take Augie because, despite his exemplary background in aviation, he was Black. Rather than have him left without a job, I said I would make the move to Eastern. I was also thinking about the chance to fly with Civil Air Transport and felt this was the right move for me now.

Eastern had good captains and beautiful stewardesses, so I thought it was all a good deal. I was flying domestic for the first time, made a good friend of the La Guardia chief pilot, and had a new girlfriend—an Eastern Airlines stewardess.

George Dole at the Harvard Club in New York called me in January 1957. He wanted to meet and discuss my working for Civil Air Transport. We made an appointment to meet, but he stood me up. A few days later he called again and asked if I could go to Washington DC on the 24th to talk to some people there. He said it was a formality and that I could count on a job.

So, here I was, enjoying life with my job, living in New York, my car, my Harley-Davidson 70, a good position at VMF-351, and my beautiful girlfriend to top it all off. Changing jobs would also mean getting rid of my Howard DGA airplane. A lot to consider, but I had wanted that CAT job since I was 18 years old, and I was not about to let my great lifestyle entrap me when adventure called. When I asked my girlfriend to go to the Far East with me, she told me I was crazy to even consider it!

I made my decision. On 24 January 1957, I flew out from Floyd Bennett in a Navy SNB to Washington DC. Several men about my age met me, asked a lot of questions that seemed to have little to do with flying and a lot to do with my military background and the Korean War. Amazing to me at the time, they already had my military records in front of them.

George Dole had not prepared me for this kind of meeting at all. Evidently, I answered their questions satisfactorily, because they asked me to join Civil Air Transport and said I would depart on Northwest Airlines in one week bound for Tokyo.

So, that was that. About a week later, I said goodbye to all my friends, boarded a Northwest Airlines flight and headed for Tokyo via Seattle. Looking back on it now, I believe the building where I met with those bigwigs of CAT was a CIA sub-headquarters.

During the six-hour flight to Seattle, while waiting for a connecting flight, Barney Barnes—also on his way to Civil Air Transport—somehow knew I would be on the same flight and introduced himself to me. He was a former World War II fighter pilot and knew Bong and all the other aces in the Pacific Theater of operations. He was, himself, an ace, flying the P-38 Lightning fighters.[11] He was pulled out of combat early, though, to sell war bonds in the states. He was also court-martialed for doing a buzz job (called flat-hatting in the Navy) in the P-38. As a result, he was not promoted or allowed to return to combat in the Pacific. En route to Tokyo, he told me about his stint with a C-46 after the war and how he had quit flying to go into the woodworking business, but now, just like me, here he was joining CAT.

His heavy social drinking, as well as being married while I was single, kept us in different social circles. He was very likable, though, and we became good friends for a while.

It was late in the evening when we departed Seattle. With the rain falling, it reminded me of our approach into Tsingtao, China, all those years before. I was about to fulfill my dream of flying with Civil Air Transport. Adventure called, and I was on my way.

Chapter 8.

CAT, INC.

Late January 1957: At last I had fulfilled my China-days' dream. I was now on my way to become a member of Civil Air Transport (CAT).[1] I had picked up enough of information from my Washington DC interview and letter from Comer to know a bit more about the company. CAT was flying commercial routes throughout Asia, serving as a privately-owned commercial airline but was,

CAT large baggage sticker

simultaneously, under the guise of CAT, Inc., providing flights for the Secret Service's intelligence operation in the Far East. Its home in Japan was on the far outskirts of Tokyo. I thought CAT would suit me fine as I wanted to live and fly in Asia.

After a long delay at Shemya[2] in the Aleutian Islands, Alaska, Barnes and I arrived in Tokyo on another rainy evening. It seemed like I was always arriving in the Far East either in the rain or during a rainy season. During the approach to Tokyo, Barnes explained to me about Oshima Island[3] in Tokyo Bay, and I could again see Mt. Fuji in the distance.

When we landed at Haneda Airport, Warren Comer and John Brown were there to meet us. Brown was a new navigator and former Northwest Airlines employee. Warren suggested I declare a Lincoln Continental while going through customs, then later ship it and make a lot of money that way. I declined, not being at all interested. Besides, I told him I had no idea where I would be based or what I would be doing. And, by this time, I knew Comer well enough to take what he said with a grain of salt.

We drove to Tachikawa Airbase and checked in at the Air Force BOQ. The next morning Barney and I walked to the CAT, Inc. complex on the base which was only a short distance away. CAT was allocated a few buildings and a ramp for its planes. In looking over the complex with such a large communications center, a mailroom struck me as a little odd. Chinese radio operators were always busy on the code keys. Turns out, that it was a direct communications system to all of CAT's operations as well as the head office at No. 46, Section 2, Zhongshan N Rd, Zhongshan District,[4] Taiwan (Formosa).

There we met Doug Smith, better known as "Snuffy" Smith, chief pilot of CAT, Inc., Tachikawa. Doug gave us a tour of the operation, handed us a C-46 manual, and told us we would be flying with him on 2 February, which was just a few days later. It seemed to me that, rather than landing in the middle of a civilian airline company, I was right in the middle of a U.S. Air Force operation. Snuffy told us we would be going to Taipei in a week or so for further indoctrination.

I went on liberty with Comer and Brown the next evening. They promised me a tour of Tachikawa city. Adjacent to the airbase, it catered to the off-duty Air Force personnel and their dependents. It was virtually a night-club city with plenty of cabarets, night clubs, and hostess bars. It was hard to believe that such a small town could have so many clubs, about 50 in all! Each club or bar was filled with hostesses available and, for 200 yen (at that time, 360 Japanese yen equaled one U.S. dollar), they would join our table and dance and drink with us until their colored sugar-water ran out. We could buy beer, Coke, or mixed whiskey. Once we stopped buying drinks, though, the girls would move on to another table.

It would not have been far off the mark to call Tachikawa at that time a super-sin city. It was truly an open city and vice seemed to be its motto then. Most of the women there had either been sold or were runaways or had been kicked out of their homes. Incest between fathers and daughters was quite common at this time and was certainly one of the reasons so many of these young girls ran away. Arriving from all parts of Japan, they either stayed with the night club owners or lived off base with an airman or officer.

CAT Curtiss C-46D Commando in Indochina (USAF - National Museum of the U.S. Air Force photo 110224-F-XN622-005, Public Domain 1950-54)

Comer and Brown had already taken up residence off-base, renting a Japanese house and paying a *josei* a monthly wage to live with them; but the josei continued to work as a hostess in one of the bars from 5:00 p.m. to 11:00 p.m. at night. Military curfew was 2300 hours until 0800 hours sharp. No Air Force or associated personnel, including CAT, Inc. pilots and personnel, were allowed on the streets of Tachikawa during those hours.

As scheduled on 2 February, Chief Pilot Doug Smith loaded a Curtiss Commando C-46 (#B-148) with sand bags to increase gross weight and simulate a loaded aircraft, which also actually made it a loaded aircraft. I was at the controls from Tachikawa to Haneda Airport for a training flight. We performed some instrument approaches and then started to make takeoffs and landings, called TGLs (touch-and-go landings). On my second takeoff, we lost number-two engine due to high cylinder temperature. Snuffy feathered the engine and got on the radio, which was both VHF and HF, to call Tachikawa operations to inform them of our situation and that we would be returning. At this point, I told Snuffy that it was not possible for me to climb and return as he had ordered me to do. It was taking more than METO (maximum-except-takeoff) power to stay above the safe single-engine speed. The only option I had open now was an immediate landing at Haneda. He and I exchanged a few words on the subject and then he took control from the right copilot's seat. He was going to return to Tachikawa Airbase—until he realized that Bravo 148 would not climb, not even a few feet, unless takeoff power was used, and that was not an option.

I asked Snuffy which runway he wanted, and he selected 33 but overshot it in his turn. That put us on a sea-effect (similar to ground-effect) very close to the waters of Tokyo Bay. Sea effect and ground effect are relatively the same.

A cushion of air roughly equal to the wingspan above the water or the ground. Because the good engine was being taxed rather severely, we barely made it to Runway 22. The temperature was rising close to the red line, and I had more than a few choice words to say to Snuffy during the approach—how the approach should be made with flaps and power, etc. We made it, but from then on, I had one enemy in CAT that I certainly did not want or need. It was not a good beginning.

Someone had misjudged how much sand was loaded. There was no question about it—there was too much. We were lucky we did not have to swim home that day.

On 3 February Barney and I were deadheaded to CAT headquarters in Taipei to be indoctrinated into CAT, receive our uniforms, and take our written exams for China Airlines transport pilot licenses. Just arriving in Taipei was an experience! It seemed as if China itself had been moved there. As far as the work and people, it was another Tsingtao, except pedicabs had replaced the rickshaws. The currency had also changed—new Taiwanese dollars. The Chinese food was the same and very good. My favorite dinner had always been Szechuan duck and still was.

On the first morning, we went to CAT headquarters on Zhongshan Road. There we met CAT's Chief Pilot Eddie Sims and the VPO (vice president of operations), Capt. Robert E. "Bob" Rousselot.[5] Later we were measured for uniforms: blue pants, navy flight jacket and a blue hat with the CAT emblem. Capt. Sims' secretary said we would take the Chinese written exam the next afternoon, but to arrive about 10:00 a.m. so she could give us the most likely questions and answers. I should not have, but I believed her.

We had a Chinese dinner at our hotel and toured the city. The next morning Barney and I showed up for the promised exam preview. She informed us that it was lost. I told her that I had not studied because of her promise and that it would surely be her fault if I failed the exam. Well, I passed with flying colors. Barney, seeing no point in studying a sure thing, did not make it on the navigation part.

When we returned to the head office, Capt. Sims told us I had made his secretary cry. He said she was from a very important family, and I was no longer welcome in CAT! Enemy number two and both chief pilots. I decided then and there to return to the USA and asked to see the VPO, Capt. Rousselot. He immediately calmed me down and explained Sims' temperament.

Despite my run-ins with both chief pilots, Capt. Rousselot encouraged me to stay, assuring me I would have a good job in CAT if I went back to Japan and did the best to stay clear of Doug Smith or at least stay on his good side.

The next day we were scheduled to go to Tainan Airbase to tour CAT's contract maintenance facilities. Tainan is south of Taipei in southern Formosa, and CAT had daily flights there (called Round Island flights) from Taipei using a C-46. We were also scheduled to spend a day on CAT's LST (landing ship transport) supply barge, which CAT had purchased while still on the mainland. It had docked at Kaohsiung, about 185 miles south of Taipei and a few miles south of the maintenance compound at Tainan.

Captain Robert E. Rousselot
(Photo by Stephen Pingry / Tulsa World)

Chapter 8. CAT, INC. | 105

Both the LST and the maintenance compound at Tainan were impressive. I first noticed how immaculately clean all of CAT's airplanes were. The maintenance was also superb, something I was to experience many times in the future. Tainan City itself was typically Chinese except that it was more tropical. Its excellent climate allowed all kinds of fruit to be purchased for a small sum, especially bananas and pineapples.

CAT had a compound in Tainan City, away from the maintenance facilities, where crew and guests stayed and where all social activities for American and Australian maintenance employees took place. It was also open to all of CAT's Chinese employees and U.S. Air Force officer-personnel based in Tainan.

CAT's maintenance base was called AirAsia and overhauled all sorts of aircraft for the U.S. Air Force (its main customer) including the latest jet fighters. Although the supervisors were mostly American and Australian, there were workers from other parts of the world, as well. I found the Chinese employees to be very skilled and able to maintain everything from a small aircraft to an airliner.

They had one Civil Air Transport pilot based fulltime at Tainan as a test pilot. His job was to test aircraft coming out of maintenance programs. I now understood that Civil Air Transport was composed of three entities: CAT; CAT, Inc.; and AirAsia—different companies sharing the same pilots, roster, and seniority system. I was assigned to CAT, Inc. and would be based in Tachikawa, Japan, for the time being, according to my boss, VPO Capt. Bob Rousselot. Later CAT, Inc. changed its name to Air America.

After my indoctrination trip to Taipei and Tainan, I returned to Tachikawa Airbase and on 11 February 1957, I was scheduled on CAT, Inc.'s DC-4 to Taipei, Kadena, Okinawa, and back to Naval Air Facility Atsugi in Japan, near Tachikawa. The flights were classified as MATS (military air transport service) flights and flew to military, as well as civilian bases. During February, March, and April, I made numerous flights to Okinawa, Taipei, Manila, Saigon, Vientiane, Guam, and Saipan.

I was doing what I had wanted to do; the flights were interesting, and I was flying in the Far East for CAT, Inc., the company I wanted to work for. I continued to live at the BOQ in Tachikawa and was issued an ID card stating that I was an employee of CAT, Inc., accorded all the military-base privileges of an officer, and governed and protected by military laws.

I again took up the study of the Japanese language during my off-duty time and rented a house off the airbase in nearby Fussa, a small Japanese town a few miles west of Tachikawa. I did this for several personal reasons. I wanted to get a better understanding of the Japanese culture and learn the language. I also loved Japanese food. Contrary to most of my friends at Tachikawa, though, I did not take up housekeeping with a Japanese girl. I preferred to be independent and have more associations before making those kinds of arrangements and decisions. I suppose it was also in the back of my mind that Tachikawa was not likely to be my permanent personal base. According to Capt. Rousselot, I could expect to be moved in a few months at most.

Although it was not a Lincoln Continental, I did buy a Buick from an Air Force officer based there and started to tour nearby towns. I went to Karuizawa, a resort village in the mountains north of Tokyo, right at the foot of the volcanic Mt. Asama.[6] Besides being a beautiful place to visit, Karuizawa is also a hot-springs resort and a favorite place for many foreigners based or living in Tokyo. I spent all my nights there in the Green Hotel, that is until I became acquainted with the Kulihara family. Mr. Kulihara was a Japanese farmer, and he and his family invited me to stay with them.

I was becoming much more engrossed in the Japanese way of life and language now. I had told Chief Rousselot that I did not want to be based in Japan but, to my own amazement, I was beginning to really like living there. I did not like Tachikawa Airbase and was not too keen on the MP enforcing the curfew, but it did have its good points—post exchange privileges, movie theaters, the officers club, etc. I began to think that by being a civilian airline pilot based in Japan, I could have my cake and eat it too.

So, I maintained my BOQ and the small Japanese house I rented in Fussa. However, I spent most of my free time during the winter of '57 with Kulihara San and family. He sold me a one-acre plot of land, and I camped out on it until I later built a home there. Kulihara had a Setter bird dog and was a real Japanese mountain man who liked country life as much as I did. I always felt at home in the mountains of Japan. The hunting opportunities surpassed those back in the lower 48 states.

In September 1957, I joined the Air Force Flying Club at nearby Showa Airfield. I was a flight instructor and got to know many Air Force personnel based at Yokota and Tachikawa airbases. The manager of the club was Master Sergeant Luther; his Japanese girlfriend was named Yoko. Luther was an ex-officer in the Air Force who accepted a master sergeant rating to serve his full 20 years for retirement. He was a good man, but I lost contact with him after I departed Japan for another assignment.

I had several friends at Tachikawa. Upon my arrival I had become friends with CAT's senior captains, all superb pilots: Randall Richardson, William "Bill" Gaddie, John Plank, and Stu Dew. Warren Comer, Jessie Walton, Herb Liu (a Chinese American), and Al Bond were also close friends at Tachikawa.

Also, during this time, I became close friends with Capt. Woody Forte who lived with a Japanese girl just off the base and made many trips to Karuizawa with me. Some of my earliest flights were with him in the Curtiss C-46 Commando. I experienced an exciting flight with Woody between Itazuke Airbase in Japan and Pusan, Korea, during the winter of '57. Our C-46 carburetors iced up, and I had to backfire the engines to clear them while over the sea. We lost 2,000 feet from our cruising altitude, and I wasn't sure we wouldn't be going in for a swim. I thought I had learned my lesson from Snuffy Smith about trusting other peoples' abilities and authority. After this, though, that lesson really sunk in. Woody had been flying DC-3s out of Bangkok for the last three years and was a bit unfamiliar with both the cold Korean winters as well as the critical aspects of the C-46. We made it this time but, sorry to say, Woody bought the farm in Laos a few years later. I missed him very much.

I flew to Saipan and Guam on many trips during the summer of that same year. Saipan is one of the most beautiful places on earth. When I stayed there, I went deep-sea fishing and scuba diving. I swam among the sunken Japanese warships from World War II. Many Japanese aircraft still lay where they had gone down. It was an eerily interesting exploration, looking them over, pondering the fate of their pilots.

Chapter 9.

INDONESIA

I spent as much time as possible with Kulihara San during October and November of 1957. We hunted pheasants and ducks. The hunting in Japan was an experience I shall never forget. I managed to hunt there for many years and never tired of it.

I also flew various routes in the Far East in the DC-4 and Curtiss C-46 during the first three months of the next year. The DC-4 trips were mainly to Okinawa, Taipei, Tainan, Guam, and Saipan. The C-46 flights were to different points in Korea and throughout Japan including Chitose, Misawa, Itazuke, and Itami. I also made some flights to Cubi Point in the Philippines.

In March 1958, I applied for one-month active duty at the Naval Air Station in Oakland, California (NAS Alameda) where I could get more flight training and obtain more endorsements. Chief Rousselot approved this temporary leave from CAT without hesitation.

I boarded a Navy transport R5D for NAS Alameda and was allowed to fly copilot most of the way as I was already checked out in the R5D. Besides, the Navy commander

Lockheed T-33 Shooting Star
(U.S. Air Force Photo/Alejandro Pena)

was a friend of mine from Pensacola days.

In Oakland, I checked out and qualified in the Navy SNB utility transport, the T-33 Navy TV-2,[1] and F2H,[2] the Navy's twin-engine jet fighter. One of the lieutenant colonels was also a federal civil examiner, so I took a check ride with him in the R5D, which was also called the DC-4, to obtain my civilian type rating, which qualified me to fly command on the four-engine aircraft. Before this, I only had my DC-3 and C-46 captain endorsements. I was happy to get this endorsement on my license, remembering how Doug Smith, my chief at Tachikawa, had refused to let me take the check ride in a CAT aircraft.

Douglas A-26 Invader

I also knew that Snuffy wanted to get me thrown out of CAT. Assistant Chief Pilot, Capt. Gaddie knew the situation between us, though, and told me not to worry as he would personally write the VPO and explain everything. This took place after I returned to Tachikawa and resumed my regular CAT flights.

On 11 April 1958, I had a flight to Taipei and Tainan, Formosa, where I was introduced to what CAT called the Black Bird, the two-engine A-26 attack bomber.[3] During the remainder of that month, I spent my time flying the A-26 and C-46 out of Manila, Clark Field, and the Celebes.

For the next six months I was based out of Clark and Tainan with an American copilot. Now I commenced to fly covert flights to Indonesia. The flights were of resupply and night covert operations in nature. While at Clark, much of my off time was spent enjoying the various avenues for nightlife available outside the airbase and in the nearby towns. On one daytime mission, my copilot failed to show up, so I took the flight myself, along with the plane kicker (cargo dropper or loadmaster)[4] and radio operator. I am certain Chief Rousselot would have canned him for good—probably me too if he had known about it. But then, perhaps Rousselot knew more than we realized.

I had a close call in the Celebes after we landed at Manado[5] one night. We had made a perfect dark-night landing with the aid of only two flares, one at each end of the runway. I went to the back door of the plane, opened it and put the ladder down, intending to identify and take on the agents we were directed to pick up and take back to Clark Field. I had told my copilot to get in the left seat and keep both engines at idle power while I made contact with the agents.

I couldn't identify the agents, however, with all the machine guns and rifles pointing directly at my face—about a dozen or so I think. Arranging the signal beforehand, I was going to flash my flashlight twice as a signal to my copilot that all was okay. I flashed it anyway—even though nothing was okay just then. I didn't want him to leave me behind in a surge of power. He just happened to be in a takeoff position, and anything was possible at that moment. (He told me later that he was scared stiff and wasn't about to trust those agents. He had every intention of taking off with the ladder down and the door open if I didn't signal that all was kosher.)

Well, three agents and I got back on board while the rest of the welcoming party just faded back into the jungle. The three escorted me to the cockpit, guns still raised. I sat down in the copilot's seat and gave him the thumbs up. We made a quick takeoff and departure. I still did not know what those agents' intentions were or what would happen in the cabin. They remained seated, but I did expect a visit to the cockpit with guns pointing at any time after takeoff. It never happened.

Afterwards, finding out that the copilot would have left me behind if he deemed it necessary when I had not signaled, I never trusted him again. That was the last of his covert career.

In April 1959, I was introduced to the Helio aircraft and to Maj. Harry C. "Heinie" Aderholt.[6] He called himself Heinie, as did everyone who knew him. I liked Heinie immediately and worked under him for the next few years. Rousselot sent me and another new hire to Kadena, Okinawa, where we met Heinie and had breakfast with him. Heinie informed me he wanted us to fly a new type of aircraft hidden in an Air Force hangar at Naha AFB. What I saw seemed like an unusual aircraft. He told me it was called a Helio, and I believe this one was designated the Helio-1.[7] It did not seem all that impressive when it was rolled out of the hangar for our preflight, but it did have a lot of high-lift devices. Heinie explained briefly how to fly it before flying us back to Kadena in it. He got us priority traffic at Kadena, so I decided this was to be a special-project aircraft of some significance. After a few demonstration takeoffs and landings, Heinie turned it over to me. It was easy to fly and certainly had the controlled takeoff and landing ability he said it did.

Brig. Gen. Harry C. "Heinie" Aderholt

Then he turned it over to the new hire who promptly had a lot of trouble flying it. He wasn't familiar with the slats, flaps, large aileron, and interceptors for controlling the aircraft. I advised Heinie about this over lunch at the officers' club. Nevertheless, Heinie sent us to Okuma Beach to practice takeoffs and landings that same afternoon. I told Heinie again the I did not want to fly with this new-hire and that I planned to ride in the back after I completed my practice flight. The new hire crashed the brand-new Helio on his second attempt at landing. The landing gear collapsed after the hard landing, and we skidded to a halt. Fortunately, we got out with only a few bruises.

Helio Courier (Photo Credit Tom Lum)

I called Heinie from Okuma and told him the I-told-you-so news. He seemed very unhappy with the new-hire but not upset with me, as I reminded him of our conversation before the new-hire and I departed.

The next day we were deadheaded to Taipei where I would have a lot of explaining to do to Rousselot. That ended my Helio introduction, as well as the new-hire's tour in Asia. He was promptly sent back to CONUS (the continental United States). Despite the new-hire's ineptitude, it turned out to be a good experience for me as, later, I would fly and come to appreciate many of the Helio's unique characteristics.

I returned to Tainan where I met another new hire named Bill Beale.[8] Bill became my best friend. He was a can-do and will-do man. He knew everyone in the CAF (Chinese Air Force) at Tainan and enabled us to even put one over on Rousselot, our boss, and fly on an actual mission with the CAF. Beale was a man who liked action and adventure and would later lead the B-26s at the Bay of Pigs invasion in Cuba.[9] Rousselot liked and trusted Beale as did I, and that meant a lot.

Beale and I flew together in F-86 Sabres,[10] F-100s,[11] B-26s, and C-46s, as well as other aircraft. Before joining CAT, he was a lieutenant colonel in the U.S. Air Force and had had quite a career as a B-24 Liberator pilot flying missions out of the Aleutians during World War II. Along with many other tours of duty, he later flew F-86 fighters from Elmendorf AFB in Anchorage, Alaska where, during his off-time, he flew the L-20 Beaver on floats. He told me many stories about the fishing and hunting in Alaska and of his war adventures with the B-24 during those hard and dangerous missions against the Japanese.

Bill somehow managed to get an assignment with the CAF as an advisor in Formosa. After his friend (a Chinese colonel) was killed, Bill fell in love with and married the colonel's Chinese wife and adopted his daughter. This was shortly before he joined CAT at Tainan.

Bill did not exactly make a hit with the other CAT pilots, but Rousselot respected him and put him in charge of some covert operations. It seemed Bill and his wife knew everyone in the CAF. Being a former Air Force colonel, Bill sought both respect and power in Air America and sensed he needed it, and, at least as far as the VPO was concerned, he received both.

North American F-100 Super Sabre

Capt. Don Teeters of CAT gave me some takeoff and landings in the PBY Catalina at Tainan. After Don went back to Taipei, I scheduled myself for local takeoffs and landings as well as local flights. Someone reported to the office that Sutphin was flying the PBY. Rousselot put a quick stop to it, and Beale got me out of the jam with flying colors. He was the only pilot in Air America to tell Rousselot straight from the shoulder what he thought. Beale and I continued to fly out of Tainan with most of the flights being local CEECO (Consolidated Electric

Equipment Company) or A-26 flights[12] until June 1959 when we reported to Itazuke AFB in Japan to transition and fly the F-100 Super Sabre. I was elated to have the chance to fly a supersonic fighter and relished having a break from Tainan.

Chapter 10.

TEST PILOT

Bill Beale knew the wing commander at Itazuke where we checked into the Head-Hunters 80th Tactical Fighter Squadron.[1] Bill registered as Lieutenant Commander, USAF Reserve, and I registered as Captain, USMCR. I think some of the boys in the squadron wondered why we were there as we flew but did not wear military uniforms. The wing commander interviewed us and told me that he had received instructions from Washington to let us join the 80th squadron for transition and training exercises.

I was assigned an excellent instructor, a World War II captain who had reapplied and gotten back on active duty. A former West Point man, he flew the P-47 Thunderbolt in the European theater during the war. Flying in an Air Force squadron was a new thing for me, and I looked forward to comparing the Air Force pilots with the Navy flyers. The 80th ran a tight outfit, and their flying was first-rate. After a month I felt comfortable flying with them. I flew a lot of supersonics and completed air refueling, aerobatics, and instruments, as well as Auto LABS (Automatic Low Altitude

Emblem of USAF 80th Fighter Squadron

Bombing Systems).[2] I especially liked the heavy-loaded, close-formation takeoffs that the 80th did. We had never done that in the Marine squadrons that I had flown with. The AB (afterburner) was new to me. It had the kick we needed to get airborne from the Itazuke runway.

I did not fly with Beale while with the squadron. He was assigned a different flight. On one of my final flights, I was required to take and pass an instrument check flight in an F-100F two-seater. I have long forgotten the Air Force captain's name who gave me that check, but I do remember his reputation for failing people who took check rides with him. After an hour or so during the check, he told me I was okay and that he would take control from the front cockpit and show me some local flying.

I could not believe what he did when we hit the deck (got close to the water). He started rapid rolls at high speed just above the ocean's surface. I was sure I was going to buy the farm each time he rolled. When he finally stopped, I complimented him on his ability. I was genuinely impressed and, in fact, marveled that I was still alive. Three months later, one of the 80th Squadron's F-100s stopped in Tainan for maintenance. The pilot told me that my instrument instructor had braked too hard while landing at Kadena and was killed.

After returning to Tainan, I met our North American F-100 technical representative and settled in as a test pilot on all the aircraft that were being overhauled at Tainan's AirAsia maintenance facility. My usual routine included Auto LABS flights in the F-100s, A-26 CEECO flights, or perhaps a two-plane bombing or gunnery practice flight with Beale.

The Auto LABS flights commenced over the water at 200 feet, doing 400-knots airspeed. We used a small rock about 50 miles off the coast on Tainan for an initial point to start our run in to the target, which was a small island used specifically for target practice. Everything was automatic. If something went wrong with the autopilot of the LABS during the run, we would disconnect by pushing a button on the control stick. If that failed, the only recourse was a circuit breaker behind our left elbow. Pull that if there is no response to normal control—then eject.

Doing an Auto LABS flight was more-or-less a joyride

Chapter 10. TEST PILOT | 123

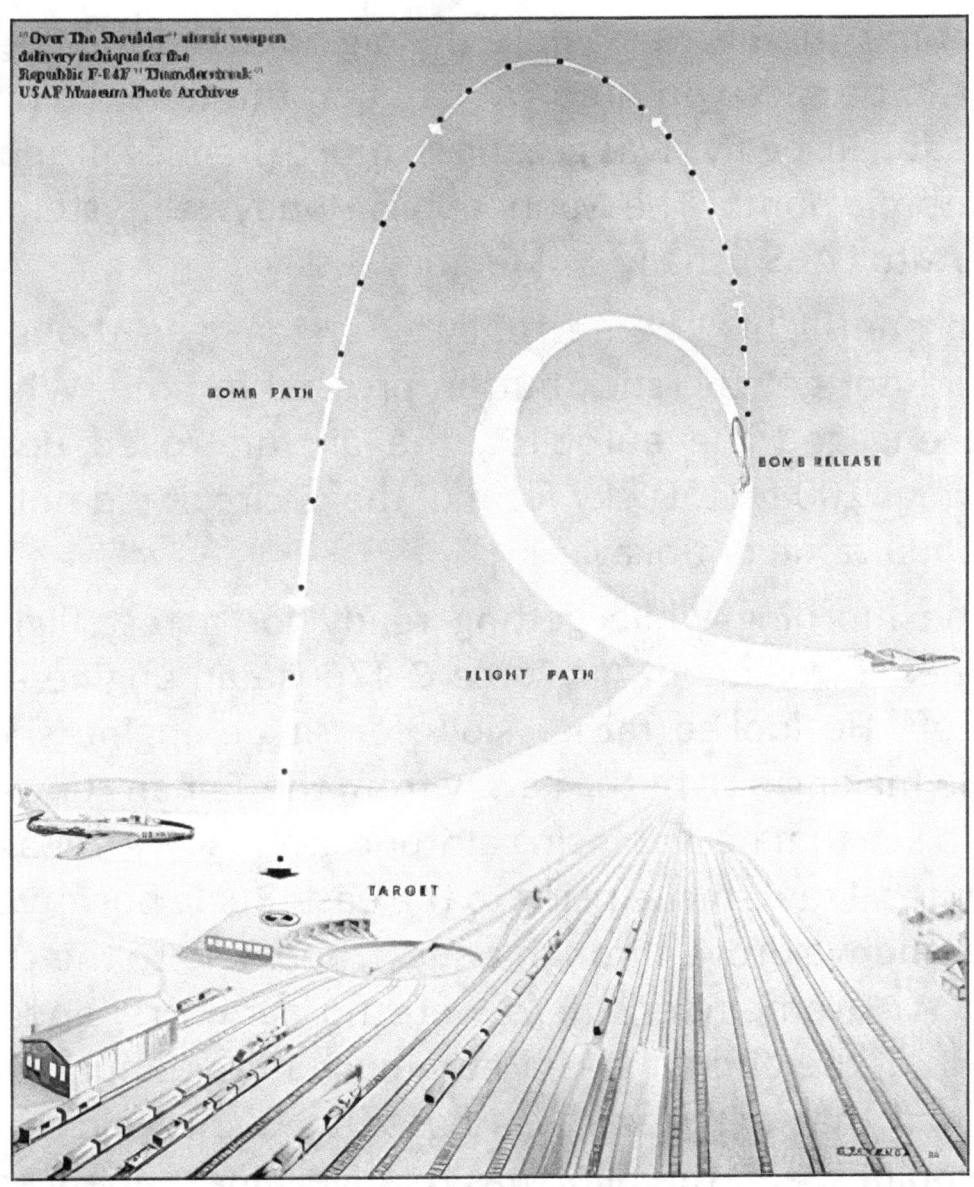

Toss- or loft-bombing with Auto LABS (U.S. military diagram of the over-the-shoulder bombing technique)

at 400 knots, 200 feet over the IP. We would wait for the target light to come on and hit the afterburner. The aircraft instantly went into almost vertical climb to 8,500 feet, the bomb release point. G-force cutback kicked in, and the airplane reversed course, rolled level, and headed for home. All this was before the big bomb hit the target. I got to be sharp on Auto LABS but, at the time, I did not question just why I was getting so much practice dropping an atomic bomb. The Minneapolis Honeywell systems in the Auto LABS usually worked flawlessly.

On one flight, I had a runaway system and thought I would not get the stick button pressed in time. When I first engaged the autopilot, the aircraft rolled upside down at 200 feet. Lucky for me, the G-circuit did not cut in, and I came out okay.

One morning while getting ready for a test flight, I happened to see an Air Force C-47 lose an engine after takeoff. He looked rather slow for single-engine speed while making a right turn away from the Tainan runway. I could see that he was losing altitude gradually. After a few minutes, I saw smoke rising to the east. Beale borrowed a jeep and we drove through a sugarcane field to the crash site. As I remember, there were no survivors, and the inside of the aircraft was pretty much burned out. I later learned that the plane was based at Clark Field in the Philippines, and the pilot was relatively inexperienced in the C-47.

At that time, I lived at the CAT hostel for pilots in the CAT Club compound. Other CAT transit pilots would overnight there when necessary. There was one houseboy who took care of the hostel, that is until I caught him stealing money from transit-pilots' wallets. The Tainan police gave him a good and fair sentence: he was made a private in the

Chinese Army and shipped to Quemoy and Matsu Islands facing the mainland where live fire was exchanged almost daily.

One day I received a message from VPO Rousselot to bring a Douglas A-26 to Taipei at 8:00 p.m. that night and pick up Hugh Hicks, his copilot and radio operator, and then fly to Tainan so he could pick up a Douglas DC-3 and fly it to Southeast Asia. The codename for Southeast Asia was just SEA.

When I got there to pick up Capt. Hicks, he let me know that he was not happy to deadhead in a bomber and especially at night. I told him it would do no good to complain to me and that he should just refuse to go, and I would return to Tainan without him—then he could take it up with Rousselot. He decided to go, but he also never stopped complaining. I arrived back over Tainan about 11:30 that night. It was fogged in solid. After holding over the Tainan beacon for about 30 minutes, waiting for the GCA to get our station, I decided to go ahead and make an approach. The weather was certainly below GCA radar minimums, but I went in anyway. I later heard that Hicks reported to everyone that I was a dangerous pilot; however, I never heard anything from Rousselot about it!

Capt. Hicks' career ended years later in the crash of a Boeing 727 at Taipei.[3]

While at Tainan, I had occasion to meet Heinie Aderholt and his Helio again. Bill Beale came to operations where

I had just landed from an F-100 test flight and told me Heinie and his Helio were about 15 miles east of Tainan Airbase in an open field. Evidently, he had the Helio aircraft transported from Okinawa in a large CAF transport and reassembled at his base; then he tested it on location. Heinie wanted me to come to the location and put on a demonstration for a few of his assembled dignitaries. I reminded Beale about the Okinawa fiasco and decided not to go. A few minutes later, however, a dispatch came from communications that I was to proceed to the field with Beale. I decided to hell with it. I would go and see what he wanted. I informed Beale, though, that I did not want to ever get assigned to such a program, because it smelled of a no-good assignment.

I did fly the Helio that day. It was a demo flight. I discovered that the Helio airplane handled better on unimproved strips and that it virtually outperformed any other STOL (short takeoff and landing) aircraft. I even performed low-altitude aerobatics, more to impress Beale than Heinie. It was great to see Heinie again, and I promptly forgot all about the Helio project after the demo flight.

One day at Tainan, a new Air America Helio arrived and was assembled there. I made the test flight and flew it locally on some other flights with Beale as I wanted to show him the outstanding capabilities of this airplane. Hugh L. Grundy, president of CAT, AirAsia, and Air America, etc., arrived in Tainan, and I was asked to fly him to Kaohsiung where the AirAsia LST (a WWII landing ship tank)[4] was docked. It was part of the AirAsia maintenance complex and was used to overhaul various aircraft parts. Al Weuste, the Tainan maintenance boss, was to accompany us on this short round trip flight. Grundy would fly as copilot with Al in the back, observing. Weuste informed me that Mr. Grundy had logged some flight time and asked me if it was possible to let him fly some. I let Grundy have control and told my company president to land it at Kaohsiung Airport. He declined; I insisted; so, he tried. Unfortunately, I had to take control back at the last moment to avoid a crash. Mr. Grundy was very unhappy about the whole episode and later tried to fire me. That did not happen, however, because Air America VPO Rousselot had no love for Grundy. Rousselot controlled all the pilots, and that was that.

Chapter 11.

LAOS AND AIR AMERICA

Chapter 11 Citation

In Ron's unfinished manuscript, most of the following chapter, Chapter 11, "Laos and Air America," is a historical background synopsis garnered directly and/or indirectly from William M. Leary's[1] treatise on the war in Laos titled: (Leary, CIA Air Operations in Laos, 1955-1974: Studies in Intelligence, Winter 1999-2000: Supporting the 'Secret War' 2007), and (Leary, Series III, Civil Air Transport (CAT). William M. Leary Papers, CA021-06, History of Aviation Archives, Special Collections and Archives Division n.d.)

William Leary's papers are well-worth researching and browsing either on the CIA website or in the History of Aviation Archives, Special Collections and Archives Division, Eugene McDermott Library, The University of Texas at Dallas.

Because Leary's work provides the historical background for events in war-torn Laos, please note that the burden of crediting each paragraph or phrase directly should be considered as cited here. Ron's phrasing remains generally as he wrote it to retain his own personal perspective concerning events as well as his contribution to Air America's activities during the Laotian Civil War. I have attempted to properly document other contributors to this chapter, as well. Allen Cates, Oden Meeker, William J. Merrigan, and Charles A. Stevenson as well as a few others I have not been able to identify have all contributed. I extend my thanks to them for all their hard work in writing this vital chapter (csn 2022; 2019).

Chapter 11. LAOS AND AIR AMERICA

To conduct covert operations in Asia in support of U.S. policy objectives, an air-transport capability was required. So, in 1950 the Central Intelligence Agency decided to bring Air America into being. In August 1950, CIA secretly purchased the assets of CAT (Civil Air Transport), an airline which began in China after World War II by General Claire L. Chennault and Whiting Willauer. Civil Air Transport would continue to fly commercial routes throughout Asia, serving in every way as a privately-owned commercial airline. At the same time, under the guise of CAT, Inc., it provided airplanes and crews for secret intelligence operations.

The CIA's air proprietary was used for a variety of covert missions during the decade. An example of this was during the Korean War, CAT, Inc. made over 100 hazardous overflights of mainland China, airdropping agents and supplies. CAT pilots could be found over Dien Bien Phu (also Dienbienphu) in 1954 supporting the doomed French garrison. In 1958, CAT provided the air force for the CIA's unsuccessful attempt to overthrow the Sukarno government of Indonesia. Beginning in 1958 and continuing in the early '60s, CAT, Inc. (now Air America as it became in 1959) was the center of a major CIA operation to train and supply anti-Communist forces in far-off Tibet. . While Air America would continue to support CIA activities throughout Asia and elsewhere during the '60s, the airline's major focus became Southeast Asia, especially the growing war in Laos.

In many ways, the Kingdom of Laos was an unlikely location for American interest. Oden Meeker, a CARE[2] man assigned to the capital of Vientiane in the mid-50s, found Laos a sleepy country with a tranquility "just this side of Rip Van Winkle."[3] The Lao people, he noted were "unambitious, nonmechanical..." Yet, "above all," he wrote, among their "host of virtues: they are...gentle and courteous. They are a smiling, whimsical people..." Inefficiency was a way of life that seemed to bother only foreigners.[4]

Still, beyond the sleepy surface, lay a stark geopolitical reality. In an age of Cold War, Laos happened to be in the wrong place at the wrong time. To Assistant Secretary of State Walter S. Robertson, Laos was "a finger thrust right down into the heart of Southeast Asia. And Southeast Asia is one of the prime objectives of international Communists in Asia because it is rich in raw materials and has excess food." Robertson painted a grim scenario for a House subcommittee in 1959. He warned that, considering the potential of the Communists gaining control of the resources of Southeast Asia, combined with the manpower of China and the industrial capacity of Japan, "we will really have to pull up stakes and come back home, because the battle will be lost."

The situation in Laos remained stable following the French departure from Indochina[5] in 1955. The United States established an operations mission in Vientiane to help the royal government with its many economic

Chapter 11. LAOS AND AIR AMERICA | 131

problems while a PEO (Programs Evaluation Office) dealt with military assistance. The first permanent CAT/Air America presence came on 30 June 1957, when Bruce Blevins arrived in Vientiane with C-47 registration Baker 817 to begin a new contract with the American embassy.[6] For the next two years Blevins flew a variety of missions, carrying embassy personnel around the country, dropping rice to outlying Lao army posts, taking photographs of drop zones, and providing logistical support for the forces of Neutralist Commander Kong Le.[7] He worked closely with

Kong Le (Lair, Bill; Ahern, Thomas; Undercover Armies, 1961-1973; Washington 2006 (Center for the Study of Intelligence, CIA) 1960s)

Jack Matthews; the CIA officer responsible for maintaining contact with Kong Le.

That fairly stable situation in Laos changed dramatically, however, in the summer of '59 when the fighting broke out between the Communist Pathet Lao and the royal government. As government positions on the strategic *Plaine des Jarres*[8] (a 30-square-mile area in the northern part of the country) became endangered, the United States dispatched special forces teams to Laos to train government troops. At the same time, the CIA called on Air America to play a much greater role in the country.

Robert Rousselot recalled that, one day in August 1959, "out of the blue," company president Hugh Grundy showed up in his office with a message from CIA headquarters directing Air America to send two pilots to Japan for helicopter training. Rousselot assumed that the helicopters would be used for a "one-time deal" but, to his great surprise, this message marked the beginning of a major long-term rotary-wing presence in Southeast Asia.

Eventually, in March 1960, four helicopters were sent to Laos. Chief Pilot Dale Williamson and three colleagues used Sikorsky H-19s[9] to fly CIA case officers around southern Laos, drop propaganda leaflets, conduct emergency medical evacuations, and perform other tasks. Restricted to areas of low elevation, the underpowered H-19s were frequently out of service. Also, the hastily trained transport pilots were unable to fully exploit even the limited potential of the H-19s.

Chapter 11. LAOS AND AIR AMERICA

Sikorsky S-55/H-19 Chickasaw in flight

The situation improved in the summer of 1960 when Clarence J. Abadie and three other experienced ex-Marine helicopter pilots replaced the original group—to their great relief. Things became even better later in the year when superior performing Sikorsky UH-34s took over for the tired H-19s.

In addition to rotary-wing capability, the CIA also asked Air America to undertake operations in Laos with STOL aircraft. The first Helio Courier arrived in Vientiane in October 1959 when Eddie Sims, the air proprietary's system chief pilot, checked out Bruce Blevins on the demanding aircraft. The STOL program got off to a poor start. The Helio's engine proved temperamental, frequently developing vapor locks on starting. In addition, the first pilots who flew it were multiengine transport pilots and did not receive adequate training on an airplane that demanded special techniques.

Air America came close to abandoning the Helio. However, Heinie, being an Air Force officer on detached service with the CIA and believing in the Helio capability, and Rousselot, who feared that the CIA would give the STOL mission to rival company, Bird & Son, if Air America proved incapable of doing the job, were able to salvage it. Early in 1960, Rousselot assigned me to the project. They both agreed that it was the "demonstration of the extraordinary capability of the STOL aircraft that saved the program."

William M. Leary wrote:

> Early in 1960, Rousselot assigned Ronald J. Sutphin, a talented light-plane pilot, to the project. Both Aderholt and Rousselot agree that it was Sutphin's skillful demonstration of the extraordinary capability of the STOL aircraft that led the CIA to greatly expand the program.[10]

In August 1960, President Dwight D. Eisenhower said in a press conference, "Laos is a very confused situation."[11]

Civil War had broken out between the neutralist forces of Kong Le and rightwing General Phoumi Nosavan.[12] The Communist Pathet Lao supported Kong Le; the U.S. Military and CIA lined up behind Phoumi. As Admiral Harry D. Felt, commander-in-chief of the Pacific Fleet, explained, "Phoumi is not George Washington. However, he is anti-Communist, which is what counts most in the sad Laos situation."

Air America transports soon began to fly guns, ammunition, and other supplies to Gen. Phoumi. In

Gen. Phoumi Nosavan

November, a C-46 engaged in this supply effort crashed on the Plaine des Jarres, killing the copilot and radio operator. These were the first Air America casualties in Laos; unfortunately, they were not the last. My good friend, Bill Beale was killed in a Beaver C-20 over Xieng Dot, Laos.[13] The aircraft exploded and burned after takeoff. I lost track of his widow and two children, though I did try to find them a few times later when I heard they had moved to Honolulu.

Heavy fighting took place in December as Gen. Phoumi drove Kong Le out of Vientiane. By the end of the year, Kong Le, who was now receiving support from a soviet airlift, had retreated to the Plaine des Jarres, securing the vital airfield complex in the area.

The appearance of the Soviets alarmed American military authorities. Adm. Felt cabled the Joint Chiefs of Staff on 29 December with this message: "With full realization of the seriousness of the decision to intervene, I believe strongly that we must intervene now or give up on Laos."

Admiral Arleigh Burke, Chief of Naval Operations, agreed. On 31 December, he told the Joint Chiefs: "If we lose Laos, we will probably lose Thailand and the rest of Southeast Asia. We will have demonstrated to the world that we cannot or will not stand when challenged." The effect, Burke warned, would soon be felt throughout Asia, Latin America, and Africa.

During his last days in office, President Eisenhower rejected direct military intervention. However, the administration did approve a recommendation from the CIA that had been endorsed by Adm. Felt and State Department officials to arm and train Hmong tribesmen in northern Laos. In January 1961, CIA paramilitary specialist James W. "Bill" Lair[14] (once described by an admiring subordinate as "a taciturn Texan—smart, sensitive and clever") met with Hmong leader Vang Pao. He found Vang Pao eager to obtain modern arms and training for the Hmong, who already had suffered greatly at the hands of the better-armed Pathet Lao. As the CIA warned to maintain a low profile in Laos, Lair arranged to have the Thai Border Police train the first one thousand Hmong recruits. A special three-day course was set up which included intensive work in map reading, tactics, demolition, and the use of WWII-era American weapons.

Hmong leader Vang Pao

With the Hmong scattered on mountainous terrain surrounding the Plaine des Jarres, Lair recognized from the beginning that effective communication was the key to effective operations. Naturally, he turned to Air America.

In the early months of 1961, Air America had only a handful of helicopters and STOL aircraft available for the task of supporting operations in Laos. This changed in early March when the new Kennedy administration became alarmed after Kong Le and the Pathet Lao captured a key road junction and threatened Vientiane and Luang Prabang. Kennedy not only placed military forces in the region on alert, but also authorized the transfer of 14 UH-34 helicopters[15] from the Marine Corps to Air America. They would be flown by Marine, Army, and Navy volunteers.

Sikorsky UH-34D helicopter (Photo Credit Tom Lum)

On 29 March 1961, Abadie led a flight of 16 UH-34s from Bangkok to Air America's new forward operating base at Udorn in northeastern Thailand, some 40 miles south of Vientiane. The helicopter force soon became involved in supporting Hmong forces engaged in a fierce battle with the Pathet Lao at Padong, a mountaintop position south of the PDJH.[16] On 30 May, the first Air America helicopter pilots died in Laos when Charles Mateer and Walter Wizbowski crashed in bad weather while attempting to land supplies to the besieged Hmong garrison at Padong. (Charles H. Mateer and Walter L. Wizbowski, 30 May 1961)[17]

In early June '61, both the United States and the Soviet Union decided to defuse the dangerous situation in Laos. At a meeting in Vienna, Pres. Kennedy and Soviet Premier Khrushchev issued a joint statement reaffirming their support "for a neutral and independent Laos." At the same time, negotiators met in Geneva to work out a settlement to the thorny problem.

By the summer of '61, the Hmong tribesmen had been trained and equipped by the CIA. As fighting diminished, Air America's role centered around supplying arms and ammunition to the 9,000 tribesmen and rice to the tens-of-thousands of Hmong refugees who had been displaced by the fighting. Most items were delivered by airdrops, but Air America also began to develop a series of airstrips, many on mountaintops or mountainsides that would form a key element in Bill Lair's transportation infrastructure for the Hmong tribe peoples.

When I arrived in Laos, the company had named the landing fields Victor One, Two, Three and so forth. I decided that the small fields and villages should be designated as "Sites" instead, similar to what they were called along the frontlines in the Korean War. They grew to encompass over 400 sites by the early 1970s.

Air America's presence in Laos grew evident with each passing month. By 1961, its personnel list recorded 163 pilots and copilots in Southeast Asia. Despite the low level of military activity, flying remained hazardous. On 12 August my neighbor and good friend crashed into the karst (mountain crest) at Pha Khao during an arms drag to Hmong forces. All five crew members—Woody Forte, Roger Sarno, David Bevan, Darrell Eubanks, and John Lewis—were killed in the crash. (Norwood N. Forte, Roger J. Sarno, David W. Bevan, Darrel A. Eubanks, and John S. Lewis, 13 August 1961.)[18]

In May 1962, the quiet in Laos was shattered when Communist troops attacked and quickly seized the provincial capital of Nam Tha in northern Laos. President Kennedy ordered 3,000 American military personnel into Thailand and, for a time, it seemed that full-scale fighting would break out. However, two months later, on 23 July 1962, Kennedy and Khrushchev met in Geneva and reaffirmed their support for the neutralization of Laos, signing the formal Declaration of Neutrality of Laos. It provided for a coalition government and withdrawal of all foreign troops from the country by 7 October 1962.

The United States complied with the agreement, pulling out its 666 military advisors and support staff. Air America arms drops also ceased. Assistant Secretary of State Averill Harriman, who was intent on ensuring U.S. compliance with the Geneva Accords,[19] allowed the CIA to retain only two men in Laos to monitor Communist compliance with the agreement.

Air America's operations declined sharply in 1963. Restricted to food resupply to the Hmong—which averaged forty tons a month by the summer of '63—the airline laid off people and mothballed planes. By May '63, the number of UH-34s assigned to Udorn had dropped from 18 to six helicopters. Flight hours, which had averaged 2,000 hours per month before the Geneva Accords, now dropped to an average of six hundred. As helicopter pilot Harry Casterlin wrote to his parents:

> "There are 37 of us over here and not enough work...We are doing virtually no flying in Laos anymore."

Despite this, reports reaching CIA headquarters from its two officers in Laos suggested that the apparent quiet was deceptive. It soon became clear that 7,000 North Vietnamese troops had not left the country. In fact, the NVA (North Vietnamese Army) was expanding its area of control, attacking both neutralist and Hmong positions throughout Laos. As Hmong ammunition stores became depleted, William Colby, head of the CIA's Southeast Asia Division, pleaded with Harriman to allow the resumption of arms shipments.

"My arguments became more forceful," Colby recalled, "reflecting the intense cables I was receiving from the two CIA officers who were still up in the hills observing and reporting on what was happening." Harriman, with great reluctance, finally approved the shipment of a small quantity of ammunition, along with strict instructions that it be used for defensive purposes only. Further shipments followed; however, as Colby points out, Harriman personally approved "each and every clandestine supply flight and its cargo."

As Hanoi sent additional troops into Laos during 1963, the Kennedy administration authorized the CIA to increase the size of the Hmong army; it reached 20,000 combatants by the end of the year.

The Hmong acted as guerrillas, blowing up NVA supply depots, ambushing trucks, mining roads, and generally harassing the stronger enemy force. Air America again took a greater role in the slowly expanding conflict. Casterlin wrote his parents in November 1963:

> "The war is going great-guns now. Don't be misled [by news reports] that I am only carrying rice on my missions, as wars aren't won on rice."

Full-scale fighting broke out in Laos in March 1964 when the North Vietnamese and Pathet Lao forces attacked across the Plaine des Jarres. By mid-May, the Communists had taken control of the strategic region, bringing an end to the already shaky coalition government. While contemplating direct American military intervention, President Lyndon Johnson ordered Navy and Air Force reconnaissance flights over the PDJ. The purpose of these flights was not only to provide intelligence, but also to send Hanoi "a message of American resolve." On 6 June, a naval reconnaissance aircraft was shot down over the PDJ. As the military services lacked search-and-rescue capability in Laos, Air America undertook the responsibility.

The unsuccessful attempt to rescue Lt. Charles E. Klusmann, who later did escape his captors, marked the beginning of what was perhaps the most demanding and hazardous of Air America's operations in Laos. The airline's pilots were neither trained nor properly equipped for the dangerous search-and-rescue tasks, but there was no one else to do it. This mission became even more difficult during the first half of 1965, when the air war expanded into the northwestern portion of North Vietnam.

That year, 1965, marked the beginning of what became known as the Secret War in Laos. Although the full extent of the conflict was not revealed to the American people until later (1969-70), the war really was not all that secret. News of the fighting frequently found its way onto the pages of the Bangkok Post and New York Times, as well as other papers around the globe.

Congress certainly was kept well informed. As former CIA Director Richard Helms pointed out, The Appropriations Subcommittees that provide funds for the war were briefed regularly. Also, several congressmen visited Laos and gave every indication of approving what was happening. They believed, Helms noted, that it was "a much cheaper and better way to fight a war in Southeast Asia than to commit American troops."

Noteworthy is that while the CIA was largely responsible for conducting military operations in Laos, the American ambassador was the man in charge. "The secret war in Laos," writes author Charles Stevenson, "was 'William Sullivan's war.' Ambassador for over four years, from December 1964 to March 1969, Sullivan insisted on an efficient, closely controlled country team. 'There wasn't a bag of rice dropped in Laos that he didn't know about,' observed Assistant Secretary of State William Bundy." Ambassador Sullivan imposed two conditions on his subordinates: First, the thin fiction of the Geneva Accords had to be maintained to avoid possible embarrassment to the Lao and Soviet governments. This meant that military operations had to be carried out in relative secrecy. Second, no regular U.S. ground troops were to become involved.[20] In general, Sullivan and his successor, G. McMurtrie Godley, successfully carried out this policy.

The early years of the war soon took on a seasonal aspect. During the dry season (October to May), the North Vietnamese and Pathet Lao went on the offensive, applying pressure among the Hmong and on government forces throughout the country. During the monsoon season (June to September), the anti-Communists took advantage of the mobility provided by Air America and struck deep into enemy-occupied territory. The situation was a mirror image of Vietnam itself. In Laos, the Communists acted as a conventional military force and were tied to roads and supply lines. The Hmong, at least

Chapter 11. LAOS AND AIR AMERICA | 145

at first, countered with guerrilla tactics.

The character of the war began to change in 1968, however. The North Vietnamese, apparently impatient with the progress of the Pathet Lao, introduced major new combat forces into Laos and took control of the year's dry-season offensive. By mid-March, they had captured the strategic valley of Nam Bak (north of Luang Prabang), successfully assaulted a key navigational facility at Phou Pha Thi[21] that was used by the USAF for bombing North Vietnam and threatened to push the Hmong out of their mountaintop strongholds surrounding the Plaine des Jarres. On 21 March, the CIA issued a Special National Intelligence Estimate to top-level policymakers in Washington on "Communist Intentions in Laos." Despite the presence of 35,000 NVA troops in the country, the CIA's analysts were relatively sanguine about the situation. Although the North Vietnamese had the capability of overrunning most of Laos in short order, the analysts concluded that Hanoi was mainly interested in protecting its supply routes to South Vietnam and did not wish to destroy the general framework of the 1962 Geneva settlement.

Events soon proved the CIA estimate to be correct. The NVA offensive ended with the onset of the monsoon in May. The Hmong, however, had suffered heavy casualties, losing over 1,000 men since January, including many top commanders. A recruitment drive turned up only 300 replacements; 30 percent of the new recruits were between the ages 10 and 14, 30 percent were ages 15-16, and the remaining 40 percent where all over 35! "Where were the ones in-between?" asked AID official Edgar "Pop" Buell[22] rhetorically. "I'll tell you! They're all dead."[23]

As the strength of the Hmong waned, the United States attempted to redress the growing imbalance of forces in the field through increased use of air power. Between 1965-68, the rate of sorties in Laos had remained constant at 10 to 20 a day. In 1969, however, the rate increased sharply, reaching as many as 300 per day.

During the wet season of 1969, Hmong leader Vang Pao[24] abandoned the use of guerrilla tactics and launched a major offensive against the NVA/Pathet Lao forces using the increased airpower to support a drive against enemy positions on the Plaine des Jarres. Largely designed to preempt an NVA/Pathet Lao attack, Operation About Face was a huge success. The Hmong reclaimed the entire PDJ for the first time since 1969, capturing 1,700 tons of food, 2,500 tons of ammunition, 640 weapons, and 25 Soviet PT-76 tanks.[25]

The victory, however, proved short-lived. In January 1970, the NVA brought in two divisions that not only quickly regained all the lost ground, but also threatened the major Hmong base at Long Tieng. For the first time, B-52s[26] were used to blunt the enemy drive.

Despite the growing NVA strength in Laos, which had now reached 67,000 men, CIA analysts continued to argue

Chapter 11. LAOS AND AIR AMERICA

Boeing B-52 Stratofortress

that the enemy did not wish to risk a decisive action. The CIA's Office of National Estimates made the following prediction in April 1970: "The Communists believe that when they obtain their objectives in South Vietnam, Laos will fall into their hands."

While U.S. prospects for success in both Laos and Vietnam diminished, Air America's presence grew. By the summer of 1970, the compound had some two-dozen twin-engine transports, another two-dozen aircraft, and some 30 helicopters dedicated to operations in Laos. Later in the year, several four-engine C-130s[27] were added. There were more than 300 pilots, copilots, flight mechanics, and air-freight specialists flying out of Laos and Thailand at that point. Air America airdropped or landed 46-million pounds of food (mainly rice) in Laos during 1970. Air America crews transported tens-of-thousand of troops and refugees, flew emergency medivac missions, rescued

Lockheed C-130 Hercules (Photo Credit Tom Lum)

downed airmen throughout Laos, inserted and extracted road teams, flew nighttime airdrop missions over the Ho Chi Minh Trail, spent long nights in Volpars[28] at altitudes of 20,000 feet monitoring sensors along infiltration routes, conducted a highly successful photo reconnaissance program over northern Laos, and engaged in numerous clandestine missions using night-vision glasses and state-of-the-art electronic equipment. The monsoon season of 1971 saw the last major offensive operations by the Hmong, who were now assisted by growing numbers

Turbo Beech Volpar (Photo Credit Tom Lum)

of Thai volunteers, themselves trained and paid by the CIA. Vang Pao once again captured the PDJ in July and established a network of artillery bases manned by Thai gunners. Vang Pao's hope of retaining the PDJ during the dry season proved abortive. On 18 December 1971, the North Vietnamese launched a coordinated assault against the artillery strongholds. Using tanks and 130mm guns that outranged the Thai artillery, the NVA recaptured the PDJ in three days.

The last days of 1971 and early months of '72 saw increased enemy pressure on the main Hmong base at Long Tieng. Air America suffered heavy losses during this period. In December, 24 aircraft were hit by ground fire and three were shot down.

On 27 December 1971 a C-123K[29] [Air America C123K (tail #6293), Flight #293 originating in Vientiane, then to Udorn Airbase and flightpath from there][30]—with Captain George Ritter, pilot; Captain Roy F. Townley, co-pilot; Edward Weissenback, kicker; and Khamphonh

Fairchild C-123 Provider (Photo Credit Tom Lum)

Saysongkham, kicker, onboard—was shot down during an arms drop. (George L. Ritter, Roy F. Townley, Edward A. Weissenback, and Khamphonh Saysongkham, all MIA.)[31] The crew remains missing in action. On 15 January, a Volpar was hit by antiaircraft fire while searching for the missing crew; the aircraft returned safely to Udorn, but Jim Rhyne lost a good portion of his right leg. On 18 March, helicopter pilot Wayne Knight was wounded during an effort to resupply Hmong troops defending Long Tieng. The next day, helicopter pilot Emmit Sullivan was shot down in northwestern Laos. On 20 March, in the same area, Porter[32] pilot Fred Connelly was wounded by ground fire. On 28 March, Tom Woosley and Izzy Friedman, flying a UH-34, were hit by 12.7mm fire as they approached Lima Site 54; the aircraft was destroyed, but the crew escaped serious injury. On 5 April, a Porter hit a mine on takeoff from Lima Site 90; the aircraft crashed and burned, injuring pilot Matt Daddio and two passengers. On 8 April, Leonard Wiehrdt crashed and was killed in a Porter. (Leonard I. Wiehrdt, 8 April 1972).[33] On 24 April, Lloyd Randell, flew a Porter into a mountainside in bad weather; the pilot and nine passengers were killed. (Lloyd Randell, 24 April 1972).[34]

That same day, Air America's vice president for flight operations sent a telex message addressed to all crew members. [In it, he noted that]:

"...the past few months have produced an appalling toll in lives and serious injuries." He urged all the flight

Pilatus Porter (Photo Credit Tom Lum)

crew members and supervisors to reappraise the factors 'which make flying in our operations a particularly unforgiving profession.' The telex continued, 'We are all called upon to perform under possibly the most difficult environmental conditions in the world considering the combination of remote, mountainous terrain, absence of modern navigation/communication and air traffic control facilities, active presence of hostile armed forces, absence of adequate means of reporting and forecasting the varied essential seasonal weather and winds, and marginal airfields and landing zones, to name a few examples.'"[35]

While Air America crew were being cautioned about the hazardous nature of operations in Laos, CIA Director Richard Helms was deciding the fate of the air proprietary. On 21 April 1972 he ended a lengthy debate within the CIA over the continued need for a covert airline capability and ordered the agency to divest itself of ownership and control of Air America and related companies. Air

America would be retained only until the end of the war in Southeast Asia.

On 27 January 1973 the Paris Agreement on Vietnam was concluded, providing for the withdrawal of American troops. The following month, a cease fire agreement was signed in Vientiane, leading to the formation of a coalition government for Laos. Although the end of the war was clearly in sight, Air America continued to lose people. Indeed, it is somewhat ironic that Air America suffered its heaviest losses in the two years following the CIA's decision to terminate the compound. Between April 1972 when Helms issued his orders and June 1974 when Air America left the country, 23 crew members died in flight operations in Laos.

At 1113 hours GMT, 3 June 1974, the last Air America aircraft crossed the border from Laos into Thailand. The end went well; Air America operations office in Vientiane informed Washington, "and the departure of AAM from Laos was without incident, although some lumps are visible in the throats of those who put so much of themselves into the operation over the years… We grieve for those missing in Laos and regret that they too could not have enjoyed today."[36]

The base at Udorn shut down at the end of June 1974. In May of '75, almost a year later, shortly after the fall of Saigon, Vang Pao left Long Tieng for the last time. Between 1960 and 1975, out of a population of 300,000, the Hmong had lost some 30,000 people.

Finally, on 30 June 1976, Air America closed its doors for good and returned well over $20 million to the U.S. Treasury.[37]

The cost of the war in Laos to Air America was extremely heavy. A long list of names on the Memorial Plaque at the University of Texas in Dallas attests to our losses. Was it all worth it? It may still be too early to tell. Historians of the next century or two will be better able to render a retrospective judgement on that question as they view the events in Southeast Asia from their distant, detached perspective.

No matter what future historians conclude, I am confident that the reputation of Air America will grow with the passing years. The compound performed superbly in that extraordinarily inhospitable and demanding environment. As one senior CIA official said, "Air America was both versatile and successful because it had a first-class assortment of deeply committed and professional crews."[38]

As for me, I was proud to be a member of the Air America crew in Southeast Asia.

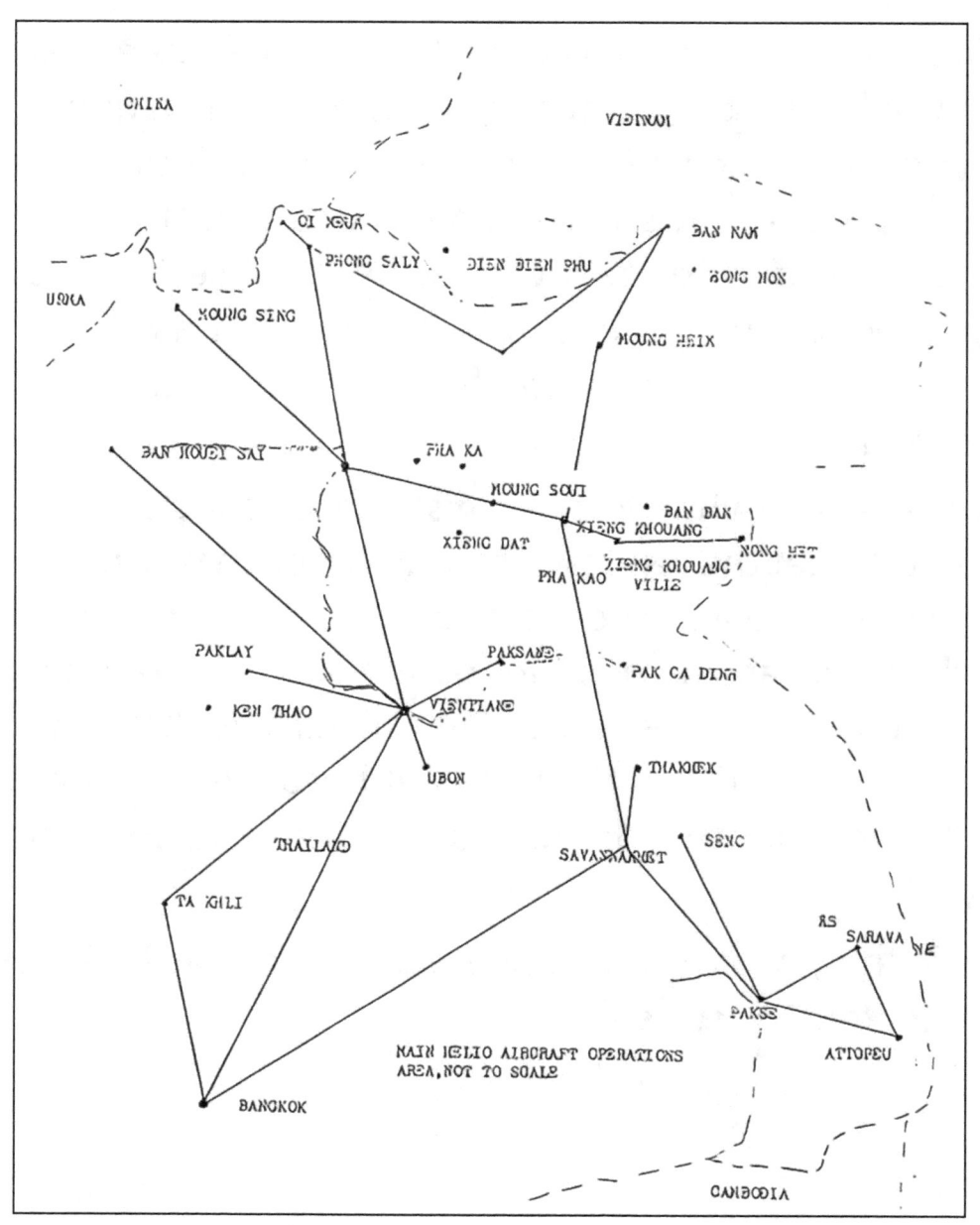

Ron's sketch of air routes over Laos

Chapter 11. LAOS AND AIR AMERICA | 155

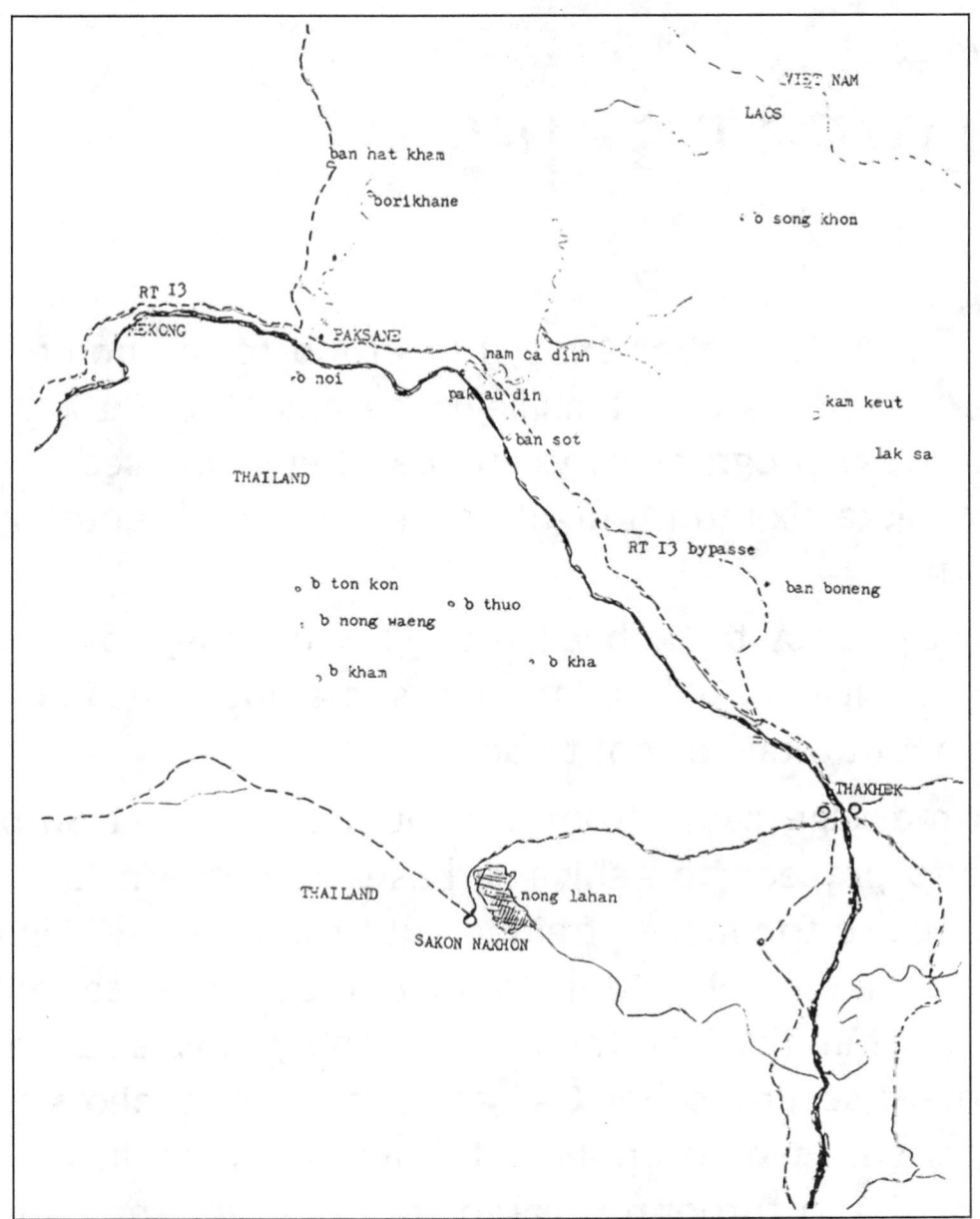

Ron's sketch of highway routes through Laos

Chapter 12.

COVERT SKIES

On 4 December 1959, I returned to my home and home base at Tachikawa because the F-100 Auto LABS test program contract was being phased out. I received a six-month flight check from my friend Snuffy Smith.

I was happy to be back at the home base, now called Air America.[1] I expected to have some duty time in Japan again, but that was not to be.

A message came from communications that Sutphin was to proceed to Ashiya Airbase in Southern Japan, a base close to where I trained with the 80th TAC Fighter Squadron. I was to report to the operations officer of the base. When I arrived the next afternoon, I was surprised to meet several other CAT and Air America pilots from Taipei who would undergo training with me in the Air Force C-130 turboprop cargo transport. At that time, I had no idea why we were being trained to fly this aircraft.

The C-130 training consisted of ground school and local transition flights. Some of the pilots were being

Chapter 12. COVERT SKIES | 157

trained as engineers and navigators. During the later stages of our training, we received training in long-range endurance flights in the western Pacific. Once training was completed, three of us proceeded to Kadena Air Force Base on Okinawa for code training, which included how to send and receive coded messages and position reports from the cockpit by Morse Code. We were assigned a safehouse during this training. It was a house isolated from the airbase and civilian population.

Once we were proficient in code and passed our tests of sending and receiving at fifteen words per minute, we boarded an Air Force 8130 for Takhli (pronounced "Tak Lee"), Thailand. Takhli lies approximately 80 miles north/northeast of Bangkok and had two runways, one asphalt and the other dirt. The nearby village of BanTakhli[2] had a population of approximately 300 people.

Years later, I became friends with Captain Ushijima when we both worked for Japan Airlines. He told me about his misadventures near Takhli.[3] He was a bomber pilot based there[4] during the war and was finally shot down and had a long walk out through the jungles. The jungle surrounding Takhli seemed to have more snakes than any place on earth! In fact, Ban Takhli was home to more king cobras than anywhere else in Southeast Asia.

We lived in tents at Takhli. Heinie was there as well, so I knew it was his operation. Heinie had his people clearing some of the old Japanese living areas which, fortunately, did push the snakes further from the immediate living area. Life there was pleasant and relatively safe if we used our mosquito netting at night.

After about ten days, we had our first covert flight. The cargo was guns, supplies, and agents who were to be dropped into Tibet. The procedures were relatively the same for all flights. We were to turn in our wallets and all identification. We were issued a money belt full of gold coins, as well as a pistol, knife, and a survival kit. Of course, the gold coins would be of no use if we went down.

I made several covert missions, all at night, during the next two months that I was at Takhli, but one stands out. This drop would be northwest of Lhasa in Tibet and would utilize two navigators and drop-tanks fitted for long range. After the usual emptying of pockets, we were issued the money belts and survival equipment, then briefed on the drop signals. At a certain time, the agent on the ground would light a fire signal. On this flight, the letter "L" would be used by creating a series of small fires on the ground. Besides me, the crew consisted of Captain Judkins, Captain Stiles (who served as the engineer), as well as Keck and Price, the navigators.

Our load was small arms, ammunition, and trained agents who were Tibetans trained on Saipan. Takeoff was at sunset and Keck hit all the check points as scheduled. We hit the IP to the minute and started our run in of 20 miles to the drop zone at 1,000 feet. The letter L came, and we made a good drop and turned for the outbound check point.

I had my sending key strapped on my knee and sent the five-letter code for drop completed. We settled down for the homebound flight and had just begun to relax when we hit unexpected weather and strong headwinds. Keck, getting high mountains on his radar, got us well off course. We surmised that we had drifted south of our planned outbound course and altered course to the left three times.

After a long wait, we suddenly oriented ourselves. We had decided to leave the low altitude and climb, regardless of possible unfriendly radar pickup. We realized we were now over Lashio in Burma (Myanmar), and the sky around us was lit up with antiaircraft fire!

I thought we were going to get shot down for sure, but with strong evasive maneuvering by diving quickly down to low altitude, we cleared the fireworks and headed away from the firing. Now oriented over Lashio, the remaining fuel was not going to get us home to Takhli, so we set course for Rangoon, Burma, hoping for the best.

As briefed before departure, we would go to an airfield about 30 miles north of Rangoon if it got to be a matter of life or death. Now it was either bail out or alter course for there. So, we changed our course. Neither Jud nor I thought a walk through the jungle would be that much fun, especially in the dark. I was briefed and knew before departure that we had a friend and agent, just in case we landed in Rangoon, so I sent a message to Takhli informing them of our intentions. From Takhli, they informed a colonel in the Burmese Air Force who was friendly to the United States.

We found the airport before daylight, thanks to good airborne radar and snaky bends in the nearby rivers. When we landed, no one was on the airfield. The field personnel evidently went to a nearby military base during the night.

We carried all the Air Force decals to glue on our C-130, so, as soon as the props stopped and while still on the runway, we got busy making our unmarked aircraft look like a real USAF transport. Luckily, we got it almost done before the first truck showed up just at daylight. The U.S. marking and the U.S. flag on the tail even looked official to us. We were an Air Force transport that had strayed from Bangkok, believe it or not.

Eventually, a Burmese colonel showed up and believed our story, but he said he must detain us because there had been some trouble that night up north, and he had to check on all matters. He said he was sure we did not fly into or over Burma on purpose and added he had been to the U.S. and had learned to fly there. Meanwhile, we could stay in some nearby small tents and were told to ignore the nearby soldiers.

We stayed in the tents for two days while the good colonel tried to clear the missing Bangkok aircraft.

Evidently, it was in the Bangkok newspaper with the headline: Air Force Transport Diverts to Burma on a Flight to India via Penang.

It was here in Rangoon that I had the biggest scare of the trip. It was during our second night there while sleeping on my cot that I awoke to find a huge, striped hyena had entered my small tent and was thoroughly looking me over at very close range—not an event I would forget quickly![5] The hyenas were extremely large in this part of Burma and had a hideous laugh.

The next night we departed for Thailand on a covert flight across Burma and arrived back in Takhli before daylight. I continued flying covert missions from Takhli during 1960 on an off-and-on basis while still being based at Tainan, Formosa, with Beale.

I was assigned to fly with Chief Pilot Eddie Sims to Vientiane, Laos, during March 1960 where the Helio aircraft B-833[6] was waiting for us on the tarmac. Eddie informed me that we had a mission to fly it up to the extreme northern part of Laos to a

"Helio B-833 on the Tarmac" (Digital Painting by Sylvia Lynne Malvoso)

place called Phongsaly (also Phong Saly/Phongsali) and would go there via Luang Prabang, the capital of Laos. We would use that field as our refueling jump-off place for the mission on 2 March to pick up our two agents.

One of our passengers spoke German, as well as English with a broken accent. We took on four Jerry cans of fuel in Luang Prabang to have enough fuel to make the return flight.

After departing, we had to fly on top of a solid overcast at 5,000 feet. Occasionally we could see the mountaintops through the low clouds. I began to be concerned that we might have to turn back or try for our alternate up the China border (Ou Neua Airfield). Before we departed, the French had reported it to have good weather.

About thirty minutes from home destination, we suddenly received a high temperature reading on our cylinder head gauge. I talked this over with Eddie and told him that we should alter our dead-reckoning course to Neua. He agreed. After a few minutes on this course, the oil temperature and pressure indicated that it would not do to go anywhere but Phongsaly and let down through the overcast. We knew the engine would fail long before we could reach Ou Neua Airfield. We seemed to be in luck that day because, at the estimated time of arrival, there was a break in the overcast, and we could see Phongsaly below.

Right then, the engine froze, so we made a circling descent through the hole in the overcast only to see about a thousand workers building a new airfield landing site where the airstrip was reported to be. With no engine noise and no landing area, we had no choice—either land in the jungle close by or take a chance on the laborers seeing the aircraft and getting clear in time. We chose the landing site and, fortunately, on our final approach, they scattered out of the way of the approaching aircraft.

The site was being constructed in steps so, frankly, I knew a crash was imminent. The aircraft hit the dirt steps, turned upside down and skidded inverted to a stop. I hurt my right leg below the knee, but I could still hobble. Otherwise, although plenty shook up, no one was hurt. Unfortunately, our aircraft was badly damaged.

Shortly after the crash, a Laotian colonel arrived and took us to his headquarters in Phongsaly, about a mile from the crash site. He spoke very little English but saw to it that my leg was bandaged. A big meal was prepared for us—brown rice (the custom was to dip your hands into the tray and pat the rice into balls), peacock, various other Laotian foods, and French wine. Everyone sat on the floor in a large circle around the food.

My leg was hurting, and I begged permission to rest after the meal. I was assigned to a large round hut with no windows and was told that I had better relieve myself before turning in as there were tigers nearby. They said they often carried off children, especially during the night. The beds were smooth boards with a wooden block for a pillow. There were no sheets or covers of any kind.

I must have slept very well, but when I woke up it was

still dark. I lay there for what seemed like a very long time. I needed to relieve myself but didn't want to take the chance of being a tiger's meal, so I lay there in agony, biding my time until daylight. I turned over after some time and suddenly saw a very small beam of sunlight through a crack. When I opened the door, the bright sunlight hit me; it was almost 1:00 p.m.

My leg hurt badly all through the rest of the day. I did not leave the village or attend any of the meetings at the colonel's headquarters. After three days, a message came to the Laotian Army headquarters that we were to go to Ou Neua where a French plane would come and pick us up and fly us to Luang Prabang. The colonel had arranged for the four of us to go by horseback through the jungle. The distance was 50 miles as the crow flies.

A small armed escort was to accompany us—20 local armed guerrillas who knew the trail through the jungles. As the colonel explained, it would not be a safe trip as we would be subject to attack by Chinese armed bands, as well as North Vietnamese guerrillas from across the border.

My leg was giving me a lot of trouble, and I did not look forward to the long trip on horseback. All I had with me was my knife and my Smith and Wesson .38-caliber pistol.

We set out mounted early the next morning: 24 armed men, eight horses, eight horse leaders, and four or five guides and interpreters who spoke Vietnamese and

Chinese. We set out on the trail northwest of Phongsaly. From there we had to ford the Nam Ou River near Ban Tang.

The locals at the river crossing had no clothes on but sported tattoos all over their lower bodies. They ferried the group across in boats and received a small amount of pay. The horses waded and swam across. I thought this was wild and beautiful country. I will never forget the flowering trees, vines, and wild orchids there.

Between the river and Ban Tang, we encountered small bands of people who would quickly fade into the jungle where they saw us. However, we did pass a clearing with a village where the inhabitants had planted some crops in a burnt area, and the women and children in the clearing did not run away. Most of the adults I saw during the trip had goiters, and I felt very sorry for them.

We spent the night at the village of Moung Ou Tai and started out about 10:00 a.m. the next morning for Ou Neua, traveling up the Nam Ou River, which flows by Ou Neua.

While going around a ridge on the narrow trail, we encountered an armed band of about fifty Chinese tribesmen. Like all the other horses, my surprised horse spooked and threw me off. There was a lot of firing and wildly running horses with and without riders. All this lasted for about three minutes with the Chinese fading away and the Laotians holding the trail. Two Chinese were killed, and one Laotian horseman was hurt in the firefight. There was nothing to do but continue the trail.

We arrived at Ou Neua after nightfall. The next day, we boarded a French plane, an L-20 Beaver, that had come for us and flew us to Luang Prabang. From there, I went to Vientiane and Bangkok on an Air America aircraft. I spent a week in the Seventh Day Adventist Hospital with a drain in my leg, as it had become infected in the jungle. I did not fly the Helio in Laos again until 25 April 1960.

Chapter 13.

HELIO OVER LAOS

"Helio B-835 in Flight"
(Digital Painting by Sylvia Lynne Malvoso)

I was still based at Tainan, Formosa and flew training flights in the A-26 attack bombers. I also continued to test military jets, the Curtiss C-46, and the Douglas DC-4 as well as various other aircraft. A new Helio aircraft No. B-835[1] showed up in Tainan in early April and by 15 April, the wings were on it and ready to fly. About that time, I started to get an uneasy feeling that I would have to fly it as I could think of no one else in the system who would or could fly it, at least at this stage of the game.

The Helio had been involved in accidents in Laos before and, to say the least, it had made a bad name for itself. In any event, I was scheduled for a test flight in it on 25 April 1960. On the test flight, however, I was happy to discover that, because of the improved engine, it was a much better aircraft. It was a pleasure to control compared to the older model.

I flew to Vientiane, Laos, the next day with the new wingless Helio loaded in the DC-4 transport plane. Once there, I acquired a room at the hotel and waited for the Filipino mechanics employed by Air America to put the wings back on the Helio. Once they did, I made two local test flights.

On 5 May I started flying with agent Jack Matthews and Lt. Vang Pao of the Laotian Army. Vang Pao, an ex-sergeant in the French Army, had risen to the rank of lieutenant in the Laotian Army. He spoke French as well as English. Later, he became a well-known general in the Laotian war.

We flew to Ban Ban, a village on Route 7, a dirt artery that runs south of the capital, east through the Phonsavan military complex, and then through Ban Ban and on to Nong Het on the Vietnam border. From there it goes through the heart of North Vietnam. Of course, this would be an invasion route from Vietnam into Laos.

After spending time in Ban Ban, we went to Nong Het for the night. There I saw a few North Vietnam prisoners who had just been captured trying to enter Laos. The next day, I saw them still standing at the same location, still at gunpoint, as they had been the day before. They had no food, no water, no shade, no nothing.

We flew back the next day following Route 7 to Phonsavan and then on a little farther west to Xieng Khouang. Upon reaching the airfield in Xieng Khouang, I noticed another aircraft entering the landing pattern at the same time as us. Vang Pao and Jack directed me to land ahead of the other pilot, which I did. The Frenchman in the Beaver aircraft took a dim view of this and pointed a pistol at my aircraft. Vang Pao saw it and came to my rescue with some armed soldiers; they took the Frenchman from Saigon away. Although I never saw him again, I did see the aircraft quite a few times afterwards in Laos.

At this early date, Jack Matthews and Vang Pao both knew that when the North Vietnamese forces (the Viet Cong) came, they would come bursting and streaming down Route 7 by the thousands. I am sure Washington got the message about the invasion route as well. For the remainder of May, I flew to many different locations in Laos. I started carrying a pouch to the French headquarters in Xeno, Laos, almost daily.

On the 27th, 28th, and 29th, I went back to Bon Neua and Phongsaly to see my friend, the Laotian colonel. Because of the kindness he had shown me after my crash, I brought him a box of cigars at that first visit as well as every other time I went to Phongsaly. On this trip, I also carried with me a Laotian general and a CIA agent. The agent explained to me that the colonel had a brother who was also a colonel in the Vietnamese Army. This brother was trying to get him to change sides and become a Viet Cong colonel and turn Northwest Laos into a Viet Cong bastion. The colonel was evidently undecided and, I suppose, wanted to be wooed by both sides.

For the next seven weeks I flew over Vang Pao's headquarters in Long Tieng with various agents. Most of the flights were along Route 7 to Nong Het except for three to Phongsaly. I usually had a Laotian general with me—Phoumi Nosavan or Vang Pao.

On 12 June I flew an American army general in to Phongsaly to have a conversation with the colonel. The weather was extremely bad. I wrote the following in my diary:

> May 20, 1960. Vientiane, Laos. 1850 hours. Moved in with Capt. Fred Walker yesterday. Today took Helio B-835 to Bon Neua, Phongsaly, Luang Prabang. Weather very bad. Flew through heavy rain and storms all day. Made one airdrop out of Phongsaly. Flight time: 9 hours 40 minutes. Very tired.

After this flight I started to get sick, but I continued to fly until 20 June. On my last flight, I went from Vientiane to Xeno, but I was very sick en route. After landing at the French military base at Xeno, I was taken to the hospital there; but when I looked around inside their facility, I decided I did not like French military hospitals. Besides,

I was feeling a little better, so I got off the stretcher and walked out. No one was trying to forcefully stop me, so I started the aircraft and departed Xeno. Once in the air, though, I again became extremely sick with a severe headache and vomiting. All the same, I managed to reach Vientiane. I was immediately evacuated from there to the Seventh Day Adventist Hospital in Bangkok where I was diagnosed with dengue fever.[2]

By 1 July I felt good enough to check out of the hospital and resume my flying in Laos. During that July, I made four more flights to Phongsaly. The remainder of the time, I patrolled Route 7 and worked with Vang Pao. I had also moved into a house in Vientiane with Fred Walker.

Capt. Fred, a Douglas DC-3 pilot, had just arrived from Taipei, and would be based in Vientiane permanently. He did not have many cargo and airdrops to make, so at his request, I began training him on Helio operations just in case I became sick again or had to depart on another assignment.

On the night of 8 August, Capt. Kong Le pulled a *coup d'état*.[3] He was a captain/paratrooper in the Laotian army. Part of that army sided with him, and the fighting went on in Vientiane and on Route 13 east of Vientiane. Air America's Helio and DC-3 escaped damage at the airfield, but for the next ten days, I stayed inside my house.

On the 18th, United States officials came to Vientiane and on the 19th, I flew the French representative to Luang

Prabang to meet with the king and different factions gathered there.[4] This was another flight I did not relish. No one onboard spoke English, I had no idea how the meeting would turn out, when it would be over, or even if I could fly back to Vientiane. Things turned out okay for me, though, as the French representative showed up at my aircraft just before dark riding in one of Kong Le's jeeps.

On the 24th, Fred and I decided to take a chance on getting to the airport and flying our planes out of Laos. After nightfall, with heavy rain falling, we made it to the airport, started the Helio and DC-3 and both aircraft departed Laos. It was a difficult flight in the Helio that night. I encountered heavy downpours and thunderstorms all the way to Bangkok.

When we got to the airport in Bangkok, though, the runway was flooded so badly that I could not land. I circled the Helio for an hour and a half until daylight came, and I could see well enough to manage a landing on a taxiway.

During September I remained at Tainan in Formosa and flew test flights on jet aircraft and gunnery flights on the A-26 attack bombers.

I returned to Laos on 1 October and moved to Pa Dong[5] with my Helio. By this time, the Pathet Lao and the Viet Cong had infiltrated south of Route 7 and were confronting the Laotians and Hmong tribesmen south of Xiengkhouang Villa (also Xieng Khouang Villa/Xiengkhoungville) on a

Chapter 13. HELIO OVER LAOS

high mountainside. The small village with its landing site was Pa Dong. I called the site, Site 15, as I had started to number all the small landing fields in Laos.

From Pa Dong we had a good field of vision. The Laotian Army had mortars shelling enemy across the valley to the north, but on my first reconnaissance flights, I observed that all the mortars seemed to be hitting one to three miles short.

A few days later, Ban Pa Dong came under mortar and small arms attack. One Laotian Beaver aircraft was destroyed, but I was airborne during the attack and no damage was done to my Helio.

The next day the Helio was rigged with one .50 caliber gun and the cargo door was removed to drop bombs. Mortar shells were rigged as bombs. These were short missions as I made the takeoffs at 4,500-feet altitude. No climbing was necessary—just fly across the valley to the north, visually spot the enemy and drop the bomb. I remained there for two weeks before being called south to Savannakhet.

At Savannakhet, I started making reconnaissance flights along Route 13 to Vientiane as Kong Le pulled his army out of Vientiane after a countercoup had started southeast. His convoy had disappeared, and our job was to find him. The Laotian army headquarters was moved to Thakhek along Route 13 to confront him if he moved that far south. It was by no means certain which way he would break out to join up with the Viet Cong and Pathet Lao troops. He could continue south or turn north to the Xieng Khouang Province at Paksane on the Mekong—or he could retake Vientiane and head north on Route 13.

I had daily flights with agents and Gen. Phoumi Nosavan, and we located Kong Le and his forces and convoys at Pak Kading Ban. Pak Kading is located 68 miles northeast of Thakhek where the Namkading River flows into the Mekong River.

On 21 October I picked up small-arms hits in my tail section while on Route 7 at Paksane. I was low on the road and flew through massed small-arms fire and, as a result, had to fly back to Thakhek with a broken rudder.

During the 22nd, 23rd, and 25th, I received heavy fire from large-caliber guns while making reconnaissance flights over Pak Kading. These flights confirmed that Kong Le had been reinforced with troops and agents from North Vietnam.

On my birthday, 3 November, I was asked to make an armed night flight to Pak Kading using rockets to sink two LCVPs tied up at the mouth of the Namkading River. Two captains and a major, U.S. Army Green Berets requested this mission, and my company approved it.

Chapter 14.

PAK KADING

On 26 October 1960, I was standing beside a company C-47 with Captain Anastasakis on the strip at Savannakhet in Laos when three men in fatigues approached and started a conversation, asking about what, if anything, I had seen on Route 7. They specifically wanted to know about Kong Le's troops. Anastasakis was making airdrops to Gen. Phoumi Nosavan's army north of us on Route 7, and he carried two kickers, a radio wireless operator, and a copilot, both of whom were Chinese. After he departed on his flight, the gentlemen asked me about the Helio and the possibility of flying night missions, something that was fine with me, but I needed prior approval from my company in Taipei. I pointed out that I could use the C-47 radio to get approval, going through the company code operator if necessary. Their requirements were no lights on the aircraft and an armed covert reconnaissance to Pak Kading.

For the next few days I monitored Route 13 as far as Vientiane. Vientiane itself was, by this time, in Gen.

Phoumi's hands again after battle and some burning in the city. I also made daylight reconnaissance flights over Vientiane during this time, taking pictures of the city. We made some practice local flights with a .50 caliber machine gun onboard as well as a rocket launcher but, in the end, decided to make the flight with only the rocket launcher and attempt to sink an LCVP if possible.

We departed Savannakhet at 11:00 p.m. on 3 November. This was my birthday mission.[1] We flew up the Mekong River at 1,000 feet above the terrain for 100 miles and then descended to a lower level. The check point IP was recognized—Ban Sot, down the Mekong from the boats and Pak Kading. As we made the run in beside the boats, it was apparent by the tracers that we had not achieved surprise. Our aircraft was hit by .50 calibers on the first pass and the engine started to cut out. I dropped flaps and set up for a water landing straight ahead on the Mekong. Then, at the last moment, I regained enough power to fly. I aborted the water landing. As I gained about 200 feet altitude, I came under attack again from numerous .50 caliber and possibly 20mm guns. I thought then that perhaps it would have been best to make the water landing rather than run this firing gauntlet.

I didn't have a whole lot of time to think about it, though, because my engine suddenly failed. I dropped flaps and set up for a crash landing in a rice paddy. We made a good landing in the paddy but crashed into an unseen bank at its end—my aircraft was wrecked.

We ran through the darkness as fast as possible for about 300 yards before finding a suitable hiding place deeper into jungle. One Army captain had been grazed on his head, and my right boot sole had been shot off, but that was all our injuries. I thought we were either lucky or very unlucky, depending on how I looked at our current situation.

The guns continued to fire in our direction after the crash, but the projectiles did not come near us or the crash site. My three companions seemed to be well prepared for escape and evasion; so, after about an hour we set off in a northeasterly direction away from Pak Kading.[2] At this time, we decided it would be best to split up to avoid capture. I later learned that the major had been killed north of Vientiane and one of the captains was a POW.

I made my way through the jungle until dawn. Then I started to look for a place to rest and decide which way to go to avoid the main Route 13 and the Mekong River. I dug in by the side of a large fallen tree and slept for about five hours then got up and started to travel through the jungle in a northwesterly direction.

The going was slow as there were no trails and the fallen, rotting trees laying crisscross on the jungle floor made progress that first day terribly slow and exhausting. By nightfall I decided to dig in again beside a dead tree and get a little rest. I slept for only a couple of hours and then started to travel again. I found it almost impossible to move anywhere, though, because of all the fallen timbers and the deep darkness of the tree canopy above.

I ended up spending a very restless night on the ground listening to the multitude of noises from the wild birds and animals. I finished eating my survival food and doctored the scratch on my elbow. I had cut it getting out of the aircraft. I had my Smith and Wesson .38-caliber pistol with fifteen rounds of ammunition and a Ka-Bar knife along with my survival kit.

As soon as I could see in the early morning light, I started to travel again. After a couple of hours, I came to a trail and followed it to a stream. Humans as well as animals used this trail, but it did not appear to have had any significant use in a while. The stream was unclear, and I could not see any fish, but I did see one or two jungle otters and water cobras. It was too deep to cross at that point, so I decided to make my way upstream towards the mountains and farther away from the Mekong.

I followed the stream a few miles until I found a place to cross on a fallen timber and, soon afterwards, was on higher terrain. With easier traveling and more trails, I could tell from my air map that I would cut across the road leading to the village of Ban Bevak[3] and, then from there, I could follow my map to the Nam Song River. By that distance, I figured I could shake off any Pathet Lao guerrilla who I was sure would be on my trail.

By nightfall, I hit a well-traveled trail that I knew would take me to the Nam Song (or Nam Xong) River. I decided to travel this trail after dark as the forest canopy was not so dense in this area, and I should have some moonlight to travel by. Sometime after midnight, I was walking slowly along with usual caution when I heard someone cough behind me. At least I thought it was a person. I quickly left the trail, waiting in the jungle for some time. There was no sound, nothing but the silent night, broken occasionally by the sound of a howling monkey or a wild bird. I started to walk again but, this time, with more caution and more worry.

After stepping back onto the trail and traveling another two- or three-hundred feet, I heard coughing again. This time I crouched down and waited, sure that a Hmong villager or someone else was behind me. After a few long minutes, my coughing stalker came into view. I could just make out the form of a magnificent clouded leopard.[4] I immediately recognized his form and knew that his habitat was in these mountainous Laotian jungles.

I had seen these live leopards before. In Vientiane, the Hotel Sombonne[5] had two caged leopards they kept in the hotel compound as pets. My friend McCann lost a finger showing me how tame they were, though. McCann was an Air America operations officer, and the only man I ever knew that put French army wine in his Corn Flakes in the morning.

My clouded leopard was standing very still, watching me with the utmost curiosity. I stood up quickly and made a scat noise, and off the trail he went. I found some rocks and sticks lying on the trail and threw them in his direction. After a while I cautiously continued my journey with no more Mr. Leopard behind me, stalking my pathway.

Before daylight, I climbed a large tree with vines all around and through it made myself a resting place. Soon I was scared awake again by the noise of large animals walking below me. Wild elephants can make a lot of noise moving along, breaking limbs off trees as they eat the foliage. I spent yet another restless night. Besides the lack of rest, I needed to find some food. That might prove difficult, though, as the sound of pistol fire could attract some very unwanted attention.

Long before dawn, I started west on the jungle trail. My trail ceased to exist after a few hours, however, having become overgrown with bushes. The trail that headed north was open, but I decided I should continue in my westerly direction.

During the morning, I came upon the fresh kill of a young water buffalo in a clearing. The mother buffalo was nearby at the edge of the clearing, making all sorts of noises and commotion. After hanging around for a while in a fallen tree and yelling at her, I decided that I would take a chance anyway and get some meat. Keeping an eye in her direction, I went to the dead calf and cut off a nice piece of water-buffalo meat to take with me. Once I had walked well away from the area, I tried to make a fire, but I could not get the wood to burn. Still hungry, I continued my trek towards the west.

Chapter 14. PAK KADING

In the afternoon, I came upon a small rise and had better success starting my fire. I roasted the meat in small pieces on a stick. The meat was a good change from the wild fruits that were making me feel bad. After eating, I lay down and went to sleep for a couple of hours.

When I awoke, I continued my trek in the direction of the Nam Song. In the late afternoon that day, I came across a large clearing of grass and small brush. It was populated by many otters living in the small streams coursing through the clearing. The ground was spongy like marsh lands. There were more cobras here, and I killed one. I skinned it, but I threw the meat away in the end. I just wasn't hungry enough yet to pack and eat snakes.

By the time I got out of the wetlands, it was getting dark. It was here in the fading light at the edge of the wetlands that I encountered my first king cobra in the wild. I had seen them several times in cages in Bangkok and in Takhli where the GIs would kill them on the runway at night by running over them while skidding their jeeps.

I had an especially bad experience at Takhli with one king. We were riding from the plane to the mess hall after a flight. It was about 10:00 p.m. and the driver was the local snake capturer and killer, sort of a hero among the other GIs. As his luck would have it, we saw a huge king on the compound road. He quickly sped up and skidded over it with the brakes locked. Suddenly and unfortunately, his engine died. We sat there wondering where Mr. King went. We could not see him anywhere in the beam of the copilot's flashlight. So, we decided best to restart the jeep and move on to the mess where we parked outside and went in to eat a hearty meal. About halfway through dinner, we heard a big commotion just outside the mess hall. Outside, we found some troops polishing off our Mr. King, who had wrapped and tangled himself up under our jeep!

King cobras are deadly. At Takhli a schoolgirl was attacked and killed by a big male king who had made his way quickly across a ditch and attacked her during the snakes' mating season. I had been briefed before about king snakes—told to stand very still when confronted and to throw a coat or hat at it if attacked, because the snake only strikes at smells and only sees moving objects. Hopefully, it would strike at the thrown clothing instead of the person.

When I encountered this large king, he was about 20 feet to my side with his head in the air. I turned toward him, stopped and, even though I thought I could move faster than he could, I did not try. I stood there thinking that the moment he moved in my direction, I would throw my hat at him and run. After a very, very long minute of face-to-face with him, his head went down, and I made a hasty retreat. That night I tried again to rest in a vined tree but gave it up after a while and finally made myself a nest on the ground by the tree's hollow trunk. I could not sleep well, however, because I got a night chill and there seemed to be an extra amount of howling-monkey and jungle-bird noises. By dawn I was stiff and hungry.

The moving was slow through the forest, and I knew I was nearing the river. I came to it late one afternoon and found a small boat with three Lao men with fishing nets. I did not run away as I could see they had no weapons. They did have quite a haul of small fish, however—a multitude of different kinds but none over eight inches long. They seemed more shocked at our meeting than I was. I greeted them in Lao and told them I was from Vientiane and wanted to go back there. I showed them 100 kip in Lao money and asked for food. They misunderstood me and offered me some fish. After more hassle, I made it plain that I wanted the food in one of the man's bags, which I knew was brown rice. He gave me two large handfuls for the 100 kip, but he did not seem especially happy about the deal. He was still scared of me as my Smith and Wesson .38-caliber pistol and the shells in my shoulder holster were clearly visible across my chest.

They agreed to take me across to the other side, but I said no until it was understood that I wanted only one man to take me across. They seemed frightened and hesitant about all this but, after a few minutes, they unloaded the boat and one man got back in it. The others quickly folded the net, grabbed their belongings, faded back from the bank, and disappeared. Once we pushed off, the one in the boat jumped out and ran frantically up the bank, screaming in Lao all the time.

With difficulty, I rowed across with the unusual oar and

left the boat high and dry on the opposite bank. I moved away as fast as I could as my location would surely be known quickly. The people I had met were most likely Pathet Lao.

I was getting a little stiff from all the walking and unusual diet, but I still had my wits about me. I knew most people get into trouble after getting shot down because they get careless after a few days. I was a graduate of an extensive escape and evasion course during the Korean War and was not about to forget my training, especially here and now.

My direction of travel that day was south towards Borikham village and then on southward to cross Route 13 and the Mekong River.

Late in the afternoon that day, though, I came upon a small village. It looked freshly and hastily deserted. The people probably heard and saw me coming. I walked through the empty village, stopping only to pick some ripe fruit. I half walked and half backed into the woodland when, at that point, I heard a lot of loud noise from nearby houses. Apparently, not all the villagers had left their homes, and they did not care for me or my fresh-fruit picking.

After this, I started to move faster through the forest using little caution. I thought that I had had too much contact at the river and at the village. By the time it started to get dark, I was completely worn out. That night, I went into a deep sleep, unbothered this time by any of the night sounds around me.

The next morning, as I was on my knees taking a long drink out of a small stream, I heard a noise and looked up at the nearby bank. I had been surrounded by well-armed, well-uniformed soldiers. Their leader spoke English and said he was with Thailand Special Forces, and they were sent to bring me in.

Ron (with walking stick) on or about 18 November 1960. Heinie Aderholt is next to Ron, and surrounding them are the Thailand Special Forces soldiers, sent to bring him in. (Family Photo)

Ron wrote on the back of the photo: Northern Laos, Moung [sic] Soui. This was taken right after I walked out after being shot down. I lived on the jungles for 2 weeks evading the enemy so I was very sick & no food. I live 1000 years in 14 days. (Family Photo, back)

Chapter 15.

VIENTIANE BURNING

Late in November 1960, I resumed Helio aircraft operations from Bangkok in the extracted and repaired Helio B-835. At that time I started to refer to the small villages at which I would land as "sites," like they were called in the Korean War around the 38th Parallel. But I did not start to number them until October '61. The site numbers became official after I received a letter from Rousselot on 27 November.

I no longer based the Helio at Vientiane because of the unstable situation as well as the fact that my two Filipino Helio mechanics had been taken prisoners during Kong Le's coup d'état, capturing the city. As prisoners, Frigi and Nabone were subject to harsh treatment. They were eventually turned loose but with their thumbs cut off so they could never again work on aircraft.

Kong Le fled east along Route 13 when Gen. Phoumi's army recaptured the city. During those last two weeks of November, I flew along Route 13 to keep track of the Kong Le army and to make flights to Luang Prabang and

Phongsaly.

On 9 December, a new Helio pilot reported to me in Bangkok. Tucker would take my place temporarily so I could return to Tainan. On the 13th and 14th of December, we made a local training flight from Bangkok to acquaint Tucker with the flying characteristics of the Helio aircraft. Then we started to fly the Route 13 area to Ban Ban and Nong Het.

On 17 December, I conducted an observation flight with an agent named Leroy, an army officer. Tucker, my trainee, went along as an observer. When we approached Vientiane, we could see it was burning,[1] so I took some pictures before returning to Savannakhet for debriefing.

The next day I flew to Wattay Airbase, the Vientiane airport, to check its conditions and status. It was deserted. After engine shutdown, Tucker and I heard outgoing artillery fire nearby. As I began to restart my engines to leave Vientiane, I noticed an Air America C-46 on its final approach to the airport. I decided to wait for him to land and see what he was doing in Vientiane.

The captain's name was Bigoney, a CAT, Inc. captain based in Taipei. As I was talking to him about the deserted airport, incoming mortar and artillery fire started landing on the airport. Bigoney made a hasty departure without taking any hits. My Helio took two hits in the right wing and flap area as we were taking off. We headed for Savannakhet to break the news on the status of things at

Chapter 15. VIENTIANE BURNING

Wattay Airbase.

After arriving back in Savannakhet, Mr. Tucker decided that being an Air America pilot was not for him and requested transportation to CONUS.

The next day it was decided I would change my base of operations to the capital of Laos, Luang Prabang. I would also have a new agent: Pat. We did not go back to Vientiane until the end of December, though, by which time the Kong Le forces had moved west along Route 13 through Vientiane and were about twenty-air-miles north of Vientiane, around Ban Na Kha.

Chapter 16.

DROP SITES OVER VIETNAM AND LAOS

Back in Tainan, I resumed my duties as a test pilot on F-100 fighters and an assortment of other aircraft. Almost every day I had a practice flight in the A-26 attack bomber, logging 42 hours flight time in it during the month of February. I also had a lot of gunnery practice on the Rangoon south of Taipei.

I also obtained a house in downtown Tainan and was able to spend a lot of time with my friend Bill Beale. Bill was also flying the A-26 almost daily; we suspected that we would soon be called to fly it somewhere else besides Formosa.

On 22 March 1961, I started flying the Curtiss C-46 Commando transport again and departed Tainan for SEA (Southeast Asia) in a Chinese-registry B-154. Again, I began making airdrops of ammunition and rice to covert operations in Northern Laos. Then, on 29 March, I returned once more to Tainan and started flying A-26 bombers on practice missions.

Chapter 16. DROP SITES OVER VIETNAM AND LAOS

In the middle of April, Capt. Beale and I were sent to Takhli, Thailand. I commenced operations in a military Helio H-555, flying in Thailand for General Aderholt. During my tour at Takhli, I was sent to Naha, Okinawa to lead a flight of eight A-26 bombers on a nonstop flight into Takhli. Beale was also dispatched to lead a flight, and Captain Barnes was leader of yet another flight.

We were to lead air strikes into Laos. Captain Beale was set to strike Xieng Khouang Airbase; I was to hit Phonsavan, and Barney's target was Ban Ban. The air strike was called off, however, due to political reasons. I did continue to fly the A-26 at Takhli and took Al White's place in a photo recon B-26 mission after he was terminated for a wheels-up landing. My total training as a photo-recon pilot lasted all of five hours, taking pictures of Takhli Airbase.

I did get one flight back to Tainan in Al's wheels-up B-26. It was damaged but made ferryable. I made a terrible landing at Tainan, though, when one airbrake locked. I had no choice but to skid the other brake, barely managing to stop on the right side of the runway. I was happy to leave that B-26 for repair.

After three days in Tainan, I returned to Takhli and resumed flying the B-26 and Helio H-555. I was training a new Helio pilot, Capt. "Andy" Andersevic. Andy proved to be a good Helio pilot and for a time would become the chief Helio pilot in Vientiane. He was a veteran and well suited for jungle warfare in SEA.

I continued to train Andy until May. Then, for the next two months, I flew the Curtiss Commando on airdrops to Northern Laos, most of my flights were to resupply mountaintop outposts. During August, September, and October of '61, I used the DC-4 for larger airdrops north of the Plaine des Jarres.

During November, I started training new Helio pilots and flew a total of 130 hours and 43 minutes, including a night-cover flight into North Vietnam. A flight attempted by a C-47 transport a few days before was shot down. Now it was my turn, along with Capt. "Doc" Johnson. It was low-level all the way with a full moon to navigate by. Since I was familiar with most of the route, I was selected to fly the mission. Johnson was along because of his vast experience in these types of flights.

Navigation at low level in a C-46 on a moonlit night goes very well in the dry season. The bends of the rivers had been clearly and accurately drawn on the French air maps I used and were easily identified even at low-level. The chances of being picked up by radar were small if we stayed extremely low all the way in and out. Winds were almost always calm, and visibility was just enough to evade enemy aircraft if we were intercepted. The most danger came from trees or water impact. With our good flight plan and navigator, the rivers were hit on schedule. The drop signal was a burning X-1. The ground agents would keep the fire signal lit for only five minutes, so our timing was critical.

Chapter 16. DROP SITES OVER VIETNAM AND LAOS

We hit the initial run in three miles from the drop zone. Climbing to 1,000 feet above the terrain, we dropped our agents their supplies right on the drop zone. Once we had pulled up to 1,000 feet, our three kickers in the back said they could see the distant lights of Hanoi.

After the drop, Johnson wanted to increase our power. He wanted to leave the area, but I was at the controls, and he let me have my way. I preferred a low-noise and low-level exit, a 90-degree turn to the left, and the mountainous route on the return to Takhli.

After we landed and went through our debriefings, picked up our wallets and personnel things, we departed for Bangkok with Doc Johnson now flying. He went to sleep after leveling off with the autopilot on. As a bad joke, I let him overfly Bangkok by about five miles before waking him. I still am not sure why I did such a thing; tricks in airplanes usually turn sour on anyone pulling them. Later in the war, I found out that all the agents on this drop site were either killed or captured.

In December, I continued to fly the Helio and C-46 aircrafts and logged 183 hours that month alone. On 15 December 1961, I again started to fly from Savannakhet on search missions in the Nong Het and Ban Ban area along Route 7. On 27 December, I pulled out of Savannakhet and went to Bangkok. The next day I moved back to the capital, Luang Prabang, and started to track the movement of Kong Le forces north of Vientiane. I also continued flying patrols in the Nong Het area along Route 7. During the first part of January 1962, I started patrolling and observing the Thathom area. Early in the morning, while eating breakfast at Muang Sing, we came under mortar and artillery attack. It was a hasty departure; I took off in the Helio in the compound area with only slight shrapnel damage to the aircraft.

We returned to Luang Prabang and spent the night there. Pat, the agent, was most anxious to depart the next morning. Suspecting a big offensive had started, he wanted to search for the Kong Le army. On 5 January, while searching along the route to Kiengkhum, we could see a large convoy of trucks hidden off the road in the jungle-green foliage. We spotted them about 10 miles from Xieng Khouang, the main artery base of Phoumi's army.

Flying very low at full power, I headed for the Xieng Khouang airport to alert the authorities of the impending attack which, I felt, would come at any moment. Four of my company's aircraft were on the flight ramp while unloading ammunition, and Pat told me to warn them. I directed them to close the door and depart immediately, which they did. Outgoing mortars were now being fired, and I was also directed to depart and wait at Xieng Khouang Villa, a small airport about 10 miles to the southwest.

I forced another Air America C-46 cargo plane away from the airport. Captain Plank was determined to land despite all the chaos on the ground. I forced him to abort his landing by flying straight at him! For some reason, he

Chapter 16. DROP SITES OVER VIETNAM AND LAOS

was not monitoring the company VHF radio frequency.

After landing at the villa, I waited for Vang Pao's family and troop; they evacuated 16 of them to a safe area. With dusk approaching, I returned to Plaine des Jarres to meet Vang Pao in my Helio. A short time after landing and conferring with Vang Pao, a Howitzer shell whistled in overhead, spraying the side of the Helio with clay and shrapnel.

Although my aircraft was leaking oil and had a flat tire, I departed with Vang Pao again to Xieng Khouang Villa. After padding the flat tire with grass and clothing, I flew the aircraft back to Vientiane that night. The next day I met with Captain Rousselot. He told me that I was assigned to a different project and informed me that I should proceed to Takhli, Thailand, to await further instructions.

After arriving at Takhli, I started flying covert missions into Laos in a C-46 transport aircraft. Most of the flights were airdrops of ammunition, rice, and either Thai or Laotian people. I flew 25 of these missions before eventually returning to my base at Tainan, Formosa.

I had one additional night-covert mission with Johnson in January, logging 200 hours, 21 minutes total during those two months.

I had been training in the Dornier (a small, two-engine STOL aircraft), and I had also completed training quite a few good Helio pilots by this time. Capt. Joe Hazen and Don Cocker were two of the outstanding pilots of the war, and I would be associated with them again as 747 captains for JAL (Japan Airlines) years later.

During a full moon on one mission that January in '62, we departed Takhli for the Ho Chi Minh Trail in North Vietnam. The idea was to cut the trail at a specific location with trained paratroopers. This mission was to go low-level to avoid detection. Johnson served as the second captain onboard.

We found the IP on time and started to climb and make the run in to drop. I found out later that this clearing in the jungle was relatively small, and some of the troopers that night landed in the trees—I believe only a few survived the war.

I resumed flying the B-26 bomber in March 1962 and logged 48 hours and 12 minutes. In April, I logged 122 hours but only 20 hours and 12 minutes in the B-26. I had resumed flying airdrops in the C-46, and, during this month, I was hit at Plaine des Jarres in the right wing and cockpit by small arms and .50 calibers. As a result, we started streaming fuel from the right side and fully expected the aircraft to burn. An hour and a half later, however, we were really relieved to be on the ground at Vientiane. The tension was high during that return flight because the copilot and kickers were constantly urging me to order us to bail out. I didn't; we made it.

During April, I flew the B-26 a total of 20 hours and 20 minutes; the rest of my time was spent in the C-46,

Chapter 16. DROP SITES OVER VIETNAM AND LAOS

dropping arms and supplies into Northern Laos.

In May of that year, I was assigned to fly the C-123 Provider, an aircraft like the Lockheed C-130 in that you could open the rear cargo door and dump the complete air load of supplies and ammunition all at once. During this month, I also logged 14 hours, 5 minutes in the B-26 and 50 hours making airdrops in the DC-4 and C-46. I ended up the month with 67 hours in the C-123.

Capt. Walker was assigned to give me eight hours of dual training in this aircraft at Hua Hin, Thailand, a resort city south of Bangkok. The city was by the sea. It had a very nice hotel and was also the home of my friend, Bill Lair. Bill kept a pet black panther. I was there five days with Fred and was able to pet the panther every day. It was very friendly, although most people were afraid to pet it.

After the check out, I went back to Vientiane and picked up another C-123 to take to Takhli where I commenced making daily airdrops into Laos. During June, I logged 112 hours, 35 minutes flying C-123s out of Takhli. I flew the B-26 bomber 14 hours and 2 minutes and then went to Vientiane where I checked out pilots in the Dornier.

During July, I logged 165 hours over Laos in the C-46, Helio, Dornier, and C-123. While making an airdrop at Muang Soui, close to the Plaine des Jarres, I was shot up by small arms, but no one onboard was hurt. During this month, I was hit again in the Helio at Ban Si[1] village but made it back to Vientiane safely. I made one night- and two day-covert missions in the C-123. I also flew the DO-28 on one flight and demonstrated the Helio a few times at Vientiane. September was a month of covert missions and resupply and observation flights; I flew 147 hours in a mixture of aircraft including the DC-4, C-46, Helio, DO-28, C-123, and the B-26 bomber. During October, I continued to fly the same aircraft but, thanks to a good friend, the VPO—I also checked out in the DC-6 transport at Taipei.

I departed Takhli one December night on a moonlit-covert in the C-123. If this mission was successful, I would be scheduled for a second flight to the same location in North Vietnam, close to the famous French holdout of Dien Bien Phu. All this country and route were very familiar to me, so the flight went off without any problems. After we crossed into Laos from Thailand, the route was toward Phongsaly at low-level altitude. Prior to the flight's departure, I had requested Phongsaly as one of the final checkpoints to find the IP or initial run-in point, in Vietnam. After passing Phongsaly, we had to fly by instruments for three or four minutes at low-level. As things turned out, though, we were close enough to correct the heading and hit the IP close enough for the final run-in.

We missed the drop zone because no fires were burning on the IP, but the copilot spotted them being lit as we were departing. I made a turn, and we made a successful drop after all. The remainder of that mission on return

Chapter 16. DROP SITES OVER VIETNAM AND LAOS

was uneventful, except for some very heavy smoke from jungle fires which fortunately provided us with additional concealment.

Unfortunately for others, one of the closest calls I had in Laos centered around a canceled Xieng Khouang flight. I had been assigned to lead several C-46 and C-123 aircraft into Xieng Khouang with a Laotian colonel onboard who was talking on the VHF radio with his friends on the airfield. If everything was okay, we would land and talk on the ground then signal the other aircraft to land. I had made two flights with the colonel onboard within the last week and did not feel too apprehensive about my assignment that morning.

I departed from Takhli before sunrise loaded with ammo and explosives. My newly assigned American copilot and I chatted all the way to Vientiane. Landing there about 7:00 a.m., we had taken the Laotian colonel onboard and refueled, then contacted the other C-46s and the C-123 sitting on the ramp waiting for me to depart. I was to lead the flight with the interpreter onboard.

As we were about to depart, however, a jeep pulled up to my aircraft with a new, low-flight-time captain, Capt. Fred Riley, hoping out. He came onboard. I had known Fred Riley for the two or three months he had been my copilot. He had been promoted to captain in the C-123 and had almost immediately gotten himself grounded because of a taxi incident at Vientiane. Then a message from the VPO had come there during the night, un-grounding him.

When he received this good news, he immediately went to Fred Walker, now Chief Pilot, Vientiane, and persuaded Walker to give him "Sutphin's flight, because Sutphin had a lot of flight time already this month."

Walker, being no friend of mine ever since a dustup we had a month before, must have thought this would be a suitable time to get even, so he assigned Riley to lead the flight. Walker had not realized that I had known this Laotian colonel for two years now and this was no ordinary flight—certainly not one for Riley to jump into unexpectedly.

After some discussion, I relented and turned the flight over to Fred, but I did notify the other waiting transports over the radio that I was not going to lead this flight and that anything might happen. The colonel expressed his dislike for the "change of menu," and they all soon decided to take off and leave their new leader, Fred Riley, behind.

Riley took off in the rear but, throughout the flight, used maximum power of the aircraft to overtake them and gain the lead. He finally succeeded in getting the lead about 10 miles south of Xieng Khouang. He made a fast, straight-in approach to the runway, perhaps ignoring the colonel's communications with his safety ground contact. Sadly, shortly before landing, the 20mms opened up on him and shot him out of the sky. (Frederick J. Riley, 27 November 1962.)[2]

Relieved of my flight, I went to a hostel in downtown

Vientiane. I was almost asleep when the officials came, got me up, and asked me why I had not taken the flight that had been set up for me. I told them the story, and off they went, grumbling to themselves. That was when it struck me that— regardless of the colonel and his communications—Xieng Khouang gunners were there, all set, prepared to shoot down the first plane coming in that morning. Fortunately, the other aircraft did escape back to Vientiane. I got to thinking then that I should go thank Captain Walker for his help, but I never did.

Fate is the hunter, I suppose.

Capt. Ronald J. "Ron" Sutphin Handwritten on the back: me VTE, Laos 1960 I picked up 231 holes this flight. (Family Photo)

Afterword

Ron's manuscript abruptly ends here, but his story as aviator and adventurer certainly does not. He went on to fly commercially for Japan Airlines in their 747 fleet of aircraft. He was a test pilot and instructor. He married and owned cattle, as well as numerous small aircraft on his ranch in Oregon. As a hobby, he and his wife, Kat, would fly into the Alaskan wilderness, repairing and salvaging downed aircraft.

I may never discover all the details of the remainder of his time with Air America, but I believe he has ended this, his story, intentionally or unintentionally, quite well. Ron is listed in CAT Association files as a First Officer, Senior Grade from Jan57 to 19Aug68 when he resigned.[1]

Fate is the Hunter[2] is Ernest Gann's autobiographical novel of life as one of those daring pioneers in commercial aviation. I think Ron must have loved his story.

Addendum

Air America®

In Remembrance of Ron Sutphin (November 3, 1930 – October 3, 2007)
October 25, 2007

In Memoriam: Ron Sutphin, CAT, and Air America Pilot Ron Sutphin, who helped introduce STOL aviation to Southeast Asia, and who logged over 40,000 hours during a long, varied, and highly accomplished aviation career, died in a plane crash on his ranch in eastern Oregon on October 3, 2007. During his life, the aircraft he flew ranged from Stearman biplanes to F-86 and F-100 combat jets to 747s.

Though not a gregarious man, he was liked and highly respected by those he flew for, including Robert Rousselot of CAT and Air America, Gen. Heinie Aderholt of the U.S. Air Force, and Bill Lair of the CIA.

Ronald J. Sutphin was born in modest circumstances in rural Virginia, in the Blue Ridge region. In 1947 he enlisted in the Marines. In his spare time, he took college correspondence courses as well as private flying lessons. When he was transferred from Camp Pendleton, California, to Quantico, Virginia in 1950, he flew himself across country in his own Piper Cub. By the time he began a naval aviation cadet program in 1952, he already had his multi-engine transport rating and was a flight instructor on weekends.

He flew combat missions in the Korean War and learned to speak basic Korean. (Later he would speak basic Lao and would become fluent in Japanese.) While he continued to fly in the naval reserve, the G.I. Bill paid for his commercial pilot training, and in 1956, he flew for Pan American and then for the smaller Seaboard & Western Airlines, until he finally got the job he wanted in Asia with Civil Air Transport, and later Air America. His missions included covert flights to Indonesia and resupply flights to Tibet.

He learned to fly the Helio Courier STOL plane from Heinie Aderholt an Air Force officer on loan to the CIA. Sutphin played a key role in modifying and improving the Helio, as the first models were difficult to fly. He flew Bill Lair of the CIA from Bangkok to Savanna khet, Laos, in 1960 on the flight that began Lair's involvement in the Laos war, as well as the involvement of the Thai Paru special-ops unit. He also located Gen. Vang Pao, the Hmong leader, for Lair when the Plain of Jars fell, and from this incident began the CIA's Hmong operation, one of the largest in Agency history.

Sutphin exited the Laos war relatively early, leaving behind stories of his aviation feats, such as flying in the front and out the back of an aircraft hangar with his wings nearly touching the doors, and flying upside down into the Long Tieng valley. Though the stories may or may not have been true, there was little doubt that Sutphin was technically capable of achieving feats of that kind. He was an extraordinarily talented pilot who liked nothing better than testing planes' capabilities without going beyond them (as I discovered for myself when he took me canyon-flying in Oregon; there was a strange sensation of being completely safe, even when one wingtip was nearly touching the boulders on the canyon floor while the other wingtip nearly touched the canyon walls). He was Air America's test pilot for several years in the early 1960s before deciding to transition back to commercial aviation. Eventually, he became a 747 instructor-pilot for Japan Airlines.

Sutphin [taught] his wife, Katariina...to fly, and she became an instructor pilot in STOL planes such as Super Cubs in Alaska, where the couple spent much of their time. After retiring from JAL, Sutphin had a sideline business of repairing crashed STOL planes in the Alaskan bush, and then flying them out to proper repair facilities, where the planes would be fully refurbished. Both in Alaska and when he bought his ranch in Oregon, he bought and sold STOL planes, and he usually seemed to have three or four of his own. He raised cattle on his ranch in the remote sagebrush country of eastern Oregon and used his planes to spot and even help herd cattle for the annual roundup. Ron Sutphin was 76 years old when he died. The NTSB has not yet finished its investigation of the accident.

— Roger Warner

In remembering Ron Sutphin, I always think of a "logbook error" story he told me many years ago. For those of you that knew our Chief of Flight Operations,

Captain Robert E. Rousselot, you will remember that he was as tough as nails. Someone remarked that Rousselot left the U.S. Marine Corp because it was too soft. Captain Rousselot was "death" on logbook errors. If you made an addition error in filling out the aircraft logbook you would receive a personal hand-written note of reprimand from Captain Rousselot. Ron Sutphin was telling me of such a hand-written note he received from Captain Rousselot, that read:

"Dear Captain Sutphin, Sad, sad, sad, evidently you can fly, but you cannot add." Signed Capt. Rousselot.

Ron Sutphin read the letter and noted that Capt. Rousselot had misspelled the word "evidently." Ron wrote back to Capt. Rousselot:

"Dear Capt. Rousselot, Sad, sad, sad, evidently you can add, but you cannot spell." Signed Capt. Sutphin.

(Warner, In Remembrance of Ron Sutphin 2007).

The Helio Courier

At the same time that Air America was trying to develop a rotary-wing capability in Laos, the company also was taking steps to introduce STOL aircraft into the country. Maj. Harry C. Aderholt, a U.S. Air Force detailee with the CIA, had supervised the development of the Helio Courier while serving with the Agency's air branch. Convinced that the aircraft could survive the short, rugged airstrips often found in remote areas, he became the foremost advocate for Air America's adoption of the Helio Courier.

Air America obtained a Helio for trials in Laos in the fall of 1959. The STOL program got off to a poor start. The Helio's engines proved temperamental, frequently developing vapor locks on starting. Mud, rocks, and gravel tended to block the aircraft's crosswind landing gear. The rudder needed modification so that it would not jam. Also, the first pilots who flew the airplane were used to multiengine transports and did not receive adequate training on an airplane that demanded special handling techniques.

Air America came close to abandoning the Helio. It was saved by Aderholt, who believed in the aircraft's capability and was determined to see it work, and by (Robert E. "Bob") Rousselot, who feared that the CIA would give the STOL mission to a rival company--Bird & Son--if Air America proved incapable of doing the job. Early in 1960, Rousselot assigned Ronald J. Sutphin, a talented light-plane pilot, to the project. Both Aderholt and Rousselot agree that it was Sutphin's skillful demonstration of the extraordinary capability of the STOL aircraft that led the CIA to greatly expand the program. (Leary, CIA Air Operations in Laos, 1955-1974: Studies in Intelligence, Winter 1999-2000: Supporting the 'Secret War' 2007).

From Simple Machines Forum, Flyhelio

Re: UF Helio's

« Reply #20 on: February 22, 2012, 01:22:24 AM »

Hi Doug,

Thanks for all of your great perseverance and diligence in tracking down all of the Helio History and sharing it with us! I greatly appreciate it; I'm catching the bug for this as well.

The Crowley Ranch H-250, which was owned by Katrina [sic] Sutphin, the widow of Ron Sutphin, was N5467E, a 1965 H-250, with c/n 2523.

Ron Sutphin was the well-known former Marine, Air Force pilot, Air America Helio Pilot and Helio military test pilot and early Helio innovator, CAT, and JAL pilot, who died Oct. 3, 2007, in a Piper Super Cub crash on his Eastern Oregon ranch while working his cattle, at the age of 76. Katariina told me that Ron wrote the Helio operating manual for Air Force and Air America operations in S.E. Asia, as well. --

Katariina Sutphin's H-250 was deregistered on 11-15-05, and the registration was canceled on 1-19-2006, -per Airport-data.com info. I believe it was Kat's first H-250. I haven't found out what happened to it after that, or any info or data on the Crowley Ranch H-295. I believe I have her email address somewhere, from contacting her a few years ago, and could try to get in touch with her again for more info, if you would like.

The Crowley Ranch airstrip picture of her N5467E H-250 which was waiting to enter next on to the Crowley Ranch strip for takeoff was probably taken in late summer or fall of 2001. The H-295 (with both red, white, and black wings and horizontal stab) is directly behind the H-250, broadside to the holding short H-250, in the left side of the photo. I looked at all of the H-295 photos on Airport-Data.com, trying to identify it that way by its paint scheme, but didn't find one that looked like it. The H-295 had a red prop spinner, the top half of the fuselage and nose was red, divided by a white stripe, and I believe the total bottom half was black. The paint looked a little old in 2001, so it was possibly re-painted by now. I told you I'm being infected with the Helio sleuth bug! But I can't complain because I love it.

Katariina's a great, classy lady who is a super ranch manager and a very experienced bush pilot and instructor, -taught by the Best, her husband Ron. She and her husband spent a lot of time for many years up in Alaska and in the N.W. on various flying adventures and aircraft salvage and bush repair missions.

One of Ron's well-loved specialties was flying in to repair downed bush planes in the field, good enough to fly them out to civilization, to salvage and/or rebuild them. Jerry Jacques...was taught to fly Helios by Ron Sutphin, as well, and very highly regards his lessons and Helio experience gained from Ron's unique special ability to transfer his Helio knowledge as a C/STOL flight instructor. We lost a true original iconic Captain Helio four and a half years ago--Ron Sutphin would have been 80 yrs. of age now, and no doubt still flying Cubs and Helios. Ron and Kat spent a lot of hours in their Cubs, Helios, other taildraggers, and even had a beautiful Grumman Goose and a T-28 for a few years. Ron checked out his wife in the T-28, too.

I believe they had one of the H-800's for a while, also. There is a picture of a beautiful H-800 in their ranch hangar. There is also a photo of the 1983 H-800, c/n H-17, N800TH, pictured at their ranch. I don't believe that is the same H-800 shown in their hangar, but I'm not 100% sure of that.

I learned from Doug Johnson's post, in which he shared his email from Jack Frye Helio Corp, on Nov. 26, 2011, that this H-800, N800TH, pictured at the Crowley Ranch, was formerly registered as the second N4104D. The first N4104D was a 1956 H-395 B, c/n 022. Jack Frye Helio Corp believes the second 4104D, the H-800 which later became N800TH, was probably renumbered by Lyn Bollinger, himself, as that N4104D number was available, and Bollinger would have done it for sentimental reasons. The email says that this H-800, N800TH crashed and was exported to Russia as a wreck. Kat Sutphin's pic of it, presumably taken on their ranch was taken before 12-19-2003.

The Sutphin's always had at least three or four taildraggers at their ranch. I believe Ron had over 40,000 hours in everything from Boeing Stearman's to JAL Boeing 747s, to piloting F-100s in the 1950s!! He's yet another legendary Helio expert I would have loved to have met and learned from, to add to the list which includes Larry Montgomery, and Robert T. Vincent III, the deceased previous owner of my Helio, and quite a few others.

Oh yeah, Doug, I'm sorry I forgot to answer your question a few months ago, to tell you that I wasn't a Laotian service Ravens pilot, when you asked me if I was associated with "The Ravens" because of my Ravens username. The S.E. Asian—Laotian Ravens very gutsy Air Force O-1 Bird Dog fire control spotter pilots working mainly in Laos. They flew with many brave Hmong tribesmen who were often their backseat spotters. There were many casualties in that vital air war specialty in the "secret war" in Laos. (Ravens 2014).

Capt. Ronald J. Sutphin

Ron Sutphin was born in the Blue Ridge region of Virginia. In 1947, he enlisted in the U.S. Marine Corps. In his spare time, he took college correspondence courses as well as flying lessons. When he was transferred from Camp Pendleton, California, to Quantico, Virginia in 1950, he flew himself across the country in his own Piper Cub. By the time he started in the naval aviation cadet program in 1951, he already had a multi-engine rating and was a flight instructor on weekends.

Ron's initial tour of duty was in Tsingtao (Qingdao), China as one of the very last of the China Marines. There he was assigned guard duty at an airbase including Civil Air Transport (CAT) pilots and their aircraft. CAT was originally a Nationalist Chinese airline created to airlift food and other supplies into war-torn China. CAT was founded by two Americans, General Claire Chennault (Ret.) and Whiting Willauer, a diplomat. Both men had long histories of service to the U.S. government and CAT was soon used to aid the Chinese nationalists in their civil war with the communists under Mao Tse-tung. CAT was sold to the US government in 1950 and was managed by the Central Intelligence Agency (CIA). It supported United States covert operations throughout Southeast Asia. Ron hoped that he would someday fly with CAT. Becoming a commercial pilot was his goal, but the military offered the training he needed through Naval Cadets at NAS Pensacola. Becoming a Marine pilot also offered aerial combat experience, not required for commercial flying but it provided adventure that Ron craved.

Ron flew combat missions in the Korean war and learned to speak basic Korean. Later he would speak basic Lao and would become fluent in Japanese. While he continued to fly in the naval reserve, the G.I. Bill paid for his commercial pilot training. He was hired as a navigator for Pan American but then met Seaboard Chief Pilot Paul Mlinar who hired Ron as a pilot. He flew for Seaboard in 1955 and 1956 on DC-4s and Super Constellations. He also flew the C-46 when it was wet-leased to Luxembourg Airlines.

Ron, however, had a desire for adventure and then got the job he really wanted, flying for CAT which changed its name to Air America in 1959. Later, Ron flew Helio Courier

STOL aircraft for Air America. He was Air America's test pilot for several years in the early 1960s and wrote the Helio Courier operating manual for Air America and for the U.S. Air Force before returning to commercial aviation. Eventually, he became a B-747 instructor pilot for Japan Airlines (JAL).

Ron taught his wife, Kat (Katariina), to fly. She became an instructor pilot in STOL planes, such as Super Cubs, in Alaska where the couple spent much of their time. After retiring from JAL, he had a sideline business repairing crashed STOL planes in the Alaskan bush and then flying them out to proper repair facilities where they would be fully refurbished. Both in Alaska and when he bought his ranch in Oregon, he bought and sold STOL planes. He raised cattle on his ranch in the remote sagebrush country of eastern Oregon and used his planes to spot and even help herd cattle for the annual roundup. He died in the crash of his Piper Super Cub. He was 76 years old and had flown more than 35,000 hours in aircraft from light planes to F-86s and F-100s, to Boeing 747s.

Ron is survived by his wife, Kat; and his sisters Bobbie Kay Trimmer, Patricia Goodyear, Kathleen Sutphin, [CS] Norwood, Loraine Kingston, and Sylvia Lynne Malvoso. He was predeceased by his brother, A.B. Sutphin, Jr., and sisters Velva I. Hudson, Ellen Fay Mack, and Elaine Edelblute.

(Kahn, Capt. Ronald J. Sutphin 2022)

Endnotes

Chapter 1: First Flight

1. C. Gilbert Taylor started the Taylor Brothers Aircraft Corporation in 1929. Production began with the Taylor E-2 Cub, with production ceasing in 1936 after a production run of about 350. In 1935, improvements to the E-2 led to the J-2 Cub, the forerunner to the Piper J-3 Cub developed in 1937. (Pilotfriend: aircraft database: aircraft manufacturers: Taylorcraft 2000) Photo [McIntyre Collection (via Tim Martin) 2022]

2. 1940 WINGS Cigarettes – Modern American Planes. The cards were produced for Brown & Williamson Tobacco Company of Louisville, Kentucky. (Chuck 2012)

3. Tailspin Tommy During 1939 and '40, Monogram Pictures released four features in which Tommy was played by John Trent, Betty Lou by Marjorie Reynolds, and Skeeter by Milburn Stone. (Markstein 2002-07)

4. Probably Joe Foss, Flying Marine: The Story of His Flying Circus, as Told to Walter Simmons. (Foss, Joe; Simmons, Walter 1943)

5. The Grumman F4F Wildcat – The F4F-4 was the first version of the Wildcat to feature a Grumman innovation, the Sto-Wing. The Sto-Wing used a novel approach using a compound angle folding-wing that was unique to Grumman. Leroy Grumman developed the idea...The F4F-4 was the first version produced in substantial numbers and made its inaugural flight on April 14, 1941. Along with the Sto-Wing, it had an increased fuel capacity of 117 gallons, a 27-gallon reserve tank, with provisions for 50 or 58 gallon drop tanks beneath the wing on hard points. It was powered by R-1830- 86 Twin Wasp engine, driving a Curtiss Electric constant-speed propeller. Armament consisted of six 0.50 caliber machine guns in the wings with 240 rounds per gun. (Dwyer, The Aviation History Online Museum 2014), Grumman F4F Wildcat.

6. (Weems 1943).

7. Ron writes Ten General Orders. I think the Marine Corps has always had Eleven General Orders. (csn 2022; 2019)

8. USS General W. A. Mann (AP-112) (1943-1949) – The U.S.S. Mann was

a General John Pope Class Transport ship, laid down in 1942 at Federal Shipbuilding and Dry Dock Co., Kearny, New Jersey, launch date unknown. The ship was acquired by the Navy and placed in partial commission on 13 October 1943. Maryland Drydocking Co., Baltimore, Maryland, did conversions for the Navy. The ship was commissioned in full as USS General W. A. Mann on 16 November 1943, under the command of Capt. Paul S. Maguire, USNR. USS Mann was assigned to Occupation and China service in the Far East from 1945 through 1953. (Priolo 2021

9. Aviation units were not the only elements of the FMF to move forward into the Pacific by December 1941. A sizable portion of the 2d Marine Division's 2d Engineer Battalion was also deployed to Oahu in the fall in order to build a camp capable of accommodating 5,000 Marines. The location of the new facility, Camp Catlin, was in the canefields east of Honolulu along the island's main highway. Its site selected by a board of Marine colonels, Catlin eventually would see tens of thousands of Marines pass through its gates into the farther reaches of the Pacific as it became the principal replacement and redistribution center for the FMF. In December it was half completed, and its Marine engineer constructors were destined to be the first members of the 2d Division to see combat in World War II. (Shaw, Opening Moves: Marines Gear Up For War 1991)

10. Curtiss C-46 Commando--At the time of its production (c. WWII), the C-46 was the largest twin-engine aircraft in the world, and the largest and heaviest twin-engine aircraft to see service in World War II. Most famous for its operations in the China-Burma-India theater (CBI) and the Far East, the Commando was a workhorse in flying over "The Hump" (as the Himalaya Mountains were nicknamed by Allied airmen), transporting desperately needed supplies to troops in China from bases in India and Burma... only the C-46 was able to handle the wide range of adverse conditions encountered by the USAAF. Unpredictably violent weather, heavy cargo loads, high mountain terrain, and poorly equipped and frequently flooded airfields proved a considerable challenge to the transport aircraft then in service, along with a host of engineering and maintenance nightmares due to a shortage of trained air and ground personnel. (Fandom Military, Curtiss C-46 Commando 2022).

11. The Northrop P-61 Black Widow, named for the American spider, was the first operational U.S. military aircraft designed specifically for night

interception of opposing aircraft, and was the first aircraft specifically designed to use radar. It was an all-metal, twin-engine, twin-boom design developed during World War II...Although not produced in the large numbers of its contemporaries, the Black Widow was effectively operated as a night-fighter by United States Army Air Forces squadrons in the European Theater, the Pacific Theater, the China Burma India Theater, and the Mediterranean Theater during World War II. (Fandom Military, Northrop P-61 Black Widow 2020).

Chapter 2: Tsingtao

1. U.S. Marines in Tsingtao, China 1945-49 – Tsingtao, China, now known as Qingdao and famous for its beer, was a German treaty port from 1897 to 1914 in Shandong Province. It is in the northeastern part of China on the east coast, north of Shanghai and southeast of Beijing. The city was occupied by Japan from 1914 to 1922 and again from 1938 to 1945. The city was under Chinese rule from 1922 to 1938. The U.S. Navy Asiatic fleet used the city as a port during the 1930s. In early June 1949 the Peoples Liberation Army entered Qingdao and took control of the city...After the end of the war with Japan on September 2, 1945, the U.S. Marines were ordered to participate in the occupation of certain areas of China primarily to assist Chiang Kai-shek's government in the surrender and disarmament of Japanese troops. As part of Operation Beleaguer, the 6th Marine Division, under the command of General Lemuel C. Shepherd (later Commandant of the Marine Corps), was ordered to carry out the mission in the Tsingtao-Chefoo area. The 6th Marine Division was deactivated on March 31, 1946, and the Tsingtao command size was sized down to become a reinforced brigade. In May 1947, after more reductions in force, the command became Fleet Marine Force, Western Pacific ("FMFWesPac"). Some Marine units remained in Tsingtao until early May 1949. Tsingtao was also the headquarters of the Western Pacific Fleet of the US Navy from 1945-1949 and the Marines provided security for the naval facility in the northwest part of the city. (Greguras 2013).

2. Foot binding – For centuries, young girls in China were subjected to an extremely painful and debilitating procedure called foot binding. Their feet were bound tightly with cloth strips, with the toes bent down under the sole of the foot, and the foot tied front-to-back so that they grew

into an exaggerated high curve. The ideal adult female foot would be only three to four inches in length. These tiny, deformed feet were known as "lotus feet." (Szczepanski 2019).

3. The Martin PBM Mariner —The PBM (Patrol Bomber, Martin) Mariner is one of the least known patrol aircraft of World War II, yet it was also one of the most successful. (S. N. Museum n.d.) There were many variants of the PBM Mariner. According to the Pilot's Handbook for Navy Model PBM-5 Airplane: The PMB-5 is a two-engine, high wing, medium range flying boat which may be used as a patrol, bomber, or torpedo airplane. (Army Air 1945). Photo: (U.S. Coast Guard photo n.d.)

4. The USS Estes was the command ship, and the USS Repose was the hospital ship that served the longest in Tsingtao. The Estes was usually at Wharf 1, Tsingtao, as the Headquarters for Commander Naval Forces, Western Pacific. The Repose, with a hospital bed capacity of 750, served as a base hospital ship in Tsingtao supporting the Marine forces in northern China. Most Marines from North China were sent to the Repose for treatment. (Greguras 2013).

5. Tsangkou Airfield. Elements of the 1st MAW were at Tsangkou (or Tsan Kou) Airfield, about 10 miles north of Tsingtao (MAGs 25 and 32). MAG-25 remained in Tsingtao until June 1946, when it returned to the U.S. The airbase had been used by the Japanese and had barracks, mess halls, hangars, and other facilities which the Marines used and expanded. This is not the current international airport which is much farther from the city than Tsangkou field. The Tsangkou airfield site is currently reportedly a China Air Force Training Center. (Greguras 2013).

6. On August 1, 1946, 1st Division directed that American forces in Tsingtao be reduced to a reinforced infantry battalion, and that the 4th Marines be returned to the United States. The regiment's 3d Battalion was to remain in China as a separate unit, in order to protect the United States and Nationalist naval bases at Tsingtao. The 12th Service battalion would also remain to continue its role of furnishing logistic support for Marine activities in Tsingtao, and a company of 3rd Battalion, 4th Marines, was assigned to guard 1st Wing facilities at Tsangkou airfield, from which VMO-6 would operate as a reconnaissance and liaison agency for 3rd Battalion, 4th Marines. (Wikipedia, Civil Air Transport 2021) By December

1948, Communist success in China was obvious. Maj. Gen. David Barracks told his superiors at the Pentagon, that...against a determined Communist advance...The complete defeat of the Nationalist Army...is inevitable." Over the next few months, the Communists gradually pushed back the Nationalists until finally capturing the capital of Nanking on April 24, 1949. The last of the Americans to leave China left Tsingtao on May 16, 1949. (Military 2021).

7. The Civil Air Transport employees liked to use the abbreviated term CAT for the company. In 1945-46 civil war broke out again between the Nationalists and the Chinese Communist Party led by Mao Tse-tung. CAT sided with the Chinese Nationalist Party headed by Chiang Kai-Shek. In 1949, the Nationalists fled China when they lost the war, and CAT helped them move to Formosa, where Chiang Kai-Shek ruled the Republic of China until he died in 1975. Once the Nationalists finished moving to Formosa, CAT no longer had a job and was nearly insolvent...until the CIA devised a plan for indirect ownership in order to use the air transport entity for their intelligence-gathering operations in China and Southeast Asia. (Cates, Air America: A Historical Synopsis from the Beginning to End 2021)

8. Also known as Higgins Boats, Landing Craft Vehicle, Personnel (LCVP) craft were used for amphibious landings in World War II and the Korean War. The first draft boat was created by Andrew J. Higgins in 1926 for use in swamp and marsh areas. The length of the wooden craft was approximately 36 feet long, could speed at 12 knots, had a crew of four, and could carry about 36 servicemen. The armament included two .30 caliber machine guns. The craft was carried by destroyers, transports, and cargo ships. (Navy n.d.)

9. He does not write much about this extraction mission, but Marines spent their time ensuring the safe evacuation of American citizens from China. By 26 May 1949, the last Marines were pulled out of China. (Marines 2022).

10. Ron writes 9 June in his manuscript. I cannot verify that he would be going back to Tsingtao on this date when all Marines were pulled out of China in May 1949. I believe he was off on the date by a month. (csn 2022; 2019)

- 16 May 1949: Company C, 3rd Marines depart Tsingtao for the U.S.

- 26 May: USS Manchester with reinforced Marine guard depart Tsingtao, ending China activities in China. (Dhaig 2014).

11. With the exception of Company C, 3d Marines, quartered ashore to patrol the harbor area, all elements of FMFWesPac were afloat by 3 February 1949...The 3d Marines and 9th Marines were left to continue evacuation operations. For more than a month, the 3rd Marines remained afloat in Tsingtao harbor, while the Communist drive gained momentum against disintegrating Nationalist opposition. On 17 March, the 3d Marines, less Company C, sailed to Shanghai to take over the mission of the 9th Marines, which left for the United States at the end of the month. While the battalion stayed on board ship at Shanghai, the Communists reached their Yangtze valley objectives, crossed the river, and on 24 April, occupied the Nationalist capital at Nanking. On the 28th, the 3d Marines left Shanghai for Tsingtao, pausing there for a few days before it left for the states. On 6 May, the 3d sailed, leaving Company C as a cruiser-borne reinforcement for Naval Forces, Western Pacific. A relief for this company, C of the 7th Marines, arrived at Tsingtao on 14 May to take over the watch, and the last element of the 3rd Marines departed. In less than a month, the 7th Marines company was also on its way home. The possibility of landing American troops in China without precipitating costly fighting was now remote, and the American fleet stood off from the Communist coast. As an instrument of American policy, the Marines were first committed to assist in the repatriation of more than a half million Japanese and to help the Chinese Central Government reestablish its sovereignty over occupied territory. Ordered to avoid involvement in the civil strife but to defend themselves if attacked, "the Marines were the balance of order" in North China, while they controlled the vital coastal cities and lines of communication. They reinforced General Marshall's attempt to secure peace, and when this failed, were given their traditional role as protectors of American lives, interests, property in China...When the defeat of the Nationalist armies forced an American withdrawal, the Marines provided a security force that ensured the escape of hundreds of foreign nationals who might otherwise have ended up in Communist prisons. Faced with a round of trying and often, dangerous assignments during the postwar years of China duty, when their full fighting power was always held in check, the Marines acquitted themselves well. The Communists, concerned solely

with their drive to conquer China, did not choose to meet the Marines head on. Once they were secure in their control of the mainland, however, the time of that encounter was not long delayed. In November 1950, they met the Marines again, this time in full-scale battle, in the rugged hills of North Korea. (Shaw, The United States Marines in North China 1945-1949 Reprinted 1968).

Chapter 3: Flight

1. Fairchild Primary Trainer (PT)...one of the most innovative and effective primary training planes ever designed, the Fairchild Primary Trainer (PT). The Fairchild PT was given its factory model number M-62 and its official name, the Cornell. The first prototype flew on May 15, 1939, and later that year won a fly-off competition against 17 other designs for the new Army training airplane. Fairchild was awarded its first Army PT contract for an initial order of 270 airplanes on September 22, 1939...Three basic variations of the Fairchild PT were produced, the PT-19, PT-23, and PT-26. All three versions used the same basic airframe. (G. W. Museum n.d.).

2. CAA (Civil Aeronautics Authority) was replaced in 1958 by the FAA (Federal Aviation Agency). (U.S. Department of Transportation n.d.).

3. The Fleet Marine Force (1) The force of marines maintained by the Major General Commandant in a state of readiness for operations with the Fleet is hereby designated as Fleet Marine Force (F.M.F.), and as such shall constitute a part of the organization of the United States Fleet and be included in the Operating Force Plan for each fiscal year. (2) The Fleet Marine Force shall consist of such units as may be designated by the Major General Commandant and shall be maintained at such strength as is warranted by the general personnel situation of the Marine Corps.

(3) The Fleet Marine Force shall be available to the Commander in Chief for operations with the Fleet or for exercises either afloat or ashore in connection with Fleet problems. (Swanson 1933).

4. American Flyers still operates six training facilities across the country in New Jersey, Florida, Arizona and three in Texas...American Flyers provides renewal certification to nearly 50% of all flight instructors. (American Flyers 2022).

Chapter 4: Naval Cadets

1. Boeing-Stearman PT-17 "Kaydet"- The USAAF had different designations based on its power plant. The PT-17 had a Continental R-670-5 engines. The Kaydet was a conventional biplane of rugged construction, with a large, fixed tailwheel undercarriage, and accommodation for the student and instructor in open cockpits in tandem. The radial engine was usually not cowled... (Wikipedia, Boeing-Stearman Model 75 2022).

2. The Cessna AT-17 "Bobcat" was a twin-engined advanced trainer aircraft designed and made in the United States ...The commercial version was the Model T-50, from which the AT-17 was developed...Dubbed the Bamboo Bomber by the pilots who flew them, it was one of the aircraft featured in the popular television series Sky King of early to mid-50's. The aircraft was replaced in later episodes by the T-50's successor, the all-metal Cessna 310. (Shupek and Ret. 1998-2020).

3. The San Carlos hotel, nicknamed "Gray Lady" due to its pearly-gray stucco exterior, sat at the corner of Palafox and Garden Streets. Built with over 150 rooms, she underwent an expansion in 1927 which brought the room total to over 500. Sadly, the Gray Lady closed in 1982, then was demolished in 1993 due to deterioration. (Trust 2021).

4. Although Ron records his name as "Peter Petterson," in his original manuscript, this is most certainly Frank E. "Pete" Petersen, Jr., Lt. Gen., USMC Retired. Peterson, who died Aug. 25 [2015] at 83, joined the Navy in June 1950 as a seaman apprentice and the next year entered the Naval Aviation Cadet Program. (Stripes n.d.).

5. North American SNJ - More American combat pilots trained in this single- engine tandem seater than in any other WW II trainer. Designed in the late 1930s, it was still being used in the Korean War on spotter missions. Known to the U.S. Air Force as a Texan, the Navy as an SNJ, and the British and Canadians as a Harvard, this low-cost trainer had high speed fighter characteristics. Almost 600 of the nearly 17,000 AT-6s built for the military are still flying today. (Fiddlersgreen: SNJ Texan: Aircraft 2022); also see: (Smithsonian National Air and Space Museum n.d.).

6. In 1943, Corry Field was designated a Naval Auxiliary Air Station (NAAS) and primary flight training was moved to other airfields in the area. For the remainder of the WWII, Corry Field hosted advanced training in multi-engine land-planes, using SNB aircraft. A transport squadron operating

R4D and R5O aircraft was located there as well...At the end of the war, Corry Field was decommissioned as a NAAS, but remained an active training field until its closure in 1958. At the time of closure, Corry Field provided the basic instrument portion of primary training in SNJ, SNB, and T-28 aircraft. (Vulcano 2016).

7. Famed woman aviator Jacqueline Cochran in 1939 wrote Mrs. Eleanor Roosevelt (wife of then-President Franklin Roosevelt) to suggest women pilots could be used in a national emergency. Aviatrix Nancy Harkness Love in 1940 made a similar proposal to the Air Corps' Ferry Command. Nothing was done until after American entry into World War II. Facing the need for male combat pilots, the situation by mid-1942 favored the use of experienced women pilots to fly U.S. Army Air Forces aircraft within the United States. Two women's aviator units were formed to ease this need and more than 1,000 women participated in these programs as civilians attached to the USAAF. These were merged into a single group, the Women Airforce Service Pilots (WASP) program in August 1943 and broke ground for U.S. Air Force female pilots who would follow in their footsteps. (National Museum n.d.).

8. In anticipation of a post-war boom in private flying, Aeronca designed a new model, the Model 7 Champion, marketed from November 1945...The Champion was the first new light aero plane to be certified after World War II. It [had] similar high-wing monoplane design as its predecessors, but the Champion was tandem dual-control configuration as standard. Variants included...the military L-16, which was used briefly in the Korean War and by the Civil Air Patrol. The Champion ceased production in 1950, but further examples were produced later by companies that acquired manufacturing rights. (Jackson 2004), 20.

9. Consolidated PB4Y-2 Privateer fulfilled a pressing need for a very long-range strategic reconnaissance aircraft. It entered production in 1943, but the type was not widely used [except] as an electronic intelligence aircraft and as a maritime patrol aircraft during the Korean War. Crew: 11; Powerplant: four 1350hp Pratt & Whitney R-1830-94 Twin Wasp 14-cylinder radial engines. The Privateer had a max speed of 287mph, a range of 2800 miles, and a ceiling of 20,700ft. Armaments could include: Twelve 12.7mm machine guns and up to 12,800 lb of bombs. (Jackson 2004), 143.

10. WAVES - Women Accepted for Volunteer Emergency Service, military unit, established on July 30, 1942, as the U.S. Navy's corps of female members...[they also served as] instructors for male pilots-in-training. Several thousand WAVES also participated in the Korean War. (Britannica, T. Editors of Encylodpaedia 2013).

11. Grumman F6F Hellcat. In the Pacific the Hellcat played a prominent role in all U S naval operations in particular the battle of the Philippine Sea, June 19-20th, 1944 in what became known as the "Marianas Turkey Shoot." American combat air patrols and anti-aircraft destroyed 325 enemy aircraft. Night fighter variants of the F6F3 were the F6F-3E and F6F-3N. The Hellcat carried a crew of 1; powerplant was a Pratt & Whitney R-2800-10W radial engine. Maximum speed was 380mph with a range of 945 miles, and ceiling of 37,300ft. Armament included six 12.7mm machine guns in the wings, or two 20mm cannon and four 12.7mm machine guns with provisions for two 1000lb bombs or six 12.7cm RPs. (Jackson 2004), 240.

12. USS Monterey (CVL-26), Independence - class light aircraft carrier... the Monterey was originally laid down as a light cruiser but following the attack on Pearl Harbor... the Monterey was reordered as an aircraft carrier. Decommissioned on February 11, 1947, the Monterey was recommissioned...15 September 1950. She departed Norfolk 3 January 1951 and proceeded to Pensacola, Fla., where she operated for the next 4 years under the Naval Training Command, training thousands of naval aviation cadets, student pilots, and helicopter trainees. (Doehring 1999-2020)

13. The Model 18 was one of Beech Aircraft's most successful and longest running production designs...[It] was designed to operate from small airfields and have a high degree of reliability and ease of repair...after the United States' entry into World War II production soared in order to meet the needs of the US military for trainers and utility transports. All branches of service flew versions of the Twin Beech, and this continued when the US Air Force came into being in 1947. [Over half] Model 18s built, were for the US military and were used to train navigators (AT-7/SNB-2), gunners and bombardiers (AT-11/SNB-1), and pilots, and for transporting cargo and personnel (C-45/SNB-5/JRB) and for aerial photography and mapping (F-2)...The Army Air Force and Navy (including Marines and Coast Guard)

had different designations for the Twin Beech. In September 1962, all surviving military Model 18s became C-45s with different letter suffixes for different versions. (C. A. Museum 2008-2022) Photo: (Coates n.d.).

14. Vought F4U/FG/F3A Corsair. The Navy awarded a contract to the Vought Company 30Jun38 to produce a new single-seat, carrier-based fighter aircraft...the series design has become legendary with a propeller of unusually large diameter and inverted gull wings which kept the main landing gear short and retractable straight back...the fuselage stayed high enough to compensate for the high blades (13 ft 3 in) driven by the Pratt & Whitney R-2800 Double Wasp, 2,000 hp engine. The Navy designated the airplane F4U. (U.S. Navy n.d.), 474.

15. Douglas A-1 Skyraider (formerly AD). The piston-engined Skyraider was designed during World War II to meet United States Navy requirements for a carrier-based, single-seat, long-range, high-performance dive/torpedo bomber, to follow-on from earlier types such as the Helldiver and Avenger. Designed by Ed Heinemann of the Douglas Aircraft Company, prototypes were ordered on 6 July 1944 as the XBT2D-1 which made its first flight on 18Mar45. In April 1945, the USN began evaluation of the aircraft at the Naval Air Test Center (NATC). In December 1946, after a designation change to AD-1, delivery of the first production aircraft to a fleet squadron was made to VA-19A. (Fandom Military, contributing n.d.). Photo: A U.S. Navy Douglas AD-4 Skyraider of attack squadron VA-195 Dambusters taking off the aircraft carrier USS Princeton (CV-37) during the Korean War. VA-195 was assigned to Carrier Air Group 19 (CVG-19) and made two deployments to Korea aboard the Princeton, from 9 November 1950 to 29 May 1951, and from 21 March to 3 November 1952. (U.S. Navy National Museum of Naval Aviation; Wikipedia 2022)

Chapter 5: Korea

1. VMA(AW)-121 (Green Knights) deployed to K-6 Airfield at Pyeongtaek, ROK to conduct strike missions in support of infantry operations. Flying missions as long as 14 hours, the Skyraider could carry 9000 pounds of ordnance...The Squadron dropped more bomb tonnage during the Korean War than any other Navy or Marine Corps squadron, devastating enemy airfields, supply dumps, bridges, and railroad yards. During the Korean War the Squadron insignia depicted Al Capp's "WolfGirl"

from the comic strip "L'il Abner." The feared "Wolf Raiders" of VMA-121 remained in South Korea for several years after the cease-fire in 1953. (VMA(AW)-121 Green Knights 2016, Association, Intruder). The VMA-121-Command Diary-Type B Report-July 1953, Korean War records state that, along with three other pilots, 2nLt. Sutphin flew MPQ Mission No. 16-A that day. Time over target was 1205 and all combat operations ceased at 2200. (Headquarters Marine Corps National Archives 1995-2021).

2. On 20 April 1952, MAG-12 made its home at K-6 Air Base, Pyeongtaek. During the war units from MAG-12, except VMA-312 which was on board the USS Bataan (CVL-29), came under the control of the Air Forces.

3. On 20 April 1952, MAG-12 made its home at K-6 Air Base, Pyeongtaek. During the war units from MAG-12, except VMA-312 which was on board the USS Bataan (CVL-29), came under the control of the Air Forces. Through the end of the Korean Conflict, the group participated successfully in numerous operations and accumulated over 80,000 effective combat sorties against enemy troops, installations, vehicles, and countless other vital targets. A second Navy Unit citation was awarded for its Korean War service. (U.S. Marine Corps 2022).

4. The Cessna L-19/O-1 Bird Dog an observation and liaison aircraft...the USAFs most widely used light aircraft. The early models saw extensive service in the Korean War. They played a prominent part as observation aircraft. (Jackson 2004), 132.

5. The Douglas R4D – The Douglas R4D (later redesignated C-117D) is a military transport aircraft developed from the civilian Douglas DC-3S or Super DC-3 airliner. It was used by the United States Navy and United States Marine Corps during the Korean War and Vietnam War. (Wikipedia, Douglas R4D-8 2022).

6. The Douglas F3D Skyknight (USA: 1948) (later designated EF-10 Skyknight) was developed in response to a 1946 U.S. Navy specification calling for an all-weather jet fighter...In use as a night intruder role in Korea, it was brought out of retirement to act as an electronic warfare aircraft during the Vietnam War, designated as EF-10. (Jackson 2004), 184. Photo: F3D-1 Skyknight carrying AAM-N-2 Sparrow I missiles during tests in early 1950s. (USN - U.S. Navy Naval Aviation News July 1954; Wikipedia

1952-1954).

7. The Grumman TBF Avenger (designated TBM for aircraft manufactured by General Motors) (USA: 1941). Five out of six Avengers were shot down during the Battle of Midway. [Even so] the Grumman TBF Avenger went on to become one of World War II's best shipborne torpedo bombers... The first production TBF-1 aircraft were delivered to Torpedo Squadron VT-8 in May42; it was this unit that suffered severe losses at Midway. The TBF Avenger carries a crew of three...Armaments include three 12.7mm and two 7.62mm (0.30in) machine guns, as well as a torpedo, bomb, and rocket load up to 2,500 pounds. (Jackson 2004), 240. Photo: A U.S. Navy Grumman TBM Avenger folding its wings after landing aboard an aircraft carrier in the Pacific, 1945. The geometric identification symbol on the wing shows that the plane was assigned to the USS Randolph (CV-15). (U.S. Navy - U.S. Navy National Naval Aviation Museum photo NNAM.1996.488.021.003 1945).

8. Perhaps he is referring to two Baekje Kingdom burial mounds: "Researchers from South Korea's Cultural Heritage Administration said the mounds at Songsan-ri may cover additional underground royal tombs dating to the Baekje era, which spanned from 18 B.C. to A.D. 660." (Baekje Kingdom Burial Mounds Recorded in South Korea 2019).

Chapter 6: American Flyers

1. For photos and details of the crash, see: (Heartsill 2019).

Chapter 7: The Road to Civil Air Transport

1. The Howard DGA-15 was a single-engine high-winged monoplane with a wooden wing and a steel-tube-truss fuselage, deeper and wider than its predecessors, allowing five people to be seated in comfort. The DGA-15P was powered by a Pratt & Whitney R-985 Wasp Junior radial engine...In the post-war years, Howard DGAs were prized more for their utility than for their clean lines. (Howard Aircraft Foundation 2017)Photo: (FlugKerl2- Own work, CC BY-SA 3.0; Wikipedia 2013).

2. The Grumman F9F/F-9 Cougar. Grumman received a Navy contract on 16Dec46 to produce a jet powered, straight wing, carried based fighter. The aircraft Grumman proposed first flew on 21Nov47 and was eventually designated and named the F9F-2 Panther. The Panther's success led

Grumman to design a swept wing derivative and propose it to the Navy. The new design retained the fuselage of the Panther but included a swept wing and tail. The Navy awarded Grumman a contract for this new aircraft on 2Mar51. It made its first flight on 20Sept and was named the Cougar but retained the F9F designation. The Cougar was first delivered to the Navy in Nov52 and remained in squadron until Feb60. The Navy accepted a total of 1,985 Cougars with the designations F9F-6, F9F-7, and F9F-8. (U.S. Navy n.d.), 485-86.

3. Douglas DC-6. Douglas was working on the DC-6 to initially be used in World War II in the mid-1940s, but the conflict soon ended. With Lockheed causing a stir in the civil scene in the post-war realm, Douglas had to shift its approach. So, it reworked the program to go head-to-head with Connie [the Lockheed Constellation] in the long-haul commercial sector... [entering] service in March 1947 with both American Airlines and United Airlines. Pan American, Delta Air Lines, National Airlines, and Braniff were all early adopters of the DC-6...the DC-6's robust and trusted Pratt & Whitney R-2800 engines allowed it to become an aviation mainstay. (Singh, How Douglas Developed The DC-6 To Compete With The Lockheed Constellation 2022) Photo: (By RuthAS - Own work 1954).

4. Douglas DC-4. Backed by four Pratt & Whitney R-2180-S1A1-G Twin Hornet 1s, the plane had a cruise speed of 200 mph (322 km/h) and a range of 1,900 NM (3,500 km). The wide-scale edition of the DC-4 was revised with a more petite build. It proved to be popular across the industry due to its efficiency and reliability. The autopilot system relayed directional hold and altitude. United entered this model into commercial service in 1942, and military variants such as the C-54 Skymaster and the R5D saw it become valued across the industry. (Singh, Experimental Aircraft: What Was The Douglas DC-4E 2022) Photo: (Kahn, Seaboard World Airlines Aircraft>Seaboard Douglas DC-4 2022).

5. The Lockheed Constellation ("Connie") is a propeller-driven, four-engine airliner built by Lockheed Corporation between 1943 and 1958 at Burbank, California. Lockheed built 856 in numerous models—all with the same triple-tail design and dolphin-shaped fuselage. Most were powered by four 18-cylinder Wright R-3350 Duplex-Cyclones. The Constellation was used as a civil airliner and as a military and civilian air transport... Its pressurized cabin enabled large numbers of commercial passengers

to fly well above most bad weather...Military versions included...the R7O R7V-1 (L-1049B)...WV-2 (L-1049B) (widely known as the Willie Victor) and many variant EC-121 designations for the Navy. (Wikipedia, Lockheed Constellation 2022) Video of last flying Lockheed Super Constellation (Stewart 2021). Photo: (Kahn, Seaboard World Airlines Aircraft>Lockheed L-1049D Super Constellation 2022).

6. Carried from India, as well as the Philippines, were thousands of monkeys for research that led to the Salk vaccine, and an end to the scourge of polio that so terrorized Americans during the 1940s and 50s. (Kahn, Seaboard World Airlines History 2022).

7. For more monkey-flight adventures, read: Monkey Business by Walter "Jorgy" Jorgensen. (Jorgensen 1997).

8. When the Chance Vought FG-1D Corsair was introduced in 1940 it boasted the most powerful engine along with the largest diameter propeller of any fighter aircraft in history. The result of this engine and propeller combination was the first fighter to exceed 400mph. Corsairs were built right up to 1952, giving the type the honor of having the longest production run of any American piston-engine fighter. The first service engagement for the Corsair was with the US Marine Corps operating from makeshift land bases across the Pacific...The Corsair proved to be a formidable air superiority fighter during World War II when she was the scourge of the skies across the Pacific and continued to deliver sterling service in later years during the Korean War. (Goodyear Corsair FG-1D [G-FGID] 2022). Photo: A Goodyear-produced FG-1D Corsair, a license-built Vought F4U-1D, during World War II. USN – U.S. Navy Naval Aviation News March 1953. (USN - U.S. Navy Naval Aviation News March 1953, Public Domain, n.d.).

9. Capt. August "Augie" Martin (8/31/19 - 7/01/68) was the first Black airline pilot in the United States. He learned to fly in the Civilian Pilot Training Program at the University of California and received his instructor's rating in 1942...In 1943, he joined the Army Air Corps and went through flight training at Tuskegee, Ala. He went on to fly B 25s and was hired by Seaboard in 1955... The August Martin High School in South Jamaica, N.Y. is named after him. In 1980, the U.S. Department of Transportation/Federal Aviation Administration published the August Martin Activities Book, a 20-page

book for minority children. It was reprinted in 1993. (August Harvey Martin 2022)

10. On November 3rd, 1955, Seaboard & Western became the first airline to hire an African American pilot, August Martin. (Kahn, Seaboard World Airlines History 2022).

11. The Lockheed P-38 Lightning was designed to meet the exacting requirements of a 1937 USAAC specification, calling for a high-altitude interceptor capable of 360mph at sea level…The Lockheed P-38 Lightning had supercharged engines, with two 1,425 hp Allison V-1710-91, 12-cylinder Vee-type engines. Its range was 2,260m, service ceiling 44,000ft. The P-38 could carry one 20mm cannon, four .50in machine guns, and an external bomb and rocket load of 4,000lb. (Jackson 2004), 306-7. Poster: (Unknown author - File:"Give us More P-38's" - NARA - 514398.jpg, Public Domain, 1941-45)

Chapter 8: CAT, Inc.

1. Civil Air Transport (CAT). was a unique airline formed in China after World War II by General Claire Lee Chennault, leader of the Flying Tigers, and Whiting Willauer of the China Defense Supplies (CDS). They purchased war surplus cargo planes, enrolled WWII veterans, and wound up with an enthusiastic, colorful group of former Flying Tiger aces and CAT airmen from the U.S. Army Air Corps, Navy, and Marine Corps. Many had been highly decorated. Operating under the aegis of the China National Rehabilitation and Relief Association (CNRRA), CAT distributed food and medicine to the interior of China where roads, railways and bridges had been destroyed by Japan's Imperial Air Force. (Smith 2012). CAT developed a reputation for being able to fly its C-46s and C-47s in hazardous conditions, and its pilots—many of them combat veterans—were renowned for getting the job done no matter what the odds. CAT began to fly missions for the CIA in October 1949, the same month that Mao proclaimed the People's Republic of China in Beijing. CIA leaders saw possibilities for contracting with CAT to support the Agency's operations to supply anti-Communist forces remaining on the mainland. The defeat of the Nationalists on the mainland in December 1949 and the retreat of the Nationalist government to Taiwan, however, left CAT near bankruptcy. CAT declined [a CIA subsidy offer in 1950]—more

personnel were let go, and its fleet of 19 C-46s was reduced to six...The outbreak of the Korean War in June 1950 spurred CIA to acquire CAT outright. On August 23, 1950, the Agency acquired the airlines' assets through a "cut- out" (a Washington area banker) and the company was reorganized as CAT Incorporated, ostensibly a private enterprise, but actually CIA's new aviation arm. (Central Intelligence Agency 2015). CAT Association website banner: "Civil Air Transport...the world's most shot at airline." (CAT Association 2012). Large baggage sticker: (Civil Air Transport (CAT); ebayimg.com n.d.).

2. Eareckson Air Station, formerly known as Shemya Air Force Base, is located on the island of Shemya, Alaska. The base was also referred to as "The Black Pearl" or "The Rock." It is the most westerly of the 11th Air Force bases and is located approximately 1,500 miles from Anchorage near the tip of the Aleutian Island chain...On 6 April 1993, Shemya AFB was renamed Eareckson Air Station. (GlobalSecurity.org 2000-2022).

3. The largest of the Izu Islands, Oshima is located east of the Izu Peninsula, around 100 kilometers from Tokyo. A large, still-active volcano dominates the island. It's a geologist's dream and an adventure for hikers and people who love the outdoors. (Tokyo Convention & Visitors Bureau 2019).

4. The 1956-1957 edition of Jane's All The World's Aircraft lists the head office address as 46 Chung Shan Road, North, 2nd Section, Taipei, Taiwan (Formosa). (Wikipedia, Civil Air Transport 2021) I cannot locate this address. Bing.com lists the address as: 46, Zhongshan North Road Section 2, Zhongshan District, Taipei City, 104, Taiwan. (Microsoft Bing; Navinfo; OpenStreetMap 2022) (csn 2022; 2019).

5. "We had a motto," Rousselot says. "First in and last out." Civil Air Transport flew 682 missions into Dien Bien Phu between March 1954 and the city's fall in May of the same year. By this time, though, Rousselot wasn't flying anymore. "I was restricted from flying because of the secrets I knew," he says. But he was handpicking the pilots who were to go. He lost two pilots in the mission, he says. Of the thousands of employees, Civil Air Transport officials count 242 casualties. The CIA counts 243. "The largest part of these losses came in Cambodia, Laos and Vietnam," Rousselot says. "They were shot down." (Parrish, Ashley [Tulsa World Staff Writer] 2001).

6. Mount Asama, Honshu's most active volcano, overlooks the resort town of Karuizawa, 140 km NW of Tokyo. It is a stratovolcano with three overlapping bodies making up this volcano. (admin 2010)

Chapter 9: Indonesia

1. The Lockheed T-33 Shooting Star (or T-Bird) is a two-seat jet trainer, with second seat instrumentation and flight controls. It was used by the U.S. Navy as a land-based trainer starting in 1949. Despite its age, the T-33 remains in service worldwide. (Fandom Military, Lockheed T-33 n.d.)

2. The McDonnell F2H Banshee went into combat in Korea for the first time on 23Aug51, when F2H-2s of VF-172 struck at targets in north-west Korea. The Banshee carried a single crew member. Specifications included a Westinghouse J34-E-34 turbojet engine, with 580mph capability, and a range of 1,170 miles. Armament capacity included four 20mm cannon with underwing racks for two 500lb or four 250lb bombs. (Jackson 2004), 334. Photo: (USN - U.S. Navy Strike Fighter Squadron 41 (VFA-41) website, Public Domain 1950s).

3. The Douglas A-26 Invader first flew in July 1962...and was the fastest U.S. bomber of World War II. The Invader, re-designated B-26B and B-26C, saw extensive service in the Korean War. (Jackson 2004), 183. Photo: (Ragnhild and Neil Crawford - flickr 2016).

4. [They were] Air Freight Specialist(s) with Air America operations in Laos. Commonly called 'kickers,' their primary job was to load aircraft with various types of cargo that included rice for refugees and ammunition for troops fighting a war against the Pathet Lao and the North Vietnamese. The task involved ensuring the aircraft was loaded according to weight and balance specifications and to unload the plane at destinations throughout Laos. Often these loads were airdropped, and the kicker's job was to kick the cargo out the back or side of the aircraft depending on the aircraft type. Thus, the nickname 'kicker.' It was a demanding and strenuous task, and they were at the mercy of the pilots hoping they knew what they were doing, and the wartime conditions in Laos. Most hits from enemy gunfire occurred in the fuselage where the kickers were located making them more vulnerable than the pilots. All of them carried parachutes, and some survived a stricken aircraft by jumping, but most perished along with

the pilots when a plane was shot down. (Cates and Bailey, beetle- bailey.pdf n.d.) Also read: Patrick Lee's novel, Kickers: a novel of the Secret War (Lee 2014).

5. Manado (Indonesian pronunciation: [Maˈnado]) is the capital city of the Indonesian province of North Sulawesi. Manado is located at the Bay of Manado and is surrounded by a mountainous area. (Wikipedia, Manado 2022) There was a general feeling that the central government was inefficient, development was stagnating, and money was being plugged into Java. In March 1957 the military leaders of both southern and northern Sulawesi launched a confrontation with the central government, with demands for greater regional autonomy…At least initially the "Permesta" (Piagam Perjuangan Semesta Alam) rebellion was a reformist rather than a separatist movement…Negotiations between the central government and the Sulawesi military leaders prevented violence in southern Sulawesi, but the North Sulawesi leaders were dissatisfied with the agreements and the movement split. Inspired, perhaps, by fears of domination by the south, the leaders declared their own autonomous state of North Sulawesi in June 1957. By this time the central government had the situation in southern Sulawesi pretty much under control but in the north, they had no strong local figure to rely upon and there were rumors that the USA, suspected of supplying arms to rebels in Sumatra, was also in contact with the North Sulawesi leaders…The rebels' few planes (supplied by the USA and flown by Filipino, Taiwanese, and US pilots) were destroyed. US policy shifted, favoring Jakarta, and in June 1958 central government troops landed in North Sulawesi. The Permesta rebellion was finally put down in mid-1961. (Blumtritt 2016) Also read: Barbara S. Harvey's, Permesta: Half a Rebellion (Monograph, No. 57). (Harvey 1977).

6. Harry Clay (Heinie) Aderholt (6 January 1920 – 20 May 2010) General Aderholt left for Okinawa in January 1960 where he became commander of the 1095th Operational Evaluation Training Group. During this assignment, he contributed to the pioneering of special air warfare techniques and was instrumental in developing the Laos airfield complex known as Lima sites. These fields were used throughout Southeast Asia as support sites for special warfare operations and as "Jolly Green" helicopter forward staging bases for rescue and recovery operations in Laos and North Vietnam. (Biographies: Brigadier General Harry C. "Heinie" Aderholt n.d.)

The Hmong were warriors in north Laos who fought against the North Vietnamese for more than 15 years. General Aderholt supported them as commander of the 56th Air Commando Wing in Thailand, flying propeller driven aircraft to conduct low-level night interdiction, as well as civic action missions. "With his passing, our nation has lost a storied member of the greatest nation, a visionary leader of combat air power, and a founding father of modern special operations," General Schwartz said. (Whitney 2010) To learn more, read Air Commando One: Heinie Aderholt and America's Secret Air Wars by Warren A. Trest (Trest, Air Commando One: Heinie Aderholt and America's Secret Air Wars 2000). Photo credit (Rossel n.d.). Ron and Heinie remained lifelong friends. (csn 2022; 2019).

7. In 1958, Aderholt heard of a short takeoff and landing aircraft developed by Otto Koppen and Lynn L. Bollinger, who'd formed the Helio Aircraft Corp. [later Helio Aircraft Co.] Aderholt arranged for a demonstration at Friendship International Airport, Md. — today known as Thurgood Marshall Baltimore-Washington International Airport — and test-flew the high-winged, fixed-gear Helio. "I knew immediately," said Aderholt. "This was what the CIA needed to exfiltrate people from hostile territory and to support partisans behind enemy lines." On April 8, 1949, Koppen and Bollinger organized the first flight of a Piper PA-17 Vagabond as a proof-of-concept ship for their high-lift flap system. The extensively modified, re-engined Piper became known as Helio-1, or, in jargon, "the helioplane." Aderholt demonstrated that the Courier could land and take off in a village that had no runway or road of any kind. Soon, a handful of CIA Couriers belonging to the agency's airline, Air America, were carrying out clandestine missions in the Laotian hinterlands. (Dorr and Borch 2013). Photo: (Lum 2014).

8. William H. "Bill" Beale, Jr. was a US military and paramilitary aviator. In the Second World War he was in the USAAF and flew bombing missions in the northern Pacific theater. In the Permesta rebellion in Indonesia in 1958 he flew bombing missions for the CIA. His career ended on a CIA covert mission in Laos when he was killed in a plane crash on 6 April 1962. (Fandom Military, William Beale [aviator] 2018).

9. Although this is what Ron was told, the reader will decide for themselves if this is factual. (J. F. Leeker, Air America at the Bay of Pigs 2021), 33-34, 36, 39, 45.

10. North American F-86 Sabre, sometimes called the Sabrejet, is a transonic jet fighter aircraft. Produced by North American Aviation, the Sabre is best known as the United States first swept-wing fighter that could counter the swept-wing Soviet MiG-15 in high-speed dogfights in the skies of the Korean War (1950–1953), fighting some of the earliest jet-to-jet battles in history. Considered one of the best and most important fighter aircraft in that war, the F-86 is also rated highly in comparison with fighters of other eras. (Fandom Military, North American F-86 Sabre n.d.) One of the greatest fighters of all time… (Jackson 2004), 528. (U.S. Air Force photo by J.M. Eddins Jr. - commons.wikimedia, Public Domain 2016).

11. The North American F-100 Super Sabre is an American supersonic jet fighter aircraft that served with the United States Air Force (USAF) from 1954 to 1971 and with the Air National Guard (ANG) until 1979…it was the first USAF fighter capable of supersonic speed in level flight. The F-100 was designed by North American Aviation as a higher performance follow-on to the F-86 Sabre air superiority fighter. (Fandom Military, North American F-100 Super Sabre n.d.). Photo: (US Air Force - U.S Air Force photo nationalmuseum.af.mil, CC BY-SA 4.0 2010).

12. CEECO [A-26/]B-26s—About 25 Douglas [A-26/]B-26s, all owned by CIA/USAF/Air Asia, were stored at Tainan, Taiwan, at various times from June 58 to about 1965. In Air America papers, these aircraft are referred to as CEECO B-26s that were to be maintained and modified by Air Asia in 1962, but the question was still open in October 62. CEECO stands for the "Consolidated Electric Equipment Company" and was an Agency proprietary. CEECO may also be identical with the USAF's Logistical Support Group, as when the remaining CEECO B-26 were to be ferried to the Congo in August 1964, the order came from the LSG293– so probably, the LSG was just another cover for the CIA. (J. F. Leeker, The History of Air America 2020-), 54.

Chapter 10: Test Pilot

1. The 80th Fighter Squadron (traditionally nicknamed the "Headhunters", and since 1971 also the "Juvats"), 7 August 1956, the Headhunters rejoined the 8th Fighter Wing, which had again moved to Itazuke. Here the squadron began flying the F-100 Super Sabre. During this time the squadron name changed again, with a 1 July 1958 redesignation as the

80th Tactical Fighter Squadron. The 80th served in combat operations in World War II, the Korean War, and the Vietnam War. Motto: Audentes Fortuna Juvat (Fortune Favors the Bold). (Battle 2010)

2. Air Force pilots developed a tactic called a "LABS Maneuver," or Low-Altitude Bombing System. As the name implies, the aircraft would come into the target area at a low altitude, and then quickly pull up. Then it performed the Immelman (or "idiot's loop"), dropping its nuclear bombs so that the trajectory of the nuclear bomb took it on a parabolic arc toward the target [away from the retreating aircraft]. This means the bomb would be flipped over backward, landing behind the plane as the plane itself backflipped. The B-47 Stratojet [or other aircraft] would continue pulling up until it was at a higher altitude before rolling over. (Team Mighty 2021) Diagram: (en:User:AaronS - http://en.wikipedia.org/ wiki/File:Overtheshoulderbomb.jpg, Public Domain 2010). For videos of the maneuver, see: (Trackrod 2014).

3. Friday 16 February 1968, Time cadet 21:20: Civil Air Transport Flight 010, Boeing 727-92C, Registration No. B-1018. The flight from Hong Kong to Taipei was commenced with a CAT Senior Pilot performing the functions of a pilot-in-command. The flight was cleared for a straight in ILS runway 10 approach. The aircraft descended below the glide slope. The radio altimeter sounded at 350 feet, but corrective action wasn't taken in time. The 727 touched down, rolled 200m and became airborne again before striking trees and a farmhouse. The Senior Pilot was properly licensed, but he was neither the assigned pilot-in-command nor a pilot under training on this flight. Total fatalities: 21 (including 3 of the 11 crew). Total occupants 63. [The database does not mention the weather conditions at the time of the accident.] The aircraft was damaged beyond repair. (Flight Safety Foundation 2022).

4. The Landing Ship, Tank, or LST, was designed to land up to twenty tanks on a beach. It did so by dropping a ramp onto the beach through a set of bow doors after the ship was deliberately grounded. The design dated to November 1941, when a British delegation to the United States asked for 200 ships and 400 craft capable of bringing tanks ashore. The former became the LST and the latter the LCT. (Budge 2006, 2008-2009, 2012, 2016-17, 2019).

Chapter 11: Laos and Air America

1. William Matthew "Bill" Leary, Jr. (May 6, 1934 - February 24, 2006) was an American academic and aviation historian. For 32 years, Leary taught at the University of Georgia from which he retired as the E. Merton Coulter Professor of History in 2005. Leary was born in Newark, New Jersey in 1934. He joined the United States Air Force and was stationed at Kadena Air Base in Japan during the Korean War where his responsibilities included filing flight plans, logging arrivals and departures, and arranging parking and service for aircraft. Leary stated that his observation of Civil Air Transport aircraft and personnel at Kadena led to a historical interest in aviation. (Wikipedia, William M. Leary, 2022; 2019)

2. CARE: Meeker identifies this as "Co-operative for American Relief to Everywhere, Inc." (Meeker 1959), 10.

3. Ibid., 35.

4. Ibid., 37.

5. Indochina, also called (until 1950), French Indochina French Indochine Française, the three countries of Vietnam, Laos, and Cambodia formerly associated with France, first within its empire and later within the French Union. The term Indochina refers to the intermingling of Indian and Chinese influences in the culture of the region. (Britannica, T. Editors of Encyclopaedia. 2022).

6. CAT's permanent presence in Laos began on 1 July 1957, when CAT pilot Bruce B. Blevins brought a C-47 to Vientiane to service a new contract with the US Embassy. Blevins found flying conditions primitive in Laos. At least Vientiane had a pierced steel plank runway and the only control tower in Laos. Elsewhere, he usually landed on dirt strips that had been built to support Japanese fighters during World War II. There were no aeronautical charts available, so he had to use French topographical maps. The only radio aid to navigation in the country was a 25-watt nondirectional beacon at Vientiane that was operated by employees of Air Laos, the country's commercial airline, who turned it on when it suited them (Leary, CIA Air Operations in Laos, 1955-1974: Studies in Intelligence, Winter 1999-2000: Supporting the 'Secret War' 2007).

7. Kong Le is a former paratrooper captain in the Royal Lao Army known

for overthrowing the government of Laos in a 1960 coup d'état. He obtained his training from the Armed Forces of the Philippines in 1957 and joined the Royal Lao Army in 1960. On August 9, Kong Le led the Second Paratroop Battalion in a nearly bloodless coup…taking over Vientiane. (Fandom Military, Kong Le n.d.).

8. The Plain of Jars [French: Plaine des Jarres] is a megalithic archaeological landscape in Laos. It consists of thousands of stone jars scattered around the upland valleys and the lower foothills of the central plain of the Xiang Khouang Plateau. The jars are mostly arranged in clusters ranging in number from one to several hundred. (Wikipedia, Plain of Jars 2022).

9. The Sikorsky S-55 (H-19 Chickasaw)…was a 12-seat utility helicopter for civil and military use…first flown on 7Nov49, and no fewer than 1026 production examples were built for the US military. The 410-448kW (550-600hp) Wright R-1340/-57 engine was located in the nose so that the long extension shaft could be carried straight up to the main 3-blade rotor-gear drive…leaving the main cabin below the flight deck free for occupancy by troops or freight. (Jackson 2004), 456-57. Photo: (U.S. Army - commons file, CC BY-SA 4.0 2017).

10. (Leary, CIA Air Operations in Laos, 1955-1974: Studies in Intelligence, Winter 1999-2000: Supporting the 'Secret War' 2007).

11. Ibid.

12. Major General Phoumi Nosavan (27Jan20 - 1985) was a military strongman…prominent in the history of the Kingdom of Laos; at times, he dominated its political life to the point of being a virtual dictator. He was born in Savannakhet, the French Protectorate of Laos. Originally a civil servant in the French colonial administration of Laos, during the last year of World War II he joined the resistance movement against the Japanese occupiers…On 25 December 1959, he took control of the capital of Vientiane and of the nation in a bloodless coup.

13. This could be Xieng Dao, Laos. As with several sites Ron mentions in his original manuscript, I cannot verify or locate this on the map. He may have misspelled the name. (csn 2022; 2019).

14. James William Lair (often referred to as Bill Lair) (4Jul24 – 28Oct2014) was an influential Central Intelligence Agency paramilitary officer from

the Special Activities Division. He was a native Texan, raised in a broken family, but a good student. He joined the CIA after serving in a combat unit in Europe during World War II, followed by a geology degree from Texas A&M. In his senior year, he was recruited by the CIA. (Wikipedia, James William Lair 2022) Roger Warner wrote of Lair in his book, Shooting the Moon: "A shy, quiet Texan, Bill Lair shaped America's war in Laos." (Warner, Shooting at the Moon: The Story of America's Clandestine War in Laos 1996), 212 [photo caption in facing page].

15. Sikorsky H-34. The Sikorsky H-34 Choctaw (Company designation S-58) was a piston-engined military helicopter originally designed by American aircraft manufacturer Sikorsky for the United States Navy for service in the anti-submarine warfare (ASW) role...It was a lengthened and more powerful version of the Sikorsky (model S-55) or UH-19 Chickasaw. Specifications: Powerplant: 1 x Wright R-1820-84, 1,525 hp radial engine; Rotor Diameter: 56'; Capacity: 2 Crew, along with 16 troops, or 8 stretchers; Top speed: 173 mph; Range 182 Nautical miles. (Cactus Air Force 2016). Additional text and photo: (Freedom's Flying Memorial; Alan Weiss 2007) Photo: (Lum 2014).

16. Possibly "Plaine des Jarres Headquarters." (csn 2022; 2019).

17. From In Memoriam, The CAT/Air America Memorial Plaque located at the Eugene McDermott Library, University of Texas at Dallas. (Leon V. LaShomb Collection, Memorial Data, Folder 14, Box 1 n.d.) and (Air America; air-america.org 2014).

18. From In Memoriam, The CAT/Air America Memorial Plaque located at the Eugene McDermott Library, University of Texas at Dallas. (Leon V. LaShomb Collection, Memorial Data, Folder 14, Box 1 n.d.) and (Air America; air-america.org 2014).

19. The 1962 Geneva accord was an agreement between the United States, the Soviet Union, China, North Vietnam, Burma, Cambodia, Thailand, South Vietnam, France, India, Poland, Canada, and Laos. All U.S. troops departed Laos, but the North Vietnamese remained in violation of the Accord and were using neutral Laos to transport military troops and supplies along the Lao-Vietnam border into South Vietnam to kill Americans and South Vietnamese troops. America faced three bad choices: overtly attack North Vietnamese troops in Laos and be publicly

excoriated for violating the Accord; walk away and risk losing the Pacific Rim to communism; or conduct covert and clandestine operations in an attempt to halt the traffic. They chose the latter, but they needed logistical support and couldn't retain secrecy while using the U. S. military. The solution once again was Air America. (Cates, Air America: A Historical Synopsis from the Beginning to End 2021).

20. (Stevenson 1972), 208-9.

21. Phou Pha Thi (Phathi) is a "sacred mountain" in Laos "believed... inhabited by great "phi", or spirits and used for the clandestine Lima Site 85 military installation during the Vietnam War. The lightly defended installation was destroyed by North Vietnamese attackers in the 10-11 March 1968 Battle of Lima Site 85. (Wikipedia, Phou Pha Thi 2021).

22. Edgar "Pop" Buell (1913-1980), a humanitarian aid worker in Laos, worked as farmer until the age of 47. In 1958 he joined the International Voluntary Services, a precursor to the Peace Corps, which offered him a job as an agricultural adviser in Laos. Buell worked in Laos through the Laotian Civil War, organizing relief aid to refugees and isolated villages. He was forced to flee Laos in 1974 when the Communist Pathet Lao gained control of the country. (Wikipedia, Pop Buell 2021).

23. "A short time ago we rounded up 300 fresh recruits. Thirty percent were 14 years old or less, and ten of them were only ten years old. Another 30 percent were 15 or 16. The remaining 40 percent were 45 or over. Where were the ones in between? I'll tell you—they're all dead." Edgar "Pop" Buell, International Voluntary Service employee, 1968 (Buell, Edgar n.d.).

24. Gen. Vang Pao (Hmong: Vaj Pov; 1929-2011) was a major general in the Royal Lao Army. After WWII, Vang Pao was recruited by the French as an officer during the First Indochina War to combat the Viet Minh. Although French forces lost the war, Vang remained in the army of the newly independent Kingdom of Laos. He was the only ethnic Hmong to attain the rank of General officer in the Royal Lao Army, and he was loyal to the King of Laos while remaining a champion of the Hmong people. During the 1960s and 1970s, General Vang commanded the Secret Army, a highly effective CIA-trained and supported force that fought against the Pathet Lao and People's Army of Vietnam...he immigrated to the U.S. in 1975. (General Vang Pao (Vaj Pov) n.d.).

25. The PT-76 amphibious light tank entered service with Soviet Army in 1951. It was designed as a reconnaissance vehicle. (Military-Today.com 2006-2022).

26. The Boeing B-52 Stratofortress is a long-range, subsonic, jet-powered strategic bomber...The bomber is capable of carrying up to 70,000 pounds of weapons and has a typical combat range of more than 8,800 miles without aerial refueling. (Wikipedia, Boeing B-52 Stratofortress 2022). Photo: (Caputo and USAF 2014).

27. Lockheed C-130 Hercules...the most versatile tactical transport aircraft ever built...flew for the first time in 1954. It carries a crew of four, with four 4050hp Allison T56-A-7 turboprop engines. It has a maximum speed of 340mph and a range of 3820 miles. Service ceiling is 33,000ft with a payload of 42,000lb. (Jackson 2004), 312. Photo: (Lum 2014)

28. Volpar Turbo Beech: The Beech 18 has over 200 Federal Aviation Administration (FAA) approved Supplemental Type Certificates (STCs)...Air America had Volpar convert 14 aircraft to turboprop power, fitted with the Volpar tricycle undercarriage and powered by two Garrett AiResearch TPE331 engines. The modified aircraft were called Volpar Turbo Beeches. The MTOW was 10,286 lb. (Wikipedia, Beechcraft Model 18 2022) See also: (D. J. Leeker 2016). Photo: (Lum 2014).

29. The Fairchild C-123 Provider is a military transport aircraft designed by Chase Aircraft and then built by Fairchild Aircraft for the U.S. Air Force... [and] various air forces in Southeast Asia. During the War in Vietnam, the C-123 was used to deliver supplies, to evacuate the wounded, and also used to spray defoliant. (Fandom Military, Fairhchild C-123 Provider n.d.). Photo: (Lum 2014).

30. (Task Force Omega Inc n.d.) A photograph of Edward Weissenback is on this site.

31. Several Laotian or similar names are listed on the plaque as MIA, and one of these is certainly the "kicker" Ron mentions but, unfortunately, does not name here. Please see the entire name list and the photo of the memorial plaque to view all who are MIA or were killed in service with CAT and Air America. (csn 2022; 2019) From In Memoriam, The CAT/Air America Memorial Plaque located at the Eugene McDermott Library, University of Texas at Dallas. (Leon V. LaShomb

Collection, Memorial Data, Folder 14, Box 1 n.d.) and (Air America; air-america.org 2014).

32. The Pilatus PC-6 Porter (Switzerland: 1959) Designed as a high braced monoplane For STOL operation on land, sea, or ice. The initial Pilatus PC-6 Porter benefited from the early introduction of the turboprop engine in 1961. Which has been successively upgraded. Later marques. This ubiquitous design with a large Freespace aft of the cockpit has been asked, as has been used as an air ambulance. Often within a winter sports context and for survey parachuting or glider towing roles, domestic operator Mount Cook Airline has used ski equipment. Examples of the Porter for a number of years to land tours and skiers on the glaciers in South Island, New Zealand. More than 550 PC six examples have been produced. The Pilatus PC-6 Porter carries a crew of one. Powered by one 680shp Pratt & Whitney Aircraft of Canada PT6A-27 turboprop engine flat rated at 550shp. It has maximum cruising speed of 161mph, range of 652 miles, and service ceiling of 28,000ft. It has a wingspan of 49ft 8in and carries payload of up to 10 persons. (Jackson 2004), 397.

33. From In Memoriam, The CAT/Air America Memorial Plaque located at the Eugene McDermott Library, University of Texas at Dallas. (Leon V. LaShomb Collection, Memorial Data, Folder 14, Box 1 n.d.) and (Air America; air-america.org 2014).

34. From In Memoriam, The CAT/Air America Memorial Plaque located at the Eugene McDermott Library, University of Texas at Dallas. (Leon V. LaShomb Collection, Memorial Data, Folder 14, Box 1 n.d.) and (Air America; air-america.org 2014).

35. AVPFO/DFD TPE to All Chief Pilots, 27 April 1972, (Hickler n.d.), cited in: (Leary, CIA Air Operations in Laos, 1955-1974: Studies in Intelligence, Winter 1999-2000: Supporting the 'Secret War' 2007).

36. Telex, VP-NTD UTH to Chief Executive Office, 3 June 1974, (Hickler n.d.), cited in: (Leary, CIA Air Operations in Laos, 1955-1974: Studies in Intelligence, Winter 1999-2000: Supporting the 'Secret War' 2007).

37. Great effort was made to make the Air America appear as a private enterprise for plausible deniability, but all work was for the U. S. government, and when the complex company was dismantled and the assets sold, the U.S. Treasury received the profit. (Cates, Air America: A

Historical Synopsis from the Beginning to End 2021).

38. Originally accessed 2019: (Unknown, AAM61.pdf n.d.), 1. Currently (6 April 2022), unknown source and author.

Chapter 12: Covert Skies

1. Air America—the name changed on 26 March 59, primarily to avoid confusion about the air proprietary's operations in Japan. (Leary, Supporting the "Secret War": CIA Operations in Laos, 1955-74 2007).

2. In the Laotian language, the words Ban, Muong, and Van all refer to villages. Nam means a stream, and Phu refers to a mountain. (Ron).

3. For more information, read: The Forgotten Legacy of World War Two in Northern Thailand: A look back at World War II in Chiang Mai and Northern Thailand, by Aydan Stuart. (Stuart 2017).

4. Probably at Lampang, Thailand. (csn 2022; 2019).

5. Really? Kathy and I wonder how Ron parted ways with this hyena. Sad, sad, sad; one more unfinished story. (csn 2022; 2019).

6. c/n 086, B-833...c/n 086, built 04/58 as model H-391B original registry N4136D sold 04/58, Civil Air Transport inc (CAT) dereg 05/58 for export 02/59, to AirAsia rereg as B-833 Taiwan 09/59, Air America (1st Helio of 29 acquired) chartered to USOM for trials in Laos sat idle at Wattay Vientiane Laos because of Pilots dislike until 2/60, (sometime between 2/59-2/60 it was the 3rd Helio converted at Tainan to H-395 configuration with GO-480 eng using Helio mod #45 it was taken by Major Aderholt to (T-05) Takhli Thailand to serve as a courier aircraft, then Major Aderholt used for training Air America pilots convincing Air America crews that the Helio could easily land at places where most other aircraft had difficulties landing, and after demonstrating dozens of short and tricky mountaintop landings at ("Lima Sites", at that time still called "Victor Sites"), sites normally used only by helicopters, the Helio became one of Air America's work horses in Laos, accident(1) after engine failure aircraft nosed over while making an emergency landing @ (L-15) Phong Saly Laos 03/60... (Johnson 2014). ...made an emergency landing at Phong Saly (L-15), Laos, on 2 March 60, while flying under contract 57-08; the emergency landing was caused by an engine failure, during which the aircraft nosed over; the pilot (E. F. Sims), the co-pilot (R. J. Sutphin) and two passengers received minor

injuries; [Helio] taken to Tainan and repaired... (J. F. Leeker, Air America: Helio H-395 Super Couriers 2015), 450-51. Digital Painting: (Malvoso, Helio B-833 On the Tarmac 2022).

Chapter 13: Helio Over Laos

1. Digital Painting: (Malvoso, Helio B-835 In Flight 2022). For a photo of this aircraft see: (C. R.-M. Wofford 2022; 1966). To browse photos see the Terry and Robert Wofford Laotian Image Collection: (Wofford and Wofford n.d.).

2. Dengue (pronounced DENgee) fever is a painful, debilitating mosquito-borne disease caused by any one of four closely related dengue viruses. These viruses are related to the viruses that cause West Nile infection and yellow fever. (WebMD 2005-2022)

3. On August 9, 1960, Kong Le staged a coup d'état to bring down Tiao Somsanith's government that included Gen. Phoumi Nosavan as deputy- Prime Minister. The plotters asked Prince Souvanna Phouma, who had just started his term as Laos Ambassador to France, to come back and form a new government. Kong Le used a helicopter to fly to Muang Kasy and bring back the Pathet Lao leaders that ran away from jail a while ago so they could be part of the Souvanna's cabinet. Most of the Lao people were hoping and thought that Prince Souvanna Phouma's neutral government was going to seek assistance from France. They were disappointed because the coup's leaders joined hands with the Pathet Lao and the communist world instead, thereby flooding Vientiane with North-Vietnamese troops. (Unforgettable Laos 2012)

4. According to Stevenson, this meeting between Souvanna Phouma and Phoumi Nosavan occurred on 23Aug60. (Stevenson 1972), 96-7, 339-40

5. The Battle of Ban Pa Dong (31Jan-6Jun61 in Ban Pa Dong, the Kingdom of Laos. Troops from the People's Army of Vietnam (PAVN) and the Pathet Lao attacked Hmong recruits being trained as Auto Defense Choc guerrillas via Operation Momentum. Although the Hmong made the tactical error of defending a fixed position, their eventual escape from the communist invaders left their fledgling L'Armee Clandestine intact and able to wage war for the Royal Lao Government. However, they abandoned four howitzers and two mortars to the victorious Vietnamese communists. The

partisans had also set a deleterious precedent for themselves with their defense of a fixed position...There was a grass airstrip at Ban Pa Dong, and some old wooden buildings that had been built by the French. It was located on a ridgeline, at 4,500 feet. (Note: I cannot locate this site on the map.) (Wikipedia, Battle of Ban Pa Dong 2022)

Chapter 14: Pak Kading

1. Helio H-395, B-835...made an emergency landing due to engine damage caused by ground fire at Ban Khan Dia, Thailand [town/village not located on the map, and ground fire probably would not come from Thailand side of the Mekong River (csn 2022; 2019)], on 3 November 60, while flying under contract 57-08; the pilot (R. J. Sutphin) and three passengers received minor injuries (J. F. Leeker, Air America: Helio H-395 Super Couriers 2015), 452.

2. His crash site must have been just north of Pak Kading and Namkading, as he does not write about crossing the river. (csn 2022; 2019).

3. As with several sites Ron mentions in his original manuscript, I cannot verify or locate this on the map. It may no longer exist as a village, or he may have misspelled the name or used a colloquialism for an existing Laotian village (csn 2022; 2019).

4. The clouded leopard (Neofelis nebulosa), also called the mainland clouded leopard, is a wild cat inhabiting dense forests...through mainland Southeast Asia...It rests in trees during the day and hunts by night on the forest floor. Their vocalizations include a short high-pitched meow call, a loud crying call, both emitted when a cat is trying to locate another one over a long or short distance; they prusten [make a chuffing noise]; when aggressive, they growl with a low-pitched sound and hiss with exposed teeth and wrinkled nose. Although smaller than snow leopards, the clouded leopard is often referred to as a "modern-day Sabre-tooth." (Wikipedia, Clouded leopard 2022).

5. I cannot verify this is the correct name of the Hotel. It may have been spelled Somboun (csn 2022; 2019).

Chapter 15: Vientiane Burning

1. This occurred the day after the Battle of Vientiane which was fought

between 13 and 16 December 1960, the battle ended with General Phoumi Nosavan winning control of the Kingdom of Laos with the aid of the Royal Thai Government and the U.S. Central Intelligence Agency. Vientiane was left devastated by the fighting, with about 600 civilians dead, about the same number of homes destroyed, and 7,000 left homeless. The losing Forces Armées Neutralistes under Captain Kong Le retreated onto the strategic Plain of Jars, to begin an uneasy coexistence with the Pathet Lao and the invading People's Army of Vietnam. (Wikipedia, Battle of Vientiane 2023)

Chapter 16: Drop Sites Over Vietnam and Laos

1. Similar to several sites Ron mentions in his original manuscript, I cannot verify or locate this on the map. It may no longer exist as a village, or he may have misspelled the name or used a colloquialism for an existing Laotian village (csn 2022; 2019).

2. From In Memoriam, The CAT/Air America Memorial Plaque located at the Eugene McDermott Library, University of Texas at Dallas. (Leon V. LaShomb Collection, Memorial Data, Folder 14, Box 1 n.d.) and (Air America; air-america.org 2014).

Afterword

1. (CAT Association 2012).

2. (Gann 1961).

Bibliography

admin. 2010. "Asama." Oregon State University>Volcano World. May 4. Accessed March 22, 2022. https://volcano.oregonstate.edu/asama.

Air America; air-america.org. 2014. "In Memoriam for Memorial Plaque." Air America. Accessed April 5, 2022; 2019. https://www.air-america.org/memorial-plaque/in-memoriam-for-memorial-plaque.html.

2022. American Flyers. Accessed March 11, 2022. https://americanflyers.com/about/.

Army Air, Forces. 1945. "Pilot's Manual for PMB05 Mariner. pdf." Smithsonian Air and Space Museum. December 1. Accessed March 11, 2022. https://airandspace.si.edu/webimages/collections/full/Pilot's%20manual%20for%20PMB05%20Mariner.pdf.

Arndted. 2016. "Invader." Flickr. September 3. Accessed March 23, 2022; 2019. https://www.flickr.com/photos/ednorberg/37075553981/in/photolist-YueUvk-93MvqN-oDFQ56-2gDpezV-51sjfo-76GN1H-Km28wQ-57efvR-558Kb3-eGkkUH-5f1Ahk-93zenW-rGVgcF-cL-NZgE-5s1PU4-oDFKEe-acG8wc-9hKe5B-3k47B4-5s4hUD-8UPWQq-7QBtti-2eCPnVj-Km28pL-oDq8nF-93yTyJ-93uR1e.

2022. "August Harvey Martin." Seaboard & Western / Seaboard World Airlines. Accessed March 16, 2022; 2019. http://www.seaboardairlines.org/obits/martin.htm.

2019. "Baekje Kingdom Burial Mounds Recorded in South Korea." Archaeology Magazine. July 18. Accessed March 14, 2022. https://www.archaeology.org/news/7835-190718-korea-baekje-tombs.

Battle, Air Force Order of. 2010. "80th Fighter Squadron." USAF Unit History. November 10. Accessed March 17, 2022. https://ww35.usafunithistory.com/PDF/75-100/80%20FIGHTER%20SQ.pdf.

n.d. "Biographies: Brigadier General Harry C. "Heinie" Aderholt." Air Force Link, Official Web Site of the United States Air Force. Accessed March 17, 2022. https://web.archive.org/web/20090116152454/http://www.af.mil/bios/bio.asp?bioID=4478.

Blumtritt, Dr. Peter. 2016. "North Sulawesi - History." north-sulawesi.org.

January. Accessed March 16, 2022. http://north-sulawesi.org/.

Boyer, J.R.; USAG-Humpherys. 2009. "USAG- Humphreys, AD with wings folded, Long before it was calle Camp Humphr..." flickr. September 29. Accessed April 14, 2022. https://www.flickr.com/photos/usa-ghumphreys/3986216282/in/album-72157622402383507/.

Britannica, T. Editors of Encyclopaedia. 2022. "Indochina." Encyclopedia Britannica. April 10. Accessed April 11, 2022. https://www.britannica.com/place/Indochina.

Britannica, T. Editors of Encylodpaedia. 2013. "WAVES." Encyclopedia Britannica. September 27. Accessed April 11, 2022. https://www.britannica.com/topic/WAVES-United-States-naval-organization.

Budge, Kent G. 2006, 2008-2009, 2012, 2016-17, 2019. "LST Class, Allied Landing Ships." The Pacific War Online Encyclopedia. Accessed March 19, 2022. http://www.pwencycl.kgbudge.com/L/s/LST.htm.

Buell, Edgar. n.d. "Hmong Timeline." The Hmong Project, Hmong Research Center 2020. Accessed March 24, 2022. https://hmongproject.com/timeline/.

By RuthAS - Own work, CC BY 3.0. 1954. "Douglas DC-6B N6531C PAA Hathrow 09.54 - Douglas DC-6." Wikipedia, The Free Encyclopedia. September 12. Accessed April 28, 2022. https://commons.wikimedia.org/w/index.php?curid=6964037.

Cactus Air Force. 2016. "H-34 Sikorsky Choctaw." Cactus Air Force Wingsand Wheels Museum. November. Accessed March 21, 2022. http://www.cactusairforce.com/inventory_item/h34-sikorsky-choctaw/.

Caputo, Airman 1st Class Victor J., and USAF. 2014. "B-52 Stratofortress assigned to the 307th Bomb Wing (cropped) - Boeing B-52 Stratofortress." Wikipedia, The Free Encyclopedia. May 15. Accessed April 16, 2022; 2019. https://commons.wikimedia.org/w/index.php?curid=68131933.

CAT Association. 2012. Civil Air Transport (CAT) Association. Accessed March 22, 2022. https://www.catassociation.org/.

Cates, Allen. 2021. "Air America: A Historical Synopsis from the Beginning to End." Air America. November 5. Accessed March 21, 2022. https://air-america.org/air-america-history.html.

Cates, Allen, and M.A. Bailey. n.d. "beetle-bailey.pdf." Air America. Ac-

cessed March 16, 2022. https://www.air-america.org/files/documents/beetle-bailey.pdf.
Central Intelligence Agency. 2015. "Stories--CIA Acquires CAT." Central Intelligence Agency. August 24. Accessed March 22, 2022. https://www.cia.gov/stories/story/cia-acquires-cat/.
Chuck. 2012. chucksusedcards.blogspot.com. August 1. Accessed March 10, 2022. http://chucksusedcards.blogspot.com/2012/08/card-find-part-2-wings-cigarettes.html.
Civil Air Transport (CAT); ebayimg.com. n.d. "Civil Air Transport "The Orient's Own"." ebayimg.com. Accessed 2022; 2019. https://i.ebayimg.com/images/i/111805484078-0-1/s-l1000.jpg.
Coates, Ed. n.d. "Beech SNB-5 Navigator 67220." Selections from the Ed Coates' Civil Aircraft Photograph Collection. Accessed April 14, 2022. https://edcoatesaircraftphotos.com/ac6/Beech%20SNB-5.html.
Connecticut Air & Space Center. n.d. "1948 Lockheed Tv-2 / T-33 Shooting Star (57-6558)." CT Air&Space Center. Accessed April 16, 2022. https://www.ctairandspace.org/t-33.
Courtney, Donald V. 2002. "Above & Beyond: Ration of Luck." Smithsonian Magazine. November. Accessed March 17, 2022. https://www.smithsonianmag.com/air-space-magazine/above-amp-beyond-ration-of-luck-35920728/.
csn. 2022; 2019. "CS Norwood, author's note." Covert Skies: Ron Sutphin's Road to Civil Air Transport (CAT) and Covert Operations in Laos.
Dhaig. 2014. The China Marines. Accessed March 11, 2022; 2019. http://www.chinamarine.org/Chronology.aspx.
Doehring, Thoralf. 1999-2020. "USS Monterey (CVL 26)." Unofficial US Navy Site. Accessed March 12, 2022. https://www.navysite.de/cvl/cvl26.htm.
Dorr, Robert F., and Fred L. Borch. 2013. "U-10 Helio Courier Was unsung Hero in Vietnam." Defense Media Network. September 29. Accessed March 17, 2022; 2019. https://www.defensemedianetwork.com/stories/u-10-helio-courier-was-unsung-hero-in-vietnam/.
Dwyer, Larry. 2014. The Aviation History Online Museum. February 19.

Accessed March 10, 2022. http://www.aviation-history.com/grumman/f4f.html.

—. 2015. The Aviation History Online Museum. December 22. Accessed March 10, 2022. http://www.aviation-history.com/northrop/p61.html.

en:User:AaronS - http://en.wikipedia.org/wiki/File:Overtheshoulderbomb.jpg, Public Domain. 2010. "Overtheshoulderbomb - Toss bombing." Wikipedia, The Free Encyclopedia . November 27. Accessed April 17, 2022; 2019. https://commons.wikimedia.org/w/index.php?curid=12160053.

Fandom Military, contributing. 2022. "Curtiss C-46 Commando." Fandom Military Wiki. Accessed April 4, 2022. https://military-history.fandom.com/wiki/Curtiss_C-46_Commando.

—. n.d. "Douglas A-1 Skyraider." Fandom Military Wiki. Accessed March 22, 2022. https://military-history.fandom.com/wiki/Douglas_A-1_Skyraider.

—. n.d. "Fairhchild C-123 Provider." Fandom Military Wiki. Accessed March 24, 2022. https://military-history.fandom.com/wiki/Fairchild_C-123_Provider?so=search.

—. n.d. "Kong Le." Fandom Military Wiki. Accessed March 24, 2022. https://military-history.fandom.com/wiki/Kong_Le?so=search.

—. n.d. "Lockheed T-33." Fandom Military Wiki. Accessed March 23, 2022. https://military-history.fandom.com/wiki/Lockheed_T-33.

—. n.d. "North American F-100 Super Sabre." Fandom Military Wiki. Accessed March 23, 2022. https://military-history.fandom.com/wiki/North_American_F-100_Super_Sabre?so=search.

—. n.d. "North American F-86 Sabre." Fandom Military Wiki. Accessed March 23, 2022. https://military-history.fandom.com/wiki/North_American_F-86_Sabre?so=search.

—. 2020. "Northrop P-61 Black Widow." Fandom Military Wiki. January 30. Accessed April 12, 2022. https://military-history.fandom.com/wiki/Northrop_P-61_Black_Widow?so=search.

—. 2018. "William Beale [aviator]." Fandom Military Wiki. May 19. Accessed March 17, 2022; 2019. https://military-history.fandom.com/wiki/William_Beale_(aviator)#.

2022. Fiddlersgreen: SNJ Texan: Aircraft. Accessed March 11, 2022.

http://www.fiddlersgreen.net/models/Aircraft/North-American-Texan.html.

Flight Safety Foundation. 2022. "Aviation Safety Network>Database." Flight Safety Foundation. Accessed March 19, 2022. https://aviation-safety.net/database/record.php?id=19680216-1.

FlugKerl2 - Own work, CC BY-SA 3.0; wikipedia. 2013. "Howard DGA15P - Howard DGA-15." Wikipedia, The Free Encyclopedia. August 4. Accessed April 15, 2022; 2019. https://commons.wikimedia.org/w/index.php?curid=27999626.

Foss, Joe; Simmons, Walter. 1943. Joe Foss, Flying Marine: The Story of His Flying Circus, As Told to Walter Simmons. New York: Books, Inc.

Freedom's Flying Memorial; Alan Weiss. 2007. "Aircraft Specifications: Sikorsky HUS (UH-34) "Sea Horse"." Freedom's Flying Memorial. Accessed March 21, 2022; 2019. http://www.freedomsflyingmemorial.org/aircraft-specs.htm.

Gann, Ernest K. 1961. Fate is the Hunter. New York: Simon & Schuster.

n.d. "General Vang Pao (Vaj Pov)." Learn Hmong Lessons & Traditions. Accessed March 24, 2022. http://hmonglessons.com/the-hmong/hmong-leaders/general-vang-pao-vaj-pov/.

GlobalSecurity.org. 2000-2022. "Eareckson Air Station." GlobalSecurity.org. Accessed March 16, 2022. https://www.globalsecurity.org/space/facility/shemya.htm.

2022. "Goodyear Corsair FG-1D [G-FGID]." The Fighter Collection. Accessed March 16, 2022. http://fighter-collection.com/cft/goodyear-corsair-fg-1d-g-fgid/.

Greguras, Fred. 2013. That's Qingdao: Qingdao Province China. August. Accessed March 10, 2022. https://www.thatsqingdao.com/us-marines-tsingtao-china-1945/.

Hansen, Neil Graham, and Luann Plamann Grosscup. 2018. Flight: An Air America Pilot's Story of Adventure, Descent and Redemption. Palisades: History Publishing Company LLC.

Harvey, Barbara S. 1977. Permesta: Half a Rebellion (Monograph, No. 57). Ithaca, New York: Cornell University Southeast Asia Program Publications.

Headquarters Marine Corps National Archives. 1995-2021. "File 521, MAG 12 Records - Korean War Project." Korean War Project. Accessed March 29, 2022. https://www.koreanwar.org/html/usmc-korean-war-records-unit.html?pid=16.

Heartsill, Gary. 2019. "The American Flyers Crash in Ardmore." N183H.pdf. July 23. Accessed March 29, 2022. http://www.gheart.net/N183H.pdf.

Hickler, Dave. n.d. "Dave Hickler Papers, CA054-03." History of Aviation Collection, Special Collections and Archives Division, Eugene McDermott Library, The University of Texas at Dallas. https://libarchives.utdallas.edu/repositories/2/resources/8 Accessed April 06, 2022.

Historica Wiki | Fandom, contributing. 2019. "Phoumi Nosavan." Historica | Fandom. July 21. Accessed April 17, 2022. https://historica.fandom.com/wiki/Phoumi_Nosavan.

Howard Aircraft Foundation. 2017. "Aircraft>Howard DGA-15." Howard Aircraft Foundation. Accessed March 14, 2022. http://www.howardaircraft.org/aircraft/116-howard-dga-15.

Intruder. 2016. "VMA(AW)-121 Green Knights." Intruder Association. Accessed March 12, 2022; 2019. https://www.intruderassociation.org/squadrons/va121.asp.

Jackson, Robert. 2004. The Encyclopedia of Aircraft. Edited by Robert Jackson. San Diego: Thunder Bay Press.

Johnson, Doug. 2014. "FlyHelio." Simple Machines Forum. Accessed March 24, 2022; 2019. https://flyhelio.com/smf/index.php?topic=735.0.

Jorgensen, Walter "Jorgy". 1997. "Seaboard Stories - Monkey Business." Seaboard & Western / Seaboard World Airlines. Accessed March 24, 2022. http://www.seaboardairlines.org/stories/s18.html.

Kahn, Ken. 2022. "Capt. Ronald J. Sutphin." Seaboard World Airlines In Memoriam. Accessed 2022. https://www.seaboardairlines.org/obits/sutphin.htm.

—. 2022. "Seaboard World Airlines Aircraft>Lockheed L-1049D Super Constellation." Seaboard & Western / Seaboard World Airlines. Accessed March 18, 2022. https://www.seaboardairlines.org/aircraft/l1049-11.htm.

—. 2022. "Seaboard World Airlines Aircraft>Seaboard Douglas DC-4." Seaboard & Western / Seaboard World Airlines. Accessed March

22, 2022. https://www.seaboardairlines.org/aircraft/aircraft.htm.

—. 2022. "Seaboard World Airlines History." Seaboard World / Seaboard & Western Airlines. Accessed March 16, 2022. http://www.seaboardairlines.org/seabhist.htm.

Lair, Bill; Ahern, Thomas; Undercover Armies, 1961-1973; Washington 2006 (Center for the Study of Intelligence, CIA). 1960s. "KongLe - Kong Le." Wikipedia, The Free Encyclopedia . Accessed April 17, 2022; 2019. www.foia.cia.gov/vietnam/6_UNDERCOVER_ARMIES.pdf.

Leary, William M. 2007. "CIA Air Operations in Laos, 1955-1974: Studies in Intelligence, Winter 1999-2000: Supporting the 'Secret War'." CIA.gov, Center for the Study of Intelligence. April 14. Accessed March 24, 2022. https://www.cia.gov/resources/csi/studies-in-intelligence/studies-in-intelligence-winter-1999-2000/cia-air-operations-in-laos-1955-1974/.

—. n.d. "Series III, Civil Air Transport (CAT). William M. Leary Papers, CA021-06, History of Aviation Archives, Special Collections and Archives Division." Eugene McDermott Library, The University of Texas at Dallas. Accessed March 20, 2022. https://libarchives.utdallas.edu/repositories/2/archival_objects/1558.

Leary, William M. 2007. Supporting the "Secret War": CIA Operations in Laos, 1955-74. Electronic, https://biotech.law.lsu.edu/cases/natsec/Vietnam/air-america.htm. Accessed March 23, 2022; 2019. https://biotech.law.lsu.edu/cases/nat-sec/Vietnam/air-america.htm#rft15.

Lee, Patrick. 2014. Kickers: a novel of the Secret War. CreateSpace Independent Publishing Platform.

Leeker, Dr. Joe F. 2016. "Air America: Beech / Volpar Turbo Beech 18." FlipHTML5. May 15. Accessed April 17, 2022. https://fliphtml5.com/gkmg/kgxa/basic/.

Leeker, Joe F. 2021. "Air America at the Bay of Pigs." CAT/Air America Archives, History of Aviation Collection, Special Colletions and Archives Division, Eugene McDemott Library, The University of Texas at Dallas. March 15. Accessed March 26, 2022. https://utdallas.app.box.com/v/history-BayOfPigs.

—. 2015. "Air America: Helio H-395 Super Couriers." The Aircraft of Air

America, History of Aviation Collection, Special Collections and Archives Division, Eugene McDermott Library, The University of Texas at Dallas. August 24. Accessed March 26, 2022. https://utdallas.primo.exlibrisgroup.com/discovery/collectionDiscovery?vid=01UT_DALLAS:UTDALMA&inst=01UT_DALLAS&collectionId=81274130000001421.

—. 2020-. "The History of Air America." Joe F. Leeker Collection, History of Aviation Collection, Special Collections and Archives Division, Eugen McDemott Library, The University of Texas at Dallas. Accessed April 5, 2022. https://utdallas.primo.exlibrisgroup.com/discovery/collectionDiscovery?vid=01UT_DALLAS:UTDALMA&inst=01UT_DALLAS&collectionId=81274130000001421.

n.d. "Leon V. LaShomb Collection, Memorial Data, Folder 14, Box 1." History of Aviation Archives, Special Collections and Archives Division, Eugene McDermott Library, The University of Texas at Dallas.

Library, Eugene McDermott. n.d. The CAT/Air America Memorial Plaque Name List . UTDallas. Accessed 2019. https://www.utdallas.edu/library/specialcollections/hac/cataam/plaque/names.html.

Lum, Tom. 2014. "The Aircraft of Air America." Air American Association Virtual Museum. Accessed April 16, 2022. https://air-america.org/virtualmuseum-aircraft.html.

Malvoso, Sylvia Lynne. 2022. "Helio B-833 On the Tarmac." Digital Painting.

Malvoso, Sylvia Lynne. 2022. "Helio B-835 In Flight." Digital Painting.

Marines, The Official Website of U.S. Marine Corps. 2022. Heritage: 9. Beginning of the Cold War: Nationalist Chinese Liaison Officers. Accessed March 11, 2022. https://www.marsoc.marines.mil/About/Heritage/.

Markstein, Donald D. 2002-07. Toonopedia, Tailspin Tommy. Accessed March 10, 2022. http://www.toonopedia.com/tailspin.htm.

McIntyre Collection (via Tim Martin). 2022. "Aircraft Photo of G-AHGW, Taylorcraft Plus D-1 Auster Mk1." AirHistory.net. March 13. Accessed April 13, 2022. https://www.airhistory.net/photo/445864.

Meeker, Oden. 1959. The Little World of Laos. New York: Charles Scribner's Sons.

Merrigan, William J. 2009. "201109 letter from merrigan to senator webb.docx." Air America. Accessed March 24, 2022; 2019. https://www.air-america.org/files/documents/201109_letter_from_merrigan_to_senator_webb.pdf.

Metzler, Gerry. 2012 - https://www.flickr.com/photos/flyguy71/7427977930/sizes/l/in/photostream/, CC BY-SA 2.0, https://commons.wikimedia.org/w/index.php?curid=20571543 (Accessed 1 May 2024)

Microsoft Bing; Navinfo; OpenStreetMap. 2022. "46, Zhongshan North Road Section 2, Zhongshan District, Taipei City, 104, Taiwan." bing.com/maps. Accessed March 16, 2022. https://www.bing.com/maps?q=No.+46%2C+Section+2%2C+Zhongshan+N+Rd%2C+Zhongshan+District%2C++Taiwan&form=ANNTH1&refig=c529391ea83141ebafb6fc3e9c9ba0a9.

Military, Fandom. 2021. Military History, Operation Beleaguer. November 10. Accessed March 11, 2022. https://military-history.fandom.com/wiki/Operation_Beleaguer#Gallery.

Military-Today.com. 2006-2022. "PT-76 Amphibious Light Tank." Military-Today.com. Accessed March 24, 2022. https://www.military-today.com/tanks/pt76.htm.

Museum, Combat Air. 2008-2022. "Beech SNB-5 Twin Beech Model 18." Combat Air Museum. Accessed March 12, 2022; 2019. http://www.combatairmuseum.org/aircraft/beechsnb.html.

Museum, Golden Wings. n.d. Fairchild PT-23. Accessed March 11, 2022; 2019. http://www.goldenwingsmuseum.com/collection/AC-Pages/PT-23.htm.

Museum, Smithsonian National Air and Space. n.d. Collection objects: Martin PBM-5A Mariner. Accessed March 11, 2022. https://airandspace.si.edu/collection-objects/martin-pbm-5a-mariner/nasm_A19730270000.

National Museum, United States Air Force. n.d. WASP: Breaking Ground for Today's Female USAF Pilots. Accessed March 12, 2022. https://www.nationalmuseum.af.mil/Visit/Museum-Exhibits/Fact-Sheets/Display/Article/196133/wasp-breaking-ground-for-todays-female-usaf-pilots/.

Navy, National Museum of the U.S. n.d. Landing Craft, Vehicle, Personnel (LCVP). Accessed March 11, 2022. https://www.history.navy.mil/

content/history/museums/nmusn/explore/photography/ships-us/ships-usn-l/landing-craft-vehicle-personnel.html.

Parrish, Ashley [Tulsa World Staff Writer]. 2001. "Robert Rousselot." Air America. June 25. Accessed March 16, 2022; 2019. https://air-america.org/cia-citations/robert-rousselot.html.

2000. Pilotfriend: aircraft database: aircraft manufacturers: Taylorcraft. Accessed March 10, 2022. http://www.pilotfriend.com/aircraft%20performance/Taylorcraft.htm.

Priolo, Gary P. 2021. NavSource Online: Service Ship Photo Archive: USS General W. A. Mann (AP-112). September 17. Accessed March 10, 2022. https://www.navsource.org/archives/09/22/22112.htm.

Ragnhild, and CC BY-SA 2.0 Neil Crawford - flickr. 2016. "Douglas A-26 Invader." Wikipedia, The Free Encyclopedia. September 3. Accessed April 16, 2022; 2019. https://commons.wikimedia.org/w/index.php?curid=83980977.

Ravens. 2014. "Simple Machines Forum." FlyHelio. June 2. Accessed March 24, 2022; 2019. https://flyhelio.com/smf/index.php?topic=279.15.

Rossel, PR/WM Eugene D. n.d. "12qlk6-webaderholt.jpg (230x172)." Air Commando Association. Accessed March 17, 2022; 2019. http://www.specialoperations.net/images/l2qlk6-webaderholt.jpg.

2022. "Seaboard World Airlines History." Seaboard & Western / Seaboard World Airlines. Accessed March 16, 2022. http://www.seaboardairlines.org/seabhist.htm.

Shaw, Jr., Henry I. 1991. "Opening Moves: Marines Gear Up For War." Marines in World War II Commemorative Series. Accessed February 2022. https://www.nps.gov/parkhistory/online_books/npswapa/extContent/usmc/pcn-190-003115-00/sec3a.htm.

—. Reprinted 1968. The United States Marines in North China 1945-1949. Accessed March 11, 2022; 2019. https://monongahela-books.com/northchina.html.

Shupek, John, and Lt. Col. Marc Matthews MD USAF Ret. 1998-2020. Skytamer Images Archive: Cessna T-50 Crane: Twin-engine five-seat low-wing light transport/training aircraft, U.S.A. Accessed March 11, 2022. https://www.skytamer.com/Cessna_T-50.html.

Singh, Sumit. 2022. "Experimental Aircraft: What Was The Douglas DC-

4E." Simple Flying. March 13. Accessed March 21, 2022. https://simpleflying.com/douglas-dc-4e-experimental-aircraft/.

—. 2022. "How Douglas Developed The DC-6 To Compete With The Lockheed Constellation." Simple Flying. Accessed March 21, 2022. https://simpleflying.com/douglas-dc-6-development/.

Smith, Felix. 2012. "The History of a Unique "Cold War" Airline." Civil Air Transport (CAT). Accessed March 22, 2022. https://www.catassociation.org/history/.

Smithsonian National Air and Space Museum. n.d. "North American SNJ-4 (AT-6)." National Air and Space Museum. Accessed May 7, 2022. https://airandspace.si.edu/collection-objects/north-american-snj-4-6/nasm_A19610123000.

Stevenson, Charles A. 1972. The End of Nowhere: American Policy Toward Laos Since 1954. Boston: Beacon Press.

Stewart, Paul. 2021. "The last flying Lockheed Super Constellation: engine start, flaming takeoff and landing. ." Bing video. March 14. Accessed March 21, 2022. https://www.bing.com/videos/search?q=lockheed+constellation&view=detail&mid=A021AEDA5A119FE67FBBA021AEDA5A119FE67FBB&FORM=VIRE.

n.d. Stripes. Accessed 2019. https://www.stripes.com/branches/marine_corps/frank-e-petersen-jr-1st-black-marine-to-pilot-a-plane-and-pin-on-a-star-1.364855.

Stuart, Aydan. 2017. "The forgotten legacy of world war Two in Northern Thailand: A look back at World War II in Chiang Mai and Northern Thailand." Citylife, Chiang Mai. January 8. Accessed March 24, 2022. https://www.chiangmaicitylife.com/clg/our-city/history/the-forgotten-legacy-of-world-war-two-in-northern-thailand/.

Swanson, Claude A. (Secretary of the Navy). 1933. Historical Documents, Orders and Speeches: General Order No. 241. December 7. Accessed March 11, 2022. https://web.archive.org/web/20101007205106/http://www.tecom.usmc.mil/HD/Docs_Speeches/Thefleetmarineforce.htm.

Szczepanski, Kallie. 2019. The History of Foot Binding in China. November 21. Accessed March 10, 2022. https://www.thoughtco.com/the-history-of-foot-binding-in-china-195228.

Task Force Omega Inc. n.d. "Weissenback, Edward J." Task Force Omega Inc. Accessed March 24, 2022. http://www.taskforceomegainc.org/w603.html.

Team Mighty. 2021. "The 'Idiot's Loop' was a mid-air backflip done by nuclear bombers." We Are The Mighty. March 30. Accessed March 18, 2022. https://www.wearethemighty.com/popular/the-idiots-loop-nuclear-bombers/.

Tokyo Convention & Visitors Bureau. 2019. "Oshima Island." The Official Tokyo Travel Gide, GO TOKYO. December 9. Accessed March 16, 2022. https://www.gotokyo.org/en/destinations/izu-and-ogasawara-islands/oshima-island/.

Trackrod. 2014. "DCS, F-86 Sabre, LABS." Bing Video. November 15. Accessed March 18, 2022. https://www.bing.com/videos/search?q=toss+bombing+nuclear+&&view=detail&mid=F16E6FB9AE4CEB6CBB11F16E6FB9AE4CEB6CBB11&&FORM=VRDGAR&ru=%2Fvideos%2Fsearch%3Fq%3Dtoss%2Bbombing%2Bnuclear%2B%26FORM%3DHDRSC3.

Trest, Warren A. 2000. Air Commando One: Heinie Aderholt and America's Secret Air Wars. Washington and London: Smithsonian Institution Press.

—. 2000. Air Commando One: Heinie Aderholt and America's Secret Air Wars. Washington and London: Smithsonian Institution Press.

Trust, University of West Florida Historic. 2021. Historic Pensacola: POP Murals. Accessed March 11, 2022. https://historicpensacola.org/popmurals/mural-san-carlos-hotel/.

U.S. Air Force photo by J.M. Eddins Jr. - commons.wikimedia, Public Domain. 2016. "F-86 Sabre heritage flight - North American F-86 Sabre." Wikipedia, The Free Encyclopedia. March 5. Accessed April 16, 2022. https://commons.wikimedia.org/w/index.php?curid=108353417.

U.S. Army - commons file, CC BY-SA 4.0. 2017. "Sikorsky H-19 Chickasaw." Wikipedia, The Free Encyclopedia . July 31. Accessed March 17, 2022; 2019. https://commons.wikimedia.org/w/index.php?curid=61413152.

U.S. Army, USAG Humphreys; Boyer, J. R. 2019. "USAG - Humphreys: K-6." U.S. Army Garrison Humphreys, The Army's Home in Korea,

History. April 12. Accessed April 14, 2022. https://home.army.mil/humphreys/index.php/about/history.

U.S. Coast Guard photo. n.d. "File: PBM Mariner water takeoff.jpg." Wikimedia Commons. Accessed April 19, 2022. https://commons.wikimedia.org/wiki/File:PBM_Mariner_water_takeoff.jpg.

U.S. Department of Transportation. n.d. "A Brief History of the FAA." Federal Aviation Administration. Accessed April 18, 2022. https://www.faa.gov/about/history/brief_history.

U.S. Marine Corps. 2022. "1st Marine Aircraft Wing>Subordinate Units>Marine Aircraft Group 12>About." The Official Website of the U.S. Marine Corps. Accessed March 12, 2022. https://www.1stmaw.marines.mil/Subordinate-Units/Marine-Aircraft-Group-12/About/.

U.S. Navy - U.S. Navy National Naval Aviation Museum photo NNAM.1996.488.021.003. 1945. "Grumman TBF Avenger." Wikipedia, The Free Encyclopedia. January 1. Accessed April 15, 2022. https://en.wikipedia.org/wiki/Grumman_TBF_Avenger#/media/File:Grumman_TBM_Avenger_aboard_USS_Randolph_(CV-15),_in_1945_(NNAM.1996.488.021.003).jpg.

U.S. Navy. n.d. "Appendix 1.2 Aircraft Data--Technical Information and Drawings." Dictionary of American Naval Aviation Squadrons--Volume 1. Accessed March 21, 2022; 2019. https://www.history.navy.mil/content/dam/nhhc/research/histories/naval-aviation/dictionary-of-american-naval-aviation-squadrons-volume-1/pdfs/app1-2.pdf.

U.S. Navy National Museum of Naval Aviation; Wikipedia. 2022. "Douglas A-1 Skyraider, photo No. 2002.001.138." Wikipedia. March 30. Accessed April 14, 2022. https://en.wikipedia.org/wiki/Douglas_A-1_Skyraider#/media/File:AD_Skyraider_VA-195_USS_Princeton.jpg.

Unforgettable Laos. 2012. "The US Getting Involved in The Secret War in Laos." Unforgettable Laos. March. Accessed March 24, 2022. http://www.unforgettable-laos.com/fightings-of-the-1960s/us-involving-in-the-secret-war-in-laos/.

United States Senate; Church Committee. 1976. Final Report of the Select Committee to Sutdy Governmental Operations with Respect to Intelligence Activities, 1975-76. no. Final Report, S. Rep. No. 94-755. Compiled by 2nd Session 94th Congress. Washington, Washington, D.C.: U.S. Government Printing Office, April 26. 239. Accessed March 24, 2022; 2019. https://www.intelligence.senate.gov/sites/default/files/94755_I.pdf.

Unknown. n.d. "AAM61.pdf." Unknown Collection Name, History of Aviation Collection, Special Collections and Archives Division, Eugene McDemott Library, The University of Texas at Dallas. Accessed 2019. https://utdallas.edu/library/specialcollections/hac/cataam/notebooks/aam61.pdf (URL no longer extant).

Unknown author - File:"Give us More P-38's" - NARA - 514398.jpg, Public Domain, . 1941-45. "Give us More P-38s - NARA - 514398 adjusted - Lockheed P-38 Lightning." Wikipedia, The Free Encyclopedia. Accessed April 15, 2022. https://commons.wikimedia.org/w/index.php?curid=99288215.

Unknown. n.d. "The Eisenhower Administration and Laos: Chapter II." https://shodhganga.inflibnet.ac.in/bitstream/10603/20519/5/05_chapter%202.pdf . 43-89.

US Air Force - U.S Air Force photo nationalmuseum.af.mil, CC BY-SA 4.0 . 2010. "North American F-100 Super Sabre." Wikipedia, The Free Encyclopedia . March 20. Accessed April 16, 2022. https://commons.wikimedia.org/w/index.php?curid=62020116.

US Congress 86, session 1, House Subcommittee on Foreign Operations and Monetary Affairs of the Committee on Government Operations, Hearings. 1959. "United States Aid Operations in Laos." Washington, DC. 184-85. https://shodhganga.inflibnet.ac.in/bitstream/10603/20519/5/05_chapter%202.pdf.

USAF - National Museum of the U.S. Air Force photo 110224-F-XN622-005, Public Domain. 1950-54. "Civil Air Transport." Wikipedia, The Free Encyclopedia. Accessed April 15, 2022; 2019. https://commons.wikimedia.org/w/index.php?curid=13949508.

USN - U.S. Navy Naval Aviation News July 1954; Wipipedia. 1952-1954. "Douglas XF3D-1 Skyknight in flight wit four...Douglas F3D Skyknight." Wikipedia, The Free Encyclopedia. Accessed April 15, 2022. https://en.wikipedia.org/wiki/Douglas_F3D_Skyknight#/media/File:Douglas_XF3D-1_Skyknight_in_flight_with_four_AAM-N-2_

Sparrow_missiles,_circa_in_the_early_1950s.jpg.
USN - U.S. Navy Naval Aviation News March 1953, Public Domain, . n.d. "Vought F4U Corsair." Wikipedia, The Free Encyclopedia. Accessed March 30, 2022. https://commons.wikimedia.org/w/index.php?curid=3698071.
USN - U.S. Navy Naval Aviation News September 1952, cover. 1952. "USN R4D-8 from VR-23 Codfish Airline over Mount Fuji, 1952." R4D-8 VR-23 over Mt Fuji 1952-Douglas C-47 Skytrain - Wikipedia. January 1. Accessed April 12, 2022. https://en.wikipedia.org/wiki/Douglas_C-47_Skytrain#/media/File:R4D-8_VR-23_over_Mt_Fuji_1952.jpg.
USN - U.S. Navy Strike Fighter Squadron 41 (VFA-41) website, Public Domain . 1950s. "McDonnell F2H-2 Banshee." Wikipedia, The Free Encyclopedia. Accessed April 16, 2022. https://commons.wikimedia.org/w/index.php?curid=12434256.
Vulcano, Edited by Mario. 2016. The Evolution of Corry Station (1922-2016). March 18. Accessed March 12, 2022. https://stationhypo.com/2016/03/18/the-evolution-of-corry-station-1922-2016/.
Warner, Roger. 2007. "In Remembrance of Ron Sutphin." Air America. October 25. Accessed March 24, 2022; 2019. https://air-america.org/in-rememberance-1/ron-sutphin.html.
—. 1996. Shooting at the Moon: The Story of America's Clandestine War in Laos. South Royalton, Vermont: Steerforth Press.
—. 1996. Shooting at the Moon: The Story of America's Clandestine War in Laos. South Royalton, Vermont: Steerforth Press.
WebMD. 2005-2022. "Dengue Fever: Symptoms, Causes, and Treatments." WebMD. Accessed March 24, 2022; 2019. https://www.webmd.com/a-to-z-guides/dengue-fever-reference#1.
Weems, Philip Van Horn. 1943. Air Navagation, Weems. New York and London: McGraw-Hill Book Company, Inc.
Whitney, Senior Airman Ryan. 2010. "Air Commando One honored, remembered." U.S. Air Force, The official web site. July 3. Accessed March 16, 2022. https://archive.ph/20120723234733/http://www.af.mil/news/story.asp.
Wikipedia, contributors. 2022. "Battle of Ban Pa Dong." Wikipedia, The Free Encyclopedia. January 1. Accessed March 24, 2022. https://

en.wikipedia.org/wiki/Battle_of_Ban_Pa_Dong.
—. 2023. "Battle of Vientiane." Wikipedia, The Free Encyclopedia. Accessed May 19, 2023. https://en.m.wikipedia.org/wiki/Battle_of_Vientiane.
—. 2022. "Beechcraft Model 18." Wikipedia, The Free Encyclopedia. April 13. Accessed April 17, 2022. https://en.wikipedia.org/w/index.php?title=Beechcraft_Model_18&action=history.
—. 2022. "Boeing B-52 Stratofortress." Wikipedia, The Free Encyclopedia. March 16. Accessed March 24, 2022. https://en.wikipedia.org/wiki/Boeing_B-52_Stratofortress.
—. 2022. "Boeing-Stearman Model 75." Wikipedia, The Free Encyclopedia. April 6. Accessed April 14, 2022. 2022.
—. 2021. "Civil Air Transport." Wikipedia, the free encyclopedia. November 13. Accessed March 16, 2022; 2019. https://en.wikipedia.org/wiki/Civil_Air_Transport.
—. 2021. "Civil Air Transport." Wikipedia, The Free Encyclopedia. November 13. Accessed March 22, 2022; 2019. https://en.wikipedia.org/wiki/Civil_Air_Transport.
—. 2022. "Clouded leopard." Wikipedia, The Free Encyclopedia. April 3. Accessed May 5, 2022. https://en.wikipedia.org/wiki/Clouded_leopard.
—. 2022. "Douglas R4D-8." Wikipedia, The Free Encyclopedia. January 10. Accessed April 14, 2022. https://en.wikipedia.org/w/index.php?title=Douglas_R4D-8&action=history.
—. 2022. "James William Lair." Wikipedia, The Free Encyclopedia. February 11. Accessed March 20, 2022; 2019. https://en.wikipedia.org/wiki/James_William_Lair.
—. 2022. "Lockheed Constellation." Wikipedia, The Free Encyclopedia. March 19. Accessed March 21, 2022; 2019. https://en.wikipedia.org/wiki/Lockheed_Constellation.
—. 2022. "Manado." Wikipedia, the free encyclopedia. February 10. Accessed March 16, 2022; 2019. https://en.wikipedia.org/wiki/Manado.
—. 2021. "Phou Pha Thi." Wikipedia, The Free Encyclopedia. February 28. Accessed March 24, 2022. https://en.wikipedia.org/wiki/Phou_Pha_Thi.

—. 2022. "Phoumi Nosavan." Wikipedia, The Free Encyclopedia. February 2. Accessed March 20, 2022; 2019. https://en.wikipedia.org/wiki/Phoumi_Nosavan.

—. 2022. "Plain of Jars." Wikipedia, The Free Encyclopedia. February 18. Accessed March 20, 2022; 2019. https://en.wikipedia.org/wiki/Plain_of_Jars.

—. 2021. "Pop Buell." Wikipedia, The Free Encyclopedia. October 20. Accessed March 24, 2022. https://en.wikipedia.org/wiki/Pop_Buell.

—. 2022. "William M. Leary." Wikipedia, The Free Encyclopedia. March 17. Accessed March 19, 2022; 2019. https://en.wikipedia.org/wiki/William_M._Leary#cite_note-ssdi-1.

Index

Symbols
1st Marine Division, 21
2nd Battalion Headquarters, 11
3rd Marines, 11, 18, 21, 218–19
38th Parallel, 62, 187
6x6 trucks, 18, 69
80th Tactical Fighter Squadron, 120, 235

A
AB, 121
Abadie, Clarence J., 133
ACRAC, 34
Aderholt, Brig. Gen. Harry C. "Heine", iii, xviii–xix, 114–15, 125, 134, 186, 191, 203–4, 206–7, 232–33, 242. See also Heinie
Admiral, 19, 45, 49, 134, 136
    Badger, 19
    Burke, Arleigh, 136
    Felt, Harry D., 134
Advanced CQ, 49
Africa, 83, 88, 136
agents, 113–14, 129, 158, 162, 170, 174, 192–93
aileron, 116
air bases
    Ashiya Airbase, 156
    Atsugi, 106
    Chitose, 110
    Elmendorf AFB, 117
    Itami Marine Corps Air Station, 60
    Itazuke Airbase, 108
    K-6, 54–56, 59, 61–62, 66–68, 70–71, 224–25
    K-46, 69
    Kadena, 106, 114–15, 122, 157, 236
    Kelly, 81
    Misawa, 110
    Naha AFB, 114
    Pyeongtaek Airbase, 55
    Tachikawa, Japan, 105
    Tainan, Taiwan, 234
    Takhli Airbase, 191
    Udorn Airbase, 149
    Wattay Airbase, 188–89
    Yokota, 108
Air Commando One, xviii
Air Force, 23, 52, 68–69, 80–81, 91–92, 98–100, 105, 107–8, 111, 114, 117–18, 120–21, 124, 129, 134, 142, 156–57, 160–61, 203–4, 206, 208, 211, 213, 216–17, 221–23, 225, 229–30, 234–36, 238, 240
    decals, 160
    Flying Club, 108
    Squadron, 34, 43–44, 51–52, 55–56, 59, 63, 71, 79, 81, 83, 120–22, 156, 216, 221, 224, 226–27, 231, 234–35
Air Group 12, 54–55, 60, 62
air stations, 30, 43
    El Toro, 51–52, 55
    Itami Marine Corps Air Station, 60
    Taipei City, 230
AirAsia, 105, 122, 126–27, 242

aircraft, v, xi–xiv, xvi, xviii–xix, 1, 17, 20, 23, 26, 30, 33, 36, 39–45, 49, 51–52, 56–57, 59, 61–62, 66, 70–71, 79–82, 88, 101, 105, 109, 111, 114–17, 122–24, 126–27, 133–35, 138, 143, 147, 149–50, 152, 156, 160–61, 163, 166–69, 171–73, 175–76, 178, 187–88, 190, 192–204, 206–7, 209, 211, 213–17, 221–28, 230–31, 233–36, 238, 240–43
   A-26 attack bomber, 112, 167, 172, 190
   A-26 Invader, 112, 231
   Aeronca, 39, 222
   Air America C-46, 188, 194
   amphibious scout plane, 20–21
   B-24 Liberator, 117
   B-26, 117, 191, 196–98, 234
   B-52, 147, 240
   Baker 817, 131
   Bamboo Bomber, 32, 221
   Beaver, 81, 117, 135, 166, 169, 173
   Boeing, xvi, 31, 125, 147, 210, 213, 221, 235, 240
      727, 125, 235
      747, xvi, 196, 202–3, 205, 210, 213
   Bravo 148 (C-46 #B-148), 101
   C123K (tail #6293), 149
   C-123 Provider, 149, 197, 240
   Canadian Beaver, 81
   Cessna, 32, 62, 221, 225
      L-19 Bird Dog, 62
      T-50 twin-engine trainer, 32
   COD turkey, 63
   Consolidated PB4Y-2 Privateer, 222
   Constellation, 86–87, 91, 93, 212, 227–28
   Corsair, 52–53, 63, 82–83, 91, 224, 228
      AU-1, 63
      FG-1D, 91, 228
   Cougar F9F-6, 82
   Curtiss C-46 Commando, 9, 80, 108, 190, 215
      C-46, xviii, 8–9, 20, 80, 85, 96, 99, 101, 104, 108–12, 117, 135, 167, 188, 190, 192–99, 212, 215, 229–30
   Dornier, 195, 197
   Douglas, xix, 51–52, 55–57, 62–63, 65, 69, 74, 83–84, 87, 112, 125, 167, 171, 224–25, 227, 231, 234
      A-1 Skyraider, xix, 224
      A-26, 112, 119, 122, 125, 167, 172, 190–91, 231, 234
      AD, 51–52, 56, 65, 67, 224
      DC-3, 28, 55, 62, 73–75, 109, 111, 125, 171–72, 225
      DC-4, 84, 87, 106, 110–11, 167–68, 192, 197–98, 212, 227
      DC-6, 83, 198, 227
      R4D, 55, 62, 69, 71, 78, 222, 225
      R5D, 10, 71, 83, 110–11, 227
   F3D Skyknight, 63, 225
   F9F-7, 82, 227
   F-100F, 121

Index

Fairchild PT-23, 22, 25
    F4F Wildcat, 214
    F6F Hellcat, 45–46, 79, 223
    F9F/F-9 Cougar, 226
    Grumman, 2, 38, 45, 48, 64, 82, 210, 214, 223, 226–27
Howard DGA, 81, 94, 226
J-3 Cubs, 22
J-5 type Cub, 1
jet fighters, xiv, 62, 83, 105
L-20 Beaver, 117, 166
Lockheed, 62, 76, 86, 91, 111, 148, 197, 227–29, 231, 240
    C-130, 148, 156, 160, 197, 240
    Electra, 76
    P-38, 95–96, 229
    T-33, 62, 111, 231
    T-33/TV-2 jet trainer, 62
McDonnell, 231
    F2H Banshee, 231
N3613K (J-3 Cub), 23
Navy Corsairs, 91
NC42992 (Piper Cub), 26
North American, 36, 118, 122, 221, 234
    F-86, xvi, 117, 203, 213, 234
    F-100, xvi, 117–19, 122, 126, 156, 190, 203, 210, 213, 234
    SNJ, 33, 36, 40, 48, 79, 83, 221–22
P-47, 120
P-61, 10, 215–16
Patrol Bomber Martin, 16
PBM, 16, 43, 217
PBY Catalina, 118

Pilatus, xii, 151, 241
    PC-6, 241
Piper Cub, 24, 26, 35, 203, 211
PT-17, 32, 37, 73, 221
SNB, 50–51, 79, 83, 95, 111, 221–23
SNB-5, 50–51, 223
Stearman, 31–32, 37, 44, 73, 203, 210, 221
T-28, 79, 210, 222
Taylorcraft, xviii, 1, 214
TBM: Torpedo Bomber, 63
Volpar, 148, 150, 240
aircraft carrier, 30, 36, 41–42, 223–24, 226
Aircraft Fleet Marine Force Pacific, 49
Airdrome, 69
Airfields, 151, 215, 221, 223–24
    Clark Field, 112–13, 124
    Cuddihy Field, 44
    K-6 airfield, 54, 224
    Meacham Field, Texas, 72
    Ou Neua Airfield, 162
    Showa Airfield, 108
    Tsangkou Airfield, 217
airline transport license, 72
Airlines, v, xv–xvi, 55, 83, 85, 92–95, 98, 102, 157, 196, 202, 204–5, 212–13, 227–30
    Capitol Airways, 80
    Eastern, 93–94, 203, 205, 208, 213
    JAL, 196, 205, 208, 210, 213
    Northwest, 95, 98, 158, 165, 170, 216

Airport, 22–23, 25–27, 31, 37, 39, 44, 46, 61, 81, 88, 90–91, 94, 98, 101, 127, 160, 172, 188, 194, 208, 217, 233
   Beirut, 90
   Haneda Airport, 98, 101
   Island Airport, 26
   JFK Airport, 91
   Kaohsiung Airport, 127
   La Guardia, 94
   Oceanside Airport, 22–23
   Pensacola Municipal Airport, 31, 39
   Xieng Khouang airport, 194
Alabama, 42
Alaska, v, xii, xiv, 98, 117, 205, 209, 213, 230
Alaskan, 202, 205, 213
Aleutian Islands, 98
All Weather Flight, 49, 51
American, iii, 1, 24, 28, 35–36, 72–73, 75–76, 83, 89, 105, 108, 112, 118, 122, 130–31, 136–37, 140, 142–44, 152, 170, 199, 204, 212, 214–15, 217–23, 226–29, 234, 236, 238
   ambassador, 144, 243
   Australian maintenance employees, 105
   embassy, 131, 236
   Flyers, 28, 72–73, 75–76, 120, 220, 226
Anchorage, 117, 230
Annapolis, 47
anti-Communist forces, 129, 229
antiaircraft, 58, 150, 159

antiaircraft emplacement, 58
antiaircraft fire, 150, 159
Appropriations Subcommittees, 143
Ardent Goose Hunter, 65
Arizona, 91, 220
Arkansas, 26
Army, 12–13, 18, 23, 54–55, 68–69, 87, 125, 131, 138, 141–42, 164, 168, 170–71, 173–75, 177, 179, 187–88, 194, 216–20, 222–23, 228–29, 236–37, 239–40, 243, 245. See also Chinese; French; Hmong; Kong Le; Laotian
Army Air Force Cadets, 23
artillery, 149, 188, 194
Asanman Bay, 64
Asia, xiii, xv–xvi, 97–98, 116, 125, 129–30, 132, 136, 140–41, 143, 152–53, 157, 190, 203–4, 208, 212, 218, 232, 234, 240, 244
Atkinson, Mr., 23
attack pilot, 55, 71
Auto LABS, 120, 122–24, 156. See also LABS
Automatic Low Altitude Bombing Systems, 120
autopilot, 122, 124, 193, 227
Aviation Training School, 24

B
Badger, 19
Baekje Kingdom burial mounds, 226
Bahrain, 90
Ban Takhli, 157

Bangkok, 85, 109, 138, 143, 157, 160–61, 166, 171–72, 181, 187–88, 193, 197, 204
Bangkok Post, 143
Base Operations, 62–63, 68
battlefields, 27
Bay of Pigs, 117, 233
Beale, William H. "Bill", 117–18, 120–22, 124–26, 135, 161, 190–91, 233
Bednekoff, Army Sergeant, 68
Bevan, David W., 140
Bickham, Corporal, 25
Bill, 18, 73, 90, 108, 117–18, 120, 125, 131, 135–36, 139, 190, 197, 203–4, 212, 233, 236–38
Bird & Son, 134, 207
Blevins, Bruce, 131, 133
Bombay, 88
Bond, Al, 108
Bong, Richard Ira "Dick" (WWII fighter pilot), 95
BOQ, 52, 78, 86, 98, 106–7
border, 44, 137, 152, 162, 164, 168, 238
Border Police, 137
Brindisi, 90
British Isles, 85
British Navy, 20
Brooklyn, 81–82
Broom, Staff Sergeant, 4
Brown, John, 98
Brown, Staff Sgt., 22
Brownsville, 44
Brusch, George, 23
Buell, Edgar "Pop", 146, 239, 247, 262
Burma, 159–61, 215–16, 238
Burmese Air Force, 160
buzz jobs, 91

C
C-Company, 13, 21
CAA (Civil Aeronautics Authority), 27, 73, 220
Cabaret, 89, 99
California, 7, 21, 25, 49, 51, 110, 203, 211, 227–28
   Bellflower, 25
   Del Mar, 25
   Laguna Beach, 52
   Long Beach, 21, 26
   Oakland, 7, 110–11
   Oceanside, 21–23, 25–26
   San Diego, 7
   San Francisco, 7
   San Marcos Valley, 25
   Santa Ana, 49, 51
   Southern California, 25
Camp, 3, 8, 21, 24, 27–29, 54, 203, 211, 215
   Catlin, 8, 215
   Joseph H. Pendleton Marine Base, 21
   Lejeune, North Carolina, 27
   Pendleton, 21–22, 24, 26, 203, 211
CAP, 46
Captain, xi, 18, 20, 46, 52, 56, 58, 60, 73, 80, 84–86, 92, 94, 104, 108, 111, 120–21, 149, 157–58, 171, 174–75, 177, 188, 191,

194–96, 199, 201, 206, 209, 236, 245
Anastasakis, 175
Andersevic, "Andy", 191
Barney Barnes, 95
Bernier, 85
Bigoney, 188
Dew, Stu, 108
Forte, Woody, 108–9, 140
Gaddie, William "Bill", 18, 108, 112
Gray, 60
Hazen, Joe, 195
Hicks, Hugh, 125
Hosford, 80–81
Johnson, "Doc", 192–93, 195–96
Jones, Charlie, 80
Judkins, 158
Law, 46–47, 90, 106
Martin, Capt. August "Augie", 93–94, 228–29
Mlinar, Paul, 83, 85–86, 212
Plank, John, 17, 108
Reese, 52
Richardson, Randall, 108
Riley, Frederick J. "Fred", 199–200
Ritter, 149–50
Rousselot, Robert E. "Bob", 102–4, 106–7, 110, 113–14, 116–18, 125, 127, 132, 134, 187, 195, 203, 206–7, 230
Sims, Eddie (CAT's Chief Pilot), 102, 133, 161
Sledge, Chuck, 60
Smith, Doug "Snuffy" (CAT Chief Pilot), 99, 101, 103, 109, 111, 156
Steed (Flight Leader), 56, 58
Stiles (served as the engineer), 158
Teeters, Don, 118
Wray, Woody, 85
Captain in the Marines, 92
Captain, USMCR, 120
car, 42, 44, 48, 50, 57, 75–76, 81, 94
  Buick, 107
  Lincoln Continental, 98, 107
  Packard, 51
CARE, 124, 184, 236
cargo dropper, 113
Caribbean, 31
carrier qualifications (CQ), 48
Carrier Training and Qualifications, 47
Casterlin, Harry, 141
CAT, xi, xv–xvi, xviii–xix, 17–18, 68, 77, 94–112, 117–18, 124, 126, 128–29, 131, 156, 188, 202–3, 208, 211–12, 218, 229–30, 235–36, 238, 240–42, 244–45
  Air America, xi, xvi, xix, 106, 118, 126–29, 131–35, 137–45, 147, 149–53, 155–56, 166, 168, 171, 179, 188–89, 194, 202–8, 212–13, 218, 231, 233–34, 236, 238–45
  airplanes, xvi, xviii–xix, 1–2, 17, 105, 129, 193, 220
  began in China, 129
  CAT, Inc., xi, 77, 97–101, 103,

105–7, 109, 129, 188, 229
Civil Air Transport, xv, 17, 34, 68, 77, 79–81, 83, 85–87, 89, 91, 93–97, 105, 128–29, 204, 211, 217–18, 226, 229–30, 235–36, 242
   compound, 12, 17–19, 57–58, 104–5, 124, 147, 152–53, 179, 181, 194, 214
   contract maintenance facilities, 103
   senior captains, 108
   Tainan City, 105
CAT (Civil Air Transport), 68, 129
cease fire agreement, 152
CEECO (Consolidated Electric Equipment Company), 118, 122, 234
Celebes, 112–13
celestial navigation, 44, 83
Charlie Company, 11–12, 18
Chennault, Claire L., 129
Chiang Kai-Shek, 18, 216, 218
Chief of Naval Operations, 136
Chief Pilot, 74, 76, 83, 94, 99, 101–3, 112, 132–33, 161, 200, 212, 241
China, xix, 6–7, 9–10, 18–20, 22, 68, 80, 96–97, 102, 129–30, 162, 211–12, 215–20, 229, 238
China, xix, 6–7, 9–10, 18–20, 22, 68, 80, 96–97, 102, 129–30, 162, 211–12, 215–20, 229, 238
   beer, 12, 99, 216
   docks, 15–17
   Harbor, 8, 16–17, 20–21, 30, 43, 219, 223
China Marines, xix, 211
Chinese, 12–15, 17–21, 61, 98, 102–3, 105, 108, 117, 125, 164–65, 175, 190, 211–12, 216, 218–19, 236
   CAF (Chinese Air Force), 117
   employees, 105, 218, 230, 236
CIA, xvi, xix, 95, 128–29, 131–34, 136–37, 139–47, 149, 151–53, 170, 203–4, 206–7, 212, 218, 229–30, 233–34, 236–39, 241–42
   Central Intelligence Agency, xv, 129, 212, 230, 237, 245
   director, 143, 151
   Hmong operation, 204
   Southeast Asia Division, 141
City Hotel, 85, 91
Civil Aeronautics Authority, 27, 220
Civil Air Patrol, 44, 222
Civil Air Transport (CAT), xv, 17, 97, 128, 211, 229–30
civil aviation school, 28
Civil War (U.S.), 27, 32
Clark, Major, 86
Class 16, 31, 50, 52
clouded leopard, xix, 179, 244. See also leopard
Club compound, 124
coalition government, 140, 142, 152
cobra, 157, 178, 181–82
Cocker, Don, 195
code training, 157
Colby, William, 141

Cold War, 130
Comer, Warren, 30–31, 84, 93, 98, 108
Communist, xii, xv, 13, 18–19, 21, 129–30, 132, 134, 140–42, 144–45, 147, 212, 218–19, 229, 239, 243
Connelly, Fred, 150
Consolidated Electric Equipment Company (CEECO), 234
Continental United States, 117
CONUS, 116, 189
Cook, Ed, 72, 74
copilot, 18, 28, 38, 71, 75, 83–84, 86, 101, 110, 112–14, 125, 127, 135, 140, 147, 149, 175, 182, 196, 198–99
Corn Flakes, 179
Corpus Christi, 42–45, 49–52
coup, 171, 187, 237, 243
covert operations, xiv–xv, xix, 113, 118, 129, 190, 212
   airline, v, xii, xv–xvi, 28, 38, 50, 55, 72–74, 79, 83, 85–86, 92–95, 97–99, 102, 107, 129, 141, 143, 151, 157, 196, 202, 204–5, 211–13, 227–30, 233, 236, 241
   career, xvii, 38, 40–41, 114, 117, 125, 203, 233
   flights, 98, 112, 118, 121–22, 126, 142, 156–58, 167–68, 170–74, 176, 187, 192, 195, 198–99, 204
   missions, xii–xiii, xv, 35, 60, 66, 117, 129, 131, 142, 147–48, 158, 161, 173, 175, 190, 193, 195, 198, 204, 209, 212, 221, 224, 229–30, 233
   reconnaissance, 142–43, 148, 173–76, 217, 222, 240
CQ (carrier qualifications), 48–49
Cubi Point, 110

D

Daddio, Matt, 150
Dance Revue, 60
Dangjin, 70
dark-night landing, 113
deep-sea fishing, 109
dengue fever, 171
Dien Bien Phu, 129, 198, 230
Dienbienphu, 129
Dilbert Dunker, 33
Doc, 192–93
Dole, George, 94–95
Doug, 99, 101, 103, 111, 208, 210–11
draft, xi, xvii, 6–9, 218
Draper, 42
drill instructors, 4
drop zones, 131
dry season, 144, 149, 192
   (October to May), 144
   dry-season offensive, 145

E

E&E (evasion and escape), 69
Earhart, Amelia, xviii
Edgar, 146, 239
Edgewater Hotel, 19
Eisenhower, President Dwight D., 134

elephants, 180
elephants, 180
estuary, 64, 66–69
Eubanks, Darrel A., 140
Europe, 80, 85, 238
European weather, 85
evasion and escape, 69

F
fall of Saigon, 152
Far East, 85, 95, 98, 106, 110, 215
Fayetteville, 39
FCLP, 41–42, 48
feather, 88
field carrier landing practice, 41
fighter pilot, xii–xiv, 63
Filipino Helio mechanics, 187
Filipino mechanics, 168
Flater, Colonel, 67
Fleet Marine Force, 27, 49, 51–52, 71, 216, 220
Fleet Marine Force Pacific, 49, 51
Fleet Marine Forces, Pacific, 71
Fletcher, Jim, 74
Flight #293, 149
flight instructor, xii, 28, 31, 72, 74, 79, 108, 203, 209, 211, 220
Flight Leader, 40, 56, 58, 66
flight surgeons, 70
flights, 17, 24–25, 30, 36–37, 39–40, 46, 49, 52, 61, 78–80, 82, 84, 87–88, 98, 104, 106, 108, 110, 112, 118, 121–22, 126, 142, 156–58, 167–68, 170–74, 176, 187, 192, 195, 198–99, 204
Florida, 28, 43, 48–49, 72, 220

food, 20, 61, 87–88, 90, 102, 106, 130, 141, 146–47, 163, 169, 178, 180, 183, 186, 212, 229. See also Chinese; Japanese
foot binding, 13, 216
forces, xii, 19, 71, 129, 131–32, 134, 138, 140, 142, 144–46, 151, 169, 174, 185–86, 189, 193, 216–17, 219, 222, 225, 229, 237, 239–40, 245. See also Hmong; Kong Le; North Vietnamese; Pathet Lao
Formosa, 99, 103, 112, 117, 161, 167, 172, 190, 195, 218, 230
Fort Worth, 28, 72–74, 76
Forte, Norwood N., 140
Foss, Joe, 2, 214
four-engine transport, 71
France, 85, 236, 238, 243
Frankfurt, 85, 87, 91–92
Fred, 150, 170–72, 197, 199–200
French, 129–30, 162–64, 166, 168–72, 179, 192, 198, 236–37, 239, 244
  air maps, 192
  Frenchman, 169
  garrison, 129
  headquarters, 11, 19, 34, 68, 95, 102, 132, 141, 163–64, 169–70, 173, 216–17, 225, 238
  Indochina, xix, 100, 236, 239
  military base, 55, 160, 170
  representative, 122, 171–72
  wine, 60, 163, 179
Friedman, Izzy, 150
Frigi, 187

Fussa, 106–7

G
G-circuit, 124
G-force cutback, 123
G.I. Bill, 73, 204, 212
Galveston, 42, 47, 50
garrison, viii, 54, 129, 139, 257
GCA (ground control approach), 67–68, 125
General Orders, 214
Geneva Accords, 140–41, 144
Georgia, 80, 236
Germany, 12, 40, 85, 87
girlfriend, 85, 94–95, 108
Godley, G. McMurtrie, 144
Gordon, Mr., 85
Green Card, 78
Green Hotel, 107
ground effect, 101
ground troops, 144
Grundy, Hugh L., 126
Guadalcanal, 2
Guam draft, 7
guerrillas (local Lao), 164
gunners, 149, 201, 223

H
Hamburg, Germany, 12
Hamer, Mr., 85
Hamilton, Chief Pilot, 74
Hamlin, Andy, 78
Haneda, 98, 101
Hanoi, 142, 145, 193
Harley-Davidson, 33, 94
Harriman, Averill, 140
Harrisburg, 3
Harvard Club, 94
Hawaii, 6
Headhunters, 234
Headquarters, 11, 19, 34, 68, 95, 102, 132, 141, 163–64, 169–70, 173, 216–17, 225, 238
Heinie, iii, xviii–xix, 114–16, 125–26, 134, 157, 186, 203–4, 232–33. See also Aderholt, Brig. Gen. Harry C. "Heine"
Helicopter, 61, 70, 132–33, 138–39, 141, 147, 150, 223, 232, 237–38, 242–43
  H-19, 132–33, 237
  Sikorsky, 132–33, 138, 237–38
Helio, xii–xiv, xix, 114, 116–17, 125–26, 133–34, 161, 166–73, 175, 187–88, 191–95, 197–98, 204, 206–13, 233, 242–44
  B-833, 161, 242–43
  B-835, 167, 170, 187, 243–44
  biplane, 32, 44, 203, 221
  F4U, 53, 224, 228
  H-555, 191
  Helio Courier, xii, xiv, xix, 116, 133, 204, 206–7, 212–13
  multi-engine, 28, 43–44, 47, 49, 71, 203, 211
  Mustang, 9–10, 17–18, 52–53
  P-51, 9, 18, 52
Helms, Richard, 143, 151
HF (high frequency), 101
Higgins boats, 19, 218. See also LCVPs
high frequency, 59

high-speed dives, 91
hit the deck, 122
Hmong, 136–42, 144–46, 148–50, 152, 172, 179, 204, 211, 233, 239, 243
   ammunition stores, 141
   base, xiii–xiv, 7, 21, 30, 37, 43–46, 51, 55, 62–63, 68–69, 78, 81, 98, 100, 105–8, 126, 138, 146, 149, 152, 156–57, 160, 170, 189, 194–95, 215, 217, 225, 228, 230, 232, 236
   base at Long Tieng, 146, 149
   garrison, 139
   guerrillas, 142, 145–46, 243
   leader Vang Pao, 136–37
   operation, xiv–xv, xix, 17–18, 33, 59, 62–63, 66, 68, 78, 95, 98–99, 101–2, 113, 118, 125, 128–30, 133, 136–38, 141, 143–44, 146–48, 150–52, 156–57, 171, 179, 187, 189–91, 204–5, 207–8, 212, 215–16, 218–20, 223–25, 229, 231–33, 235–37, 239, 241–43
   peoples, 139
   positions, 132, 141, 146
   recruits, 3–6, 137, 145, 239, 243
   refugees, 139, 147, 231, 239
   tribesmen, 136, 139, 165, 172, 211
   villager, 179, 184
Ho Chi Minh Trail, 148, 196
Hoengseong, 69
Hoirt, 52
Hollywood Marines, 7
Hong Kong, 20, 85, 235
Honolulu, 8, 71, 135, 215
horseback, 164
Horst, 52, 60
hostel, 124, 200
hot-springs resort, 107
Hua Hin, Thailand, 197
hyena, 161, 242

I

Iberia, Louisiana, 79
Idlewild, 86, 91, 93
ILS, 92, 235
Inchon, 58
India, xix, 84, 87–89, 161, 215–16, 228, 238
Indonesia, 110–13, 115, 117, 119, 129, 204, 231, 233
initial point (IP), 40, 122
Instructors Basic Training, 79
instrument landing system (ILS), 92
instrument pilot, 73, 78
IP (initial point), 40, 123, 158, 176, 196, 198
Ireland, 83
Ishibashi 258, 60
Italy, 85, 90
Itazuke, 108, 110, 119–21, 234
Iwo Jima, 9

J

Jack, 132, 168–69, 210
Jackson Heights, 82
Jackson, Grandpa, 26
Jacques, Jerry J., v, xiv
jail, 89–90, 243
Japan, xvi, 9–10, 21, 54, 60–62, 69,

98, 100, 103, 105–8, 110, 119, 130, 132, 156–57, 196, 202, 205, 213, 216, 229, 236, 242
Japanese, 7–9, 21, 45, 55, 61, 99–100, 106–9, 117, 157, 204, 212, 216–17, 219, 236–37
   culture, 106, 236
   house, xvii, 3, 19, 60, 65–66, 72, 74, 100, 106–7, 130, 157, 171, 184, 190
   language, 61, 106–7
   people, 21
   warships, 109
   yen, 99
Jenkins, PFC, 4
Jerry cans, 162
Johannesburg, 83
Johnson, Doug, 210
Joint Chiefs of Staff, 136
jungle otters, 178

K
Kahn, Ken, v, xv–xvi
Kaohsiung, 104, 126–27
Kaohsiung Airport, 127
Karst, 140
Karuizawa, Japan, 107–8, 231
Katariina, 205, 208–9, 213
Keck (navigator), 158–59
Kennedy administration, 138, 142
Khamphonh Saysongkham, 149
Khrushchev, Soviet Premier, 139
kicker(s), 113, 149–50, 175, 193, 196, 231–32, 240
Klusmann, Charles E., 143
Knoxville, 26

Kobe beefsteak, 60
Kong Le, 131–32, 134, 136, 138, 171–75, 187, 189, 193–94, 236–37, 243, 245
   Neutralist Commander, 131
Kongse-Ri, 64
Korea, xv, 27, 34, 45, 49–52, 54–61, 63, 65, 67–69, 71–72, 84–85, 108, 110, 220, 224–26, 231
Korean, xii, xix, 27, 31, 35, 51, 54, 59–61, 63–66, 68–72, 95, 109, 129, 139, 184, 187, 204, 212, 218, 221–25, 228, 230–31, 234–36
   children, 14, 24, 63, 65, 69–70, 82, 135, 163, 165, 229
   farmers, 69
   friends, xix, 20, 44, 46, 61, 71, 73, 78, 84, 95–96, 106, 108, 157, 199, 233
   Korean War, xix, 31, 35, 51, 54, 95, 129, 139, 184, 187, 204, 212, 218, 221–25, 228, 230–31, 234–36
   language, 68–69, 71
   people, 68–69
   ring-necked pheasants, 63
   village, 2, 56–58, 64–65, 68–69, 107, 139, 157, 164–65, 168, 173, 178, 184, 187, 197, 233, 239, 242, 244–45
   winters, 48, 109
Kulihara, Mr., 107

L
LABS, 120, 122–24, 156, 235. See

Index | 275

also Auto LABS
Lair, James William "Bill", 131, 137, 139, 197, 203–4, 237–38
landing ship transport, 104
landing signal officer, 41
Laos, xii, xvi, 17, 109, 128–55, 161, 166–73, 175, 186, 189–93, 195, 197–99, 201, 204, 206–7, 211, 230–33, 236–39, 241–43, 245
Laos, xii, xvi, 17, 109, 128–55, 161, 166–73, 175, 186, 189–93, 195, 197–99, 201, 204, 206–7, 211, 230–33, 236–39, 241–43, 245
  Ban Ban, 168, 188, 191, 193
  Ban Na Kha, 189
  Ban Pa Dong, 173, 243–44
  Ban Sot, 176
  Bon Neua, 169–70
  Declaration of Neutrality of, 140
  Kiengkhum, 194
  Kingdom of Laos, 130, 237, 239, 243, 245
  Long Tieng, 146, 149–50, 152, 170, 204
  Luang Prabang, 138, 145, 161–62, 164, 166, 170, 187, 189, 193–94
  Moung Ou Tai, 165
  Muang Sing, 194
  Nam Bak, 145
  Nam Tha, 140
  Namkading River, 174
  Nong Het, 168, 170, 188, 193
  Northern Laos, 17, 136, 140, 148, 186, 190, 192, 197
  Northwest Laos, 170
  Ou Neua, 162, 164–66
  Padong, 138–39
  Pak Kading, 174–77, 179, 181, 183, 185, 244
  Paksane, 174
  Pha Khao, 140
  Phongsaly, 161–63, 165, 169–71, 188, 198
  Phonsavan, 168–69, 191
  Phou Pha Thi, 239
  Savannakhet, 173, 175–76, 188–89, 193, 237
  Secret War, xvi, 128, 143–44, 207, 211, 232, 236–37, 241–42
  Thakhek, 173–74
  Thathom, 194
  Vientiane, 106, 130–31, 133, 136, 138, 149, 152, 161, 166, 168, 170–77, 179, 183, 187–89, 191, 193, 195–201, 236–37, 242–45
  Xeno, 169–71
  Xieng, 135, 169, 172, 174, 191, 194–95, 199–201, 237
  Xieng Khouang, 169, 172, 174, 191, 194–95, 199–201
  Xieng Khouang airport, 194
  Xiengkhouang, 172
Laotian, xii, xix, 128, 163–66, 168–73, 179, 195, 199–200, 211, 233, 239–40, 242–45
  Army headquarters, 164, 173
  Civil War, 128, 134, 212, 218, 239
  colonel, 67, 111, 117–18, 160, 163–64, 169–70, 199–201, 215

language, 242
Laotian Beaver, 173. See also aircraft
Laotian colonel, 163, 169, 199–200
people, 195
Lashio in Burma (Myanmar), 159
Latin America, 136
Laurel Fork, 1, 26
LCVPs, 19, 174. See also Higgins boats
left seat, 80, 86, 113
leopard, xix, 179–80, 244. See also clouded leopard
Leroy (army officer), 188
Lewis, John S., 140
Licensed Commercial Pilot, 27
aviation, xiv–xvi, 20, 24, 28, 30, 34, 38, 40, 43, 68, 72, 76, 91, 94, 128, 202–5, 211, 213–15, 220–21, 223–28, 230, 234, 236, 240
Commercial, xi–xii, xvi, xix, 24, 26–27, 33, 38, 50, 68, 72, 92, 97, 129, 202, 204–5, 212–13, 221, 227, 236
license, 21, 26–28, 72, 85, 102, 111, 228
Lieutenant, 36, 38, 50–52, 55, 63, 65, 68–69, 71, 89, 111, 117, 120, 168
Curtiss, Dave, 63, 84
Schlung, Myron, 38
Spurr, Tom, 30–31, 37, 52, 56, 67
Stuart, 65–66, 242
Lieutenant Colonel, 111, 117
Kessler, W. M., 6
Petersen Jr., Frank E. "Pete", 35, 221
Lieutenant Commander, USAF Reserve, 120
Lima Site, 150, 232, 239, 242
Lima Site 90, 150
Lindbergh, Charles, xviii
Lisbon, 83
Liu, Herb, 108
loadmaster, 113
Lokker, Bob, 30–31
London, 83, 92
Lordsburg, New Mexico, 26
Louisiana, 79
LSO (Landing Signal Officer), 41, 49
LST (landing ship transport), 104–5, 127, 235
Lurie, Master Sergeant, 55
Luther, Master Sergeant, 108
Luxembourg, 85, 87–88, 90, 212

M
Macon, 80
MAG, 34, 59, 62–63, 68, 84, 86, 217, 225
MAG-12, 34, 59, 62–63, 68, 84, 86, 225. See also Marine Air Group 12
Marine Air Group, 54–55, 60, 62
Marine Air Group 12, 54–55, 60, 62. See also MAG-12
mainland, 20, 104, 125, 129, 220, 229, 244
Mainside, 30, 34–36, 38, 43–45, 50, 78–79
Major Clark, 86

Malvoso, Sylvia Lynne, ii, v, ix, 161, 167, 243, 253
Manado, 232
Manila, 85, 106, 112
Marine Air Group 12, 54–55, 60, 62
Marine Aviation Detachment, 72, 76
Marine Corps, xv, 3–4, 6, 13–14, 26, 34–35, 45, 49, 51–52, 54, 60, 79, 138, 211, 214, 216, 220, 224–25, 228–29
Marine Corps Institute (MCI), 6
Marine pilot, 3, 47, 52, 212
Martin, Corporal, 29
Martin, Second Lieutenant, 69
Master Sergeant, 55, 108
    Lurie, 55
    Luther, 108
Mateer, Charles, 139
MATS (military air transport service) flights, 106
Matthews, Jack, 132, 168–69
maximum-except-takeoff (METO), 101
McCann (Air America operations officer), 179
McClaugherty, Lieutenant, 36, 38
MCI (Marine Corps Institute), 6, 22
McKillop, 84
Meeker, Oden, 128, 130
Mekong River, xii, xix, 174, 176–78, 184, 244
Memorial Plaque at the University of Texas in Dallas, 153
METO (maximum-except-takeoff), 101

Midway, 35, 71, 226
military, xvi, 5, 14–15, 51, 55, 76, 87, 95, 100, 106, 120, 123, 131, 134, 136, 138, 140, 142–44, 160, 167–68, 170, 191, 208, 212, 215–16, 218, 221–25, 227–28, 231–34, 237–40
military air transport service, 106
military complex, 168
Minneapolis Honeywell, 124
Mobile, 42
mock dogfight, 52
model airplanes, 1–2
Modern American Aircraft, 1
monkey handlers, 87–88
Moore, Professor Albert, 73
Morse Code, 36, 157
mountain crest, 140
Mt. Asama, 107
Mt. Fuji, 98
Mt. Royal, 2, 87, 91
Murphy, Mrs., 82
Myanmar, 159

N
NAAS, 30, 39, 48, 221–22
    Bagdad, 30, 41–42
    Barin Field, 48
    Bronson, 30, 48
    Chevalier Field, 30, 78
    Corry Field, 30, 38, 221–22
    Naval Auxiliary Air Station, 30, 38, 41, 48, 221
    North Whiting Field, 36, 79
    Saufley Field, 30, 39
    Whiting Field, 30, 36, 38, 41, 79

Nabone, 187
Naha, 10, 114, 191
NAS, xv, 24, 42, 48–49, 86, 91, 110, 212
    Alameda, 110
    Corpus Christi, Texas, 42, 49
    Floyd Bennett, 81, 83–84, 86, 91, 95
    Naval Air Station, 36, 43, 49, 78, 81, 84, 110
    Pensacola, Florida, 28, 43, 49, 72
NAS Pensacola, xv, 24, 212
Nashville, Tennessee, 80
Nationalist troops, 19
Naval Aviation Cadet, 28, 30, 203, 211, 221, 223
Naval Aviation Cadet flight training, 28
Naval Cadets, 28–29, 31, 33, 35, 37–39, 41, 43, 45, 47, 49, 51, 53, 212, 220
NAVCADs, xv, 52
Navigation Service, 24
Navigator, 10, 24, 50, 83–84, 89, 92, 98, 157–58, 192, 212, 223
Navy, 2, 7, 14, 16–17, 20, 35–36, 38, 43, 45, 47, 49–51, 71, 78–79, 82, 86–87, 91, 95–96, 102, 110–11, 120, 138, 142, 215–18, 221, 223–29, 231, 238
    bombers and fighters, 2
    wings pinned on, 50
Navy fleet, 20
Neil, Mr., 22
neutralist, 131, 134, 141
New Delhi, 84, 87–90

New Mexico, 7, 26
New Orleans, Louisiana, 78–79
New York, xvi, 35, 81–88, 91, 93–94, 143
New York Times, 143
Nishihara, Miki, 61
Norfolk, Viriginia, 39, 223
North Africa, 88
North Carolina, 27, 39
North Korea, 58, 60, 220
North Vietnam, 143, 145, 168, 174, 192, 196, 198, 232, 238
North Vietnam prisoners, 168
North Vietnamese, 141–42, 144–45, 149, 164, 169, 231, 233, 238–39
    guerrillas, 164
    North Vietnamese Army, 141
Nosavan, Gen. Phoumi, 135, 174–75, 243
NVA, 141–42, 145–46, 149

O

Office of National Estimates, 147
Okinawa, Japan, 9–10, 16, 52, 106, 110, 114, 126, 157, 191, 232
Okuma Beach, 116. See also Okinawa, Japan
Operation About Face, 146
orders, 3, 28, 47, 49, 55, 71–72, 81, 152, 214
Osaka, Japan, 54, 60–61
Oshima, 98, 230
otters, 178, 181

P

Pacific Fleet, 134, 216
Pacific Theater, 95, 216, 233
Padre Island, Corpus Christi, Texas, 46
Pan Am (Pan American World Airways), 83
panther, 197, 226–27
Pao, 136–37, 149, 152, 168–71, 195, 204, 239
paramilitary, 136, 233, 237
Paris Agreement on Vietnam, 152
Parris Island, 3–4, 6–7
PARU, 204
Pathet Lao, xii, 132, 134, 137–38, 142, 144–46, 172, 174, 178, 184, 231, 239, 243, 245
   Communist, 132, 134, 140–42, 144–45, 147, 212, 218–19, 229, 239, 243
   guerrilla, 178
   NVA/Pathet Lao forces, 146
   people, 184
PDJ (Plaine des Jarres), 142–43, 146, 149
Pearl Harbor, 8, 21, 223
pedicabs, 102
Pennsylvania, 2–3, 87, 91
Pensacola, xv, 24, 28, 30–36, 38–39, 43–44, 47–50, 72, 76, 79, 81, 111, 212, 223
Permesta rebellion, 232–33
pheasant and rabbit hunting, 87
Philadelphia, 3
Philippines, 110, 124, 228, 237
Phouma, Prince Souvanna, 243
Phoumi, Gen., 134–36, 170, 174–76, 187, 194, 237, 243, 245
Pigman, Mrs., 75
Pigman, Reed, 28, 73, 76
pilot, iii, v, xi–xvii, xix, 1–3, 9, 16, 18, 24, 27, 33–34, 39–40, 47, 52, 55, 61, 63, 67–68, 71–74, 76–78, 80, 83, 85–86, 93–95, 99, 101–2, 105, 107, 112, 117–18, 120–25, 127, 132–34, 141, 149–50, 157, 161, 169, 171, 188–91, 200, 202–5, 207–9, 211–13, 217, 228–29, 234–36, 242, 244
Pine Bluff, Arkansas, 26
Plain of Jars, 17, 204, 237, 245
Plaine des Jarres (PDJ), 17, 135–37, 142, 145–46, 192, 195–97, 237–38
plane, iv, xii–xiii, xv–xvi, 1, 16–17, 20–21, 25–26, 45, 51–52, 55, 60, 68, 75, 88, 92, 98, 113, 122, 124, 134, 141, 164, 166, 168, 172, 181, 194, 201, 203–5, 207, 209, 213–14, 220–22, 226–27, 229, 231–33, 235
Plane Captain, 20
Polio Foundation, xix, 87
Port Royal, 4, 7
President, 102, 126–27, 132, 134, 136, 140, 142, 150, 222
   Johnson, Lyndon, 142
   Kennedy, 138–40, 142
Price (navigator), 158
Pulaski, Virginia, 2
Pusan, South Korea, 108

Pyeongtaek, South Korea, xix, 54–55, 66, 71, 224–25

Q
Quantico, 26–27, 63, 203, 211
Quemoy and Matsu Islands, 125
Quonset huts, 56

R
radio, 58, 70, 98, 101, 113, 125, 135, 175, 195, 199–200, 235–36
radio operator, 98, 113, 125, 135
Randell, Lloyd, 150
Rangoon, Burma (Myanmar), 159–61, 190
rattlesnake, 22
Reserve Captain, 92
Rhesus monkeys, xix, 87–88, 90
Rhyne, Jim, 150
rice, 10, 66, 131, 139, 142, 144, 147, 163, 176, 183, 190, 195, 231
  brown rice, 163, 183
  drops, 140
  fields, 1, 30, 37, 66, 139, 173, 232
  paddy, 10, 176
Rickenbacker, Eddie, xviii
rickshaws, 102
Robertson, Walter S., 130
Ross, Mrs., 72, 74, 76
Round Island flights, 104
Route 7, 168–72, 174–75, 193
Route 13, 171, 173–75, 177, 184, 187–89

S
Saigon, 106, 152, 169
Saipan, 106, 109–10, 158
salt beds, 64
San Antonio, Texas, 81
Sarno, Roger J., 140
Saysongkham, 150
Scandinavia, 85
Scribner, Col. Lansen, 18
scuba diving, 109
SEA (Southeast Asia), 21, 101, 109, 125, 190–91, 197, 223, 229, 241
sea-effect, 101
Seaboard & Western, v, xv, 83–88, 91–94, 204, 212, 227–29
seaplanes, 16
Seattle, Washington, 95–96
Secret Service, 98
Secret War in Laos, 143–44
Seoul, South Korea, 54, 60
Setter bird dog, 108
Seventh Day Adventist Hospital, 166, 171
shakedown flights, 82
Shannon, 83, 92
Shemya, Alaska, 230
short takeoff and landing (STOL), 126, 233
shut down, 88, 152
Siberian geese, 64
Single Engine Airline Transport Pilot, 74
sites, 8, 139–40, 187, 190–91, 193, 195, 197, 199, 201, 232, 237, 242, 244–45
soldiers, 7, 27, 69, 160, 169, 185–

86
South Africa, 83
South Carolina, 3–4
South Korea, 54, 225–26
South Vietnam, 145, 147, 238
Southeast Asia (SEA), xiii, xv–xvi, 125, 129–30, 132, 136, 140–41, 143, 152–53, 157, 190, 203, 212, 218, 232, 240, 244
Southern Japan, 9–10, 156
Soviet Union, 139, 238
Special National Intelligence, 145
Stark, Noble, 30–31, 37
State Department, 136
Stevenson, Charles A., 128
stewardess, 88, 90, 94
Stockum, Lem, 84
STOL (short takeoff and landing), xix, 126, 133–34, 138, 195, 203–7, 209, 213, 241
Sukarno government of Indonesia, 129
Sullivan, Amb. William, 144
Sullivan, Emmit, 150
Sundin, Corporal, 4
super chargers, 91
Super Constellation, 86–87, 212, 228
Sutphin, Ronald J. "Ron", iii, xi–xix, 2, 4, 6, 8, 10, 14, 16, 18, 20, 24, 26, 28–30, 32, 34, 36, 38, 40, 42, 44, 46, 48–50, 52, 56, 58, 60, 62, 64, 66, 68, 70, 74, 76–78, 80, 82, 84, 86, 88, 90, 92, 94, 96, 98, 100, 102, 104, 106, 108, 112, 114, 116, 118, 122, 124, 126, 128, 130, 132, 134, 136, 138, 140, 142, 144, 146, 148, 150, 152, 154–55, 158, 160, 162, 164, 166, 168, 170, 172, 174, 176, 178, 180, 182, 184, 186, 188, 192, 194, 196, 198, 200–214, 216, 218, 220–22, 224, 226, 228, 230, 232–34, 236–38, 240, 242, 244–45
swimming and ditching lectures, 33
Szechuan duck, 102

T
tactics, 18, 137, 145–46
Tailspin Tommy, 2, 214
Tainan, 103–6, 110, 112, 117–19, 122, 124–27, 161, 167, 172, 188, 190–91, 195, 234, 242–43
Taipei, 99, 102–4, 106, 110, 112, 116, 118, 125, 156, 171, 175, 188, 190, 198, 230, 235
Taiwan, 93, 99, 229–30, 234, 242
Taiwanese dollars, 102
Takarazuka, Japan, 60–61
Takhli, 157–61, 181–82, 191, 193, 195–99, 242
Tennessee, 26, 80
Texas, 28, 42, 44, 49, 51, 72, 81, 128, 153, 220, 238, 240–41, 245
TGLs, 101
Thai, 137, 149, 195, 204, 245
Thailand, 136, 138, 140, 147, 152, 157, 161, 185–86, 191, 195, 197–98, 233, 238, 242, 244
Tibet, 129, 158, 204
tigers, 163

Tokyo, 21, 85, 95–96, 98, 101, 107, 230–31
Tokyo Bay, 98, 101
tour of duty, xv, 12, 71, 211
Townley, Roy F., 149–50
tracers, 176
transit pilots, 124
transport pilot, 74, 102, 105, 132–33
Treasure Island Naval Base, 7
triangular sightings, 70
Triple A card, 33
troops, 7, 9, 19, 57–58, 132, 140–45, 147, 150, 152, 174–75, 182, 215–16, 219, 225, 231–32, 237–38, 243
Tsingtao (Qingdao), China, 9–10, 12–21, 96, 102, 211, 216–19
Tucker, 188–89
twin-engine transports, 147

U
U.S. Army, 54, 69, 174, 222, 229, 237
  Green Berets, 174
Udorn Airbase, 149
Udorn, Thailand, 138, 141, 149–50, 152
Uncle Forrest, 27
United States Air Force (USAF), 234, 236
United States Marine Corps (USMC), 225
USAF (United States Air Force), 8, 100, 120–21, 145, 160, 225, 234, 240

USMC (United States Marine Corps), 6, 8, 221
USS (United States Ship), 7–8, 42, 48, 50–51, 214–15, 217, 219, 223–26
  Arizona, 8
  Cabot aircraft carrier, 42
  Estes (command ship), 217
  Mann, 7–8, 214–15
  Monterey (CVL-26), 223
  Repose (hospital ship), 217

V
Vang Pao, 136–37, 149, 152, 168–71, 195, 204, 239
very high frequency (VHF), 59
VHF (very high frequency), 59, 70, 101, 195, 199
Vienna, 139
Viet Cong, 169–70, 172, 174
Vietnam, xii, 35, 79, 143–45, 147, 152, 168, 174, 190–93, 195–99, 201, 225, 230, 232, 235–36, 238–40, 243, 245
Vietnamese Army, 141, 170
Villa, 172, 194–95
VIP (very important person), 78–79
Virginia, 1–2, 26, 39, 203, 211
VMA, 52, 55, 60, 62, 64–67, 69, 224–25
  121, 55, 59–60, 62, 64–67, 121, 224–25, 228
  212, 52, 60, 212, 238
  251, 60, 69
  Marine Attack Squadron, 55
VMAT-10, 51, 54

VMF-351, 81–82, 84, 86, 91–92, 94
volunteers, 138, 149
VPO (vice president of operations), 102–3, 106, 112, 118, 125, 127, 198–99

W
Wake Island, 8
Walton, Jessie, 108
Warren, 30–31, 34, 84, 93, 98, 108, 233
Washington DC, 3, 27, 93–95, 97
Washington, George, 134
WASP (Women Airforce Service Pilots), 39, 214, 222, 224, 226
water buffalo, 180
water cobras, 178
water landing, 16, 176
Waves (Women Accepted for Volunteer Emergency Service), 44–46, 223
Weaponry
  12.7mm fire, 150
  1000-pound bombs, 57
  20mm cannon, 58, 65, 223, 229, 231
  20mm guns, 176
  20mms, 200
  250-pound bombs, 57
  BAR (Browning Automatic Rifle), 13, 35, 38, 89, 99–100, 178
  Browning automatic rifle, 13
  GPs [general purpose (bombs)], 57
  Howitzer, 195, 243
  Ka-Bar knife, 178
  M1 rifle, 6, 18
  machine gun, 113, 176, 214, 218, 222–23, 226, 229
  mortar shells, 173
  napalm, 52, 59
  napalm tanks, 59
  rocket launcher, 176
  shotgun, 18, 87
  small arms, 59, 158, 173, 196–97
  Smith and Wesson .38-caliber pistol, 164, 178, 183
  Soviet PT-76 tanks, 146
  tanks, 59, 146, 149, 158, 214, 235
Weems (Air Navigation Manual), 3, 214
Weissenback, Edward A., 150
West Point, 120
western movie set, 89
wet season of 1969, 146
  monsoon season (June to September), 144
Weuste, Al, 127
whiskey, 55–56, 99
White, Al, 191
Wiehrdt, Leonard I., 150
wild boar hunting, 85
Willauer, Whiting, 129, 212, 229
Williamson, Dale (Chief Helicopter Pilot), 132
Wings cards, 1
WINGS Cigarettes, 1, 214
Wizbowski, Walter, 139
Women Accepted for Volunteer Emergency Service (Waves), 223

Women Airforce Service Pilots
    (WASPs), 39, 222
Woosley, Tom, 150
World War II, 8, 45, 51–52, 95, 109,
    117, 120, 129, 215–18, 222–24,
    226–29, 231, 235–38, 242
    fighter pilot (WWII), 95
WWII, 2, 23, 32, 34, 39–40, 127,
    137, 215, 221, 229, 239
    era American weapons, 137

X
Xieng Dot, 135

Y
Yokohama, 21
York, Pennsylvania, 2
Young-Ja, 68–69

Z
Zhongshan Road, 102

www.ingramcontent.com/pod-product-compliance
Lightning Source LLC
Chambersburg PA
CBHW080746060526
44119CB00072B/166